Single mom, empty nest —
what to do?

I pondered that question for months before my only child left for college. And then one night, while watching *Under the Tuscan Sun* for the tenth time, a voice whispered: *Let's sell the house, move to Italy, eat gelato and write a book.*

The voice belonged to the writer-in-me, who herself has a cameo role in this memoir of our year-long adventure in Italy, where we lived in Florence on a lively street called Via Tavanti.

Our *Under the Tuscan Sun* fantasy quickly collided with the reality of living in a culture that has a formidable bureaucracy and clings to its old ways. But we soon became players in the grand comedy-drama of Italian life, surrounded by a cast of colorful characters: a maniacal Mafia princess and her no-nonsense papa from Palermo, a playboy leather merchant, the owner of Florence's most illustrious literary café, a shop girl with a big mouth, an olive thief, and an amorous Umbrian artisan who invited us into his ancient world.

We hobbled on cobbles—in the sandal steps of Dante, Michelangelo, Leonardo da Vinci and Salvatore Ferragamo—awed by the beauty and history that surrounded us. We ate tubs of gelato, wandered through sunflower fields, hung out one evening with monks in a crypt, and served up *magnifico* margaritas that our friends in Florence will never forget.

During our year in Italy, we overcame megavolt culture shock with resolve and a sense of humor. We dealt with trauma and heartache—the result of a family crisis that spun out of control back home. And we learned how much there is to gain in life simply by letting go.

We reflected on all of this, gazing at the swirling colors of a carousel, at our favorite Florence café, which is where this story begins...the day we met the playboy leather merchant who said, "It's like a fantasy"—the fateful first words of *Tales from Tavanti*.

TALES FROM
Tavanti

An American Woman's Mid-Life Adventure In Italy

Rebecca Bricker

Tales from Tavanti

ISBN: 146357276X
ISBN-13: 978-1463572761

Cover art by Mark Andresen
Cover graphic design by Elizabeth MacFarland
"Giubbe Rosse and the Carousel" sketch by Will Williams

Contents

To my friends in Italy

Author's Note

There are some characters in this story who have given me permission to use their real names. I commend them for their spirit of adventure. One even said she would be "honored" to be in this book—that would be Elena, whose apartment I rented on Via Tavanti.

As for everyone else, including those who rolled their eyes and moaned when I asked if I could reveal their identities, I've tried to give them safe haven in this author's version of a witness protection program. You know who you are. But hopefully the rest of the world won't have a clue—and if someone spills the beans, I know of a guy in Palermo…oh, never mind.

To ensure the privacy of those in the protection program, portions of this book come under the heading of "novoir"—a genre of my own invention that blends novel and memoir. But even in places where I've taken liberty with the facts, the underlying essence of the story remains true.

RB

"Giubbe Rosse and the Carousel"
Piazza della Repubblica
Florence

1

The carousel

"It's like a fantasy," he said.

His voice startled me. I was entranced by the swirling colors of the spinning carousel in the piazza. I hadn't even noticed him sitting at a nearby table. When I turned to look at him, I could tell he had already taken me in, all of me.

I had been writing in my journal at my favorite place in Florence, Piazza della Repubblica, the city's main square in Roman times. Its enormous triumphal arch looks like something out of an epic Hollywood film. At any minute you expect Charlton Heston to come riding into the piazza on a golden chariot surrounded by a thousand cheering extras, clad in togas and strappy Roman sandals.

But on that October day, Piazza della Repubblica was quiet except for the laughter of children on the carousel. The tourist season was over. I was a straggler, nearing the end of my grand tour of Italy.

I don't know how long Marcello had been sitting there, watching me. I was deeply lost in my own fantasies of Italian guys in togas.

Actually, I had been writing about a masseur, at a Tuscan villa where I had stayed, who had given me a massage I'll never forget.

Marcello was Italian, but spoke English fluently with a hint of an American accent. He owned a leather store in Florence and traveled to the U.S. on business a few times a year. His leather coats and jackets, produced at his factory, are sold at Neiman's and Bloomingdale's, he told me. He knew southern California well, especially the high-end retail locales of Newport Beach and the designer shopping mecca, South Coast Plaza. Funny, the places we had in common— I've lived in southern California most of my adult life and grew up in the suburbs of Marcello's favorite U.S. city, Chicago.

He was well dressed and good looking—about 50, I would have guessed. I noticed crutches propped next to his table. He sat back in his chair, with his right leg stretched out. He had been in a motorcycle accident several months earlier, he said, and was still recovering from surgery to mend his badly broken tibia.

We talked for a long time, and he asked me to come by his store, just a block away. He said, "I'm not a designer, but I have something in mind for you." He glanced in the direction of my derriere. I am a full-bodied woman who should have lived in another era when Rubens or Renoir surely would have glorified my curves on canvas.

"Come by the store and ask for me," he said.

Marcello gave me his card and invited me to join him for a drink that evening. We were to meet under the triumphal arch at seven.

I watched him hobble away, thinking how treacherous it would be to negotiate Roman pavers on crutches.

I stayed for a while at my table, writing. I didn't stop by Marcello's store on my way back to the hotel. A drink first, I decided, then the trunk show.

But none of that happened. When I got back to the hotel, I felt tired and achy, like I might be coming down with a cold. I took a hot shower and crawled into bed. I called Marcello and asked if we could postpone our drink. He said of course.

The next morning I felt better and walked to the Duomo, Florence's famous cathedral, which is surrounded by leather shops. I was on a mission to find the Perfect Purse.

Buying a handbag in Florence is like a courtship. The courtship is more of a hustle if you're buying at a stall on the streets or in the markets. But if you're in a shop, it's more languorous and usually starts with a cappuccino.

I had stopped in at a leather shop on Piazza del Duomo a few days earlier. The shop manager, a Middle Eastern guy who called himself Antonio, was very taken with me. He showed me a red handbag and told me how beautiful I was and wondered if my eyes could be any bluer. I sensed danger and didn't linger.

As bad luck would have it that morning on my search for the Perfect Purse, Antonio spied me from the doorway of his shop and, before I could escape, greeted me with courtly flourish. He kissed my hand and asked me to come inside and join him for a cappuccino. I was hesitant as he walked ahead of me up the stairs to the second floor where there was a sitting area, with a sofa and a postcard view of the Duomo. But mostly the upstairs space was storage for racks of jackets covered with plastic bags. Antonio served me a cappuccino and then cut to the chase. He asked me if I would go with him that evening to Piazzale Michelangelo to see the breathtaking view of Florence at sunset. His *amore* got the better of him and he leaned over and tried to kiss me. I pulled away.

"What's wrong?" he asked.

"I don't even know you!"

A bell rang as a customer entered the store. Antonio ran down the stairs. I gave him a five-second head start and then I ran down the stairs and out the door.

I could hear him calling, "Rebecca, come back!"

I hurried down the street and ducked into another leather shop. This time I was greeted by Alex from Egypt. Alex's brother Tito owned the shop, but Tito wasn't there. Alex showed me several handbags, and to prove they were genuine leather, he pulled out a lighter and tried to set one on fire. Actually, he was trying to show me that it wasn't vinyl, which would have melted instantly from the heat.

"What the hell are you doing?" I shrieked. "I was going to buy that bag."

Alex laughed. "There's no harm to it. Look, it's fine. It's real leather."

He was right. The bag was unscathed. He offered me a cappuccino and a chair in plain view of the front door. So I sat down.

Alex and I hung out together for about an hour. He told me his life story. The long and short of it was that he had come to Florence to find a wife. He was 36 and his family was pressuring him to marry.

Tito walked in and quickly looked me over. Alex introduced us. And then Tito asked me, "Are you married?"

I burst out laughing. "I'm much too old for your brother."

"How old are you?"

"Old enough to have a 19-year-old son."

"No," Tito said, giving me another once-over.

Tito and Alex gave me a great discount on two bags, with hopes that I would come back soon. While I was still in the store, my cell phone rang. It was Marcello, wanting to know how I was feeling. The thought occurred to me that if I lived in Florence, my lovers would all be leather merchants and my closets would be filled with Perfect Purses.

Marcello and I re-scheduled our drink for that evening, place to be determined. I called him back a short while later. When he heard my voice, he said, "Are you canceling on me again?"

"No, I just wondered if we could meet at La Giostra," I said. "My hotel booked a table for me there." La Giostra, which means "carousel" in Italian, was once the winter storehouse for one of the city's carousels and is now a top-rated restaurant in Florence.

"I know the owner," Marcello said. "I'll meet you there at 7:30."

I was on time and waited outside the restaurant. After about fifteen minutes, I showed Marcello's card to the hostess and asked if he might be in the back talking to the owner. He wasn't there and no one had seen him. I sat down at a table, explaining to the waiter that I was waiting for someone. He served two complimentary glasses of prosecco. At 8:15, I told the waiter, "My companion is obviously delayed. I will begin without him."

"Good for you," he said.

I drank both glasses of prosecco. My phone rang at quarter of nine. I didn't answer. Everyone was looking at me—the woman dining alone whose date had stood her up.

On the way back to the hotel, I ripped Marcello's card into tiny pieces. At ten, as I was getting into bed, my phone rang again. Marcello said he had been detained at a meeting and asked if it was too late to go out for a drink.

"Yes, it's too late," I said. "I'm leaving early tomorrow."

"Ah, that's too bad," he said. "Another time. Let me know if you're ever back in Florence."

I had no plans to return to Florence anytime soon. But even if I had, I couldn't imagine ever wanting to see Marcello again.

2

The lease

Five months later, I was on a plane back to Florence. I suppose you could say I was in the midst of a mid-life crisis. I prefer to call it a catharsis.

I had just finished writing a book—a memoir about the previous year of my life, leading up to my son's departure for college. It had started as a hopeful tale as I contemplated my options and possible adventures. I had been a single mother for ten years and had told my son, "The day you leave for college, I'm going out the door behind you with my passport in my pocket."

No empty nest for me. In fact, I sold the nest. That wasn't part of the initial plan, however. I had hoped to rent out my lovely bungalow in Pasadena while I was enjoying my gap year of globe-trotting. But I saw doomsday looming for California real estate. Days before the crash of 2008, I closed escrow on my home of twenty-two years. Two days after Lehman Brothers failed, I was on a plane to Rome. I was an exhausted wreck by the time I arrived in Italy.

After three months of wandering around Europe that fall, I returned to Pasadena, where I rented an apartment while I finished the book. As much as I love Pasadena and my many friends there, I was back in my old life, which seemed very empty without my son around.

The subtitle of my memoir was "My Journey to a New Life." Having written 116,000 words on the subject, I felt I clearly needed to make a change.

In a moment of total caprice, I made an appointment at the Italian consulate in L.A. I had wanted to spend my gap year in France, but I read online that it was easier to get an extended-stay visa in Italy than France, which, I later learned, is like saying it's easier to climb Mt. Everest with a frayed rope than no rope at all. I reasoned that Italy had played an important role in my post-traumatic stress recovery—as had that gifted Tuscan masseur—so I chose Italy.

Italy, however, was skeptical. The woman at the consulate, whom I shall refer to hereafter as Snarky Bitch, glowered at me over the top of her glasses and told me I hadn't read the directions for the visa application. I assured her I had. But then she produced another set of directions with two additional pages of fine print that said I couldn't apply for a visa unless I had proof of a place of residence in Italy. I showed her a listing of available apartments I had received from a real estate agent in Florence.

Snarky Bitch shook her head. "You need a lease."

"How can I get a lease without a visa?"

"Not my problem," she said.

That's how I ended up on a plane back to Florence. My friend Tom, who works for a major airline, had given me a buddy pass. So off I went, hoping for a sign from the universe that this was meant to be more than just a lark.

Feeling refreshed after a night in business class, I walked down the jetway with a lovely American woman named Kathryn. She had been sitting a few rows ahead of me, and I had admired her elegantly upswept gray hair, artfully secured with beautiful combs.

She looked to be in her 70s. We chatted as we waited for our luggage and ended up sitting next to each other on the bus from the Pisa airport to the Florence train station. We shared a cab to my hotel and exchanged phone numbers before she continued on to her apartment.

I had made appointments with three real estate agents in Florence who specialized in long-term rentals. In the span of a week I saw more than two dozen apartments, from the ancient city center to the banks of the Arno, the hills of the nearby villages of Fiesole and Settignano, the terraced olive groves of Bagno a Ripoli and the hamlets of Chianti. I looked at apartments in renovated Tuscan farmhouses, in villas that were once part of grand Florentine estates and in tower houses of the old city that date back to the twelfth century.

Kathryn arranged for me to see the apartment below hers which was vacant. It was beautiful, with a living room view of ancient Florence across the Arno River. The rent was high. The landlady was willing to come down a bit, but not enough. It would have been great having Kathryn for an upstairs neighbor, but she comes to Florence only a few times a year for two- to three-week stays.

Kathryn had lots of good advice. According to an article she read in *The New York Times,* there are three essentials when evaluating an apartment: location, light and a big room. "And if you want to survive a summer in Florence," she added, "you need an air conditioner and window screens to keep away the mosquitoes." Kathryn doesn't come to Florence in the summer.

Everywhere I went, people offered to assist in my search. A waiter at a café I frequented checked on possible vacancies in his building. Enrico, the kind manager of the hotel where I was staying, contacted a couple of real estate agents on my behalf and even drove me to see two properties. Enrico's assistant Susanna accompanied me on one appointment, to a modern glass house with a garden terrace accessible only by a step ladder with handrails. The walls of the bathroom were also glass, which would give the neighbors an incredible view of me taking a bath. Ever practical Susanna worried about the utility bills with so much glass around.

I soon was center stage in a grand Italian morality play called Cheating the Government. One apartment Enrico took me to see was priced at €1,300 a month, but the landlord told him he would put €800 on the contract.

Puzzled, I said to Enrico, "I don't get it."

"He'll lower the rent by €100 if you agree to do this," Enrico explained in English.

"So he can pay less tax," I said. The landlord would pay tax on rental income of only €800, the amount on the contract, instead of the €1,200 that I would actually pay him.

Enrico nodded.

I smiled at the landlord, who was smiling at me because apparently he thought he had just clinched the deal. I was smiling because I was thinking he was a money-grubbing scumbag. The apartment was full of religious art and knick-knacks. In every room, there was a portrait of Jesus or the Madonna or both. The guy had been especially pleased to show me the Madonna-and-child painting in the master bedroom. He put his finger behind the bottom of the gilded frame and the painting swung on a hinge—revealing a safe on the wall behind it.

On my first day in Florence, I stopped in at my favorite leather shop—dangerously close to amorous Antonio's—where I had bought a Perfect Purse on my previous visit. (If you must know, I bought four Perfect Purses on that trip.) When I walked in with the purse slung over my shoulder, the owner smiled.

"Do you like my handbag?" I asked him.

He laughed. His sales assistant, a friendly young woman named Nadia, whom I had not met before, wanted to know what had brought me back to Florence. Her eyes lit up when I told her I was looking for an apartment.

"I will help you find a place," she said enthusiastically. "You can go out with me and my friends. You can teach me English. And your friends will come and buy lots of handbags." Nadia is a good saleswoman. She immediately sent a text message to a real estate broker, asking if he had any rental properties. She gave me her number and told me to come back to the shop the next day.

When I returned, Nadia was ready for me. She told me she used to work at a leather shop owned by Jordanian brothers who had a number of rental properties. She made a quick call and spoke in Italian to Arman, one of the brothers. When Nadia hung up, she looked pleased. "Arman has a place for you to see. He is waiting for you at the shop." She took my map of Florence and made an X. "We are here," she said. Then she drew a large dot, a few blocks away: "You need to go here."

Off I went. It's important to mention that I was limping. I had bruised the arch of my right foot on my first day in Florence on those wretched Roman pavers. The Romans may have been expert road builders, but I'm convinced the crew that laid the sidewalks of Florence was heavily imbibing grappa.

I limped over to the dot Nadia had drawn on my map. As I entered the store where Arman was waiting, I looked up at the sign above the door and a bell went off in the alarm center of my brain.

Arman told me I needed to see his brother Kamil. "He works at a restaurant not far from here," Arman said. "He has the key to the apartment." Arman wrote the name of the restaurant on my map. I thanked him, but wished he had told Nadia for me to go directly to the restaurant.

By this point I was dragging my sore foot across those damn pavers. As I approached the restaurant, the bell in my alarm center became a blaring siren. I recognized him immediately, sitting at a table under the awning. *Shit, it's that guy*, I thought. For a second, I couldn't remember his name.

Marcello glanced at me and then did a little double-take. I suddenly remembered: the name on the sign at the store was on the card Marcello had given me the day we met—the card I tore into tiny pieces.

I quickly went into the restaurant looking for Kamil, who apologetically told me that the guy with the apartment key had gone to Arezzo and wouldn't be back for an hour. Another brother, who had been sitting with Marcello, came into the restaurant to tell me about the apartment, which was across from the Mercato Centrale, Florence's historic food market. He said the apartment was on the third floor.

My foot was throbbing. "Does the building have an elevator?" I asked.

"There are only eleven apartment buildings in Florence with elevators," he said, and this one wasn't one of them.

"Only eleven?" I asked skeptically. "Then I've already seen half of them." I didn't like this guy.

I told him that I didn't yet have a visa. "You don't need a visa if you rent from me," he said. He invited me to sit down and have a drink.

I sat at a table outside, out of Marcello's line of vision, but where I could observe him. There were two young Middle Eastern women sitting at the table next to his. I didn't know if they were with him. He barely spoke to them. At one point, he asked one of them, "What's your name?" and then didn't say anything more to her. He looked very bored.

I was scribbling away in my journal, sipping a cappuccino, when he got up to leave. I tried not to look at him, but my curiosity got the better of me. He was a few feet away, staring at me.

"I see your leg is better," I said. His crutches were gone.

"I know you," he said. "I remember your face. But I don't remember where we met."

"At the carousel," I replied. "We were at a café in the piazza last fall. I was writing in my journal—like now."

I could tell he couldn't recall. I didn't mention that he had stood me up at La Giostra. We chatted for a minute. He said his leg had healed well.

The brother I didn't like appeared and seemed impatient to go. Marcello said good-bye. I looked at my watch. I had been waiting for an hour for the key to return from Arezzo. I told Kamil I needed to leave. He apologized again.

I hobbled back to the hotel, thinking about how easy my life was in Pasadena. I drove everywhere I needed to go. My apartment building had underground parking and two elevators. No schlepping grocery bags up steep medieval staircases.

When I got back to the hotel, Enrico gave me an ice pack for my now very swollen foot. He came to my room later with a bucket full of ice. I spent most of that evening in my room, with my foot up, watching cable news and playing solitaire on my phone. I read for a while and checked my e-mails on the hotel computer. I e-mailed my dear friend Nancy, whom I've known since college. I told her I was having second thoughts about moving to Florence.

Nancy is a seasoned expat, who has lived in Berlin for the past ten years. She called me immediately and gave me a pep talk. "You're taking the first steps on your journey," she said. "You don't know where it will take you, but you have made a start."

"The first steps really hurt," I complained. "I can barely walk."

She was sympathetic, but encouraged me not to give up. "Put out your hands, palms up, and say this prayer to the universe," she told me. I repeated the prayer as she spoke it: *Perfect solutions are coming to me easily and effortlessly.*

Feeling better, I headed out the next morning, by taxi, to Piazza della Signoria, where I was to meet a real estate agent at her office. The piazza, where the Palazzo Vecchio and the Uffizi art gallery are located, is popular with tourists. It's set like a stage, with a gallery of enormous sculptures immortalizing conquerors, mythological figures and historic acts of violence such as the rape of the Sabine women. The perimeter of the piazza is ringed with cafés, including the ritzy Caffè Rivoire, where Kathryn treated me to an obscenely rich (and expensive) hot chocolate one chilly afternoon.

The numbering system of the buildings on the piazza defy logic. But that was before I learned that addresses in Florence are distinguished by black and red numbers: the red numbers are for businesses and the black numbers are for residences. I looked up from my map in exasperation and saw a man smiling at me. It was Marcello.

"We must stop meeting like this," I said.

"It's funny," he said, "but as I walked around the corner, I was thinking about you. Really, it's true. And here you are. How strange."

"The universe works in strange ways," I said, amused.

"I have a bit of a headache this morning. My mind wanders when I have a headache," he said.

Hung-over and thinking of me. I didn't exactly feel flattered.

He asked if I had seen the apartment. I told him the guy with the key never showed up.

"That's too bad," he said. "How long are you here for?"

"Probably another week."

"Would you like to meet for a drink?" he asked.

Here we go again, I thought. We exchanged cell numbers.

"Call me," he said, as he turned to walk away.

I tucked his card into my bag, thinking, *No chance of that*.

༄

A week went by. I had a few more apartments to see, but I was feeling discouraged. I hadn't seen a place in my price range that felt like a good fit for me. My favorite agent, Sofie, had arranged one last tour of properties, on the periphery of the city. Sofie is a good agent because she picks up on emotional cues. A few days earlier, she had shown me an apartment in a twelfth-century building near Piazza Santo Spirito, a charming artsy area that's a bit dodgy due to the drug dealers who hang out there. I liked the apartment, which had been renovated with contemporary furnishings. I fell in love with the view from the bedroom where the current tenant had set up her writing desk by the window.

The first apartment Sofie showed me on our final tour was near Piazza Leopoldo, about ten minutes by bus from the city center. She called the building a "skyscraper," which made me laugh. It had eight floors. The apartment was on the fifth floor with a large balcony overlooking a busy street called Via Tavanti. The building was part of a new residential-retail complex that included a supermarket, a café, a dry cleaner, an optician and a hair salon. The apartment had two bedrooms, two baths—one with a Jacuzzi tub. The second bedroom had a western view where I could sit at my desk and watch the sun set over the mountains. I especially liked that the building had two elevators and underground parking. Sofie had nailed me. I hated to admit it, even to myself: I was a wimp and a sell-out. The Old World romantic in me had lost out to the L.A. girl.

I was back at the hotel that night, contemplating all this, when my cell phone rang. It was Marcello. I hadn't seen or spoken to him since our encounter at Piazza della Signoria. Every day since then, as I shuffled through the business cards I accumulated daily, I put his at the bottom of the pile.

"Rebecca," he said, surprise in his voice. "I wasn't sure you were still here. I haven't seen you around town."

"I've hurt my foot and haven't been walking around much."

"I'm sorry to hear that," he said. "You know there's an Italian proverb—if you walk with a person who limps, you will limp, too."

"Since you're no longer limping, I should walk with you and hope my limp goes away," I said. That made him laugh.

He asked if I'd like to meet for a drink the following evening. I told him I had plans, which was true. I was meeting with the owner of the apartment on Via Tavanti.

"What about Friday?" he asked.

Give him a second chance, said a little voice in my head.

He suggested we meet near my hotel, under the arch at the end of Borgo Pinti. A man who likes to meet under arches must have some redeeming qualities, I told myself.

I was a few minutes late because I had dawdled at the hotel soaking my foot. I walked past La Giostra, which happens to be on Borgo Pinti, thinking about the warped irony of this meeting. As I approached the arch at the end of the street, there was no sign of Marcello.

When I reached the corner, he suddenly appeared. He apparently had been on time and had been scouting the bars in the neighborhood. We didn't walk far—about ten meters to an Irish pub.

We took seats at the bar and he ordered a margarita. The bartender looked at him like he was from Mars, or maybe L.A.

"We don't make margaritas," she said.

"Okay, what about a Bloody Mary," he said. I ordered one, too.

"If I move to Florence, I'll make you a margarita you won't forget," I promised. "The only problem is that people who drink my margaritas forget where they live and end up in bed with people they don't normally sleep with." Marcello liked that.

He asked if I had found a place and I told him Sofie was drawing up a lease for the apartment on Via Tavanti. "I've been having second thoughts ever since I got here," I confessed. "I have until tomorrow to back out."

He wanted to know about my writing. I told him I had been a magazine journalist for many years. "I used to write a gossip column for *People* magazine," I said. "Have you heard of it?"

"Yes, I know *People* magazine," he said.

"I love to write. It's my passion," I said. "I've written ten screenplays—nothing that's been produced—but a few of the scripts have placed in screenwriting competitions. And I've just finished a book."

"You really are a writer." He was impressed.

As we talked, a young American girl stepped up to the bar and looked wide-eyed at Marcello. She was so delighted to see him that she was nearly jumping up and down. He didn't notice her at first—he was looking at me with his back to her.

Finally, I said to him, "I think there's someone who'd like to get your attention."

He turned toward her. "Becky!" he said. "I wondered what happened to you."

"I'm Becky," she said, shaking my hand.

"And I'm Rebecca."

"How do you spell it?" she asked.

"One B, two C's."

She gave me a thumbs-up and introduced me to her girlfriend. Two American girls from Kansas.

The bartender asked Becky for an ID.

I said to Marcello, "Are they carding her?"

He laughed. "Not in Italy. They just want to see her student ID so she can get a discount."

"You can drink in Italy from the time you're 5," Becky said.

"You're 21, right?" Marcello asked her. I squelched a giggle, wondering if she was a notch on his belt.

"I'm 23," she said, trying to sound sophisticated.

I had to smile. I remember having a fling at her age with an "older" man, who was all of 30.

The girls wandered off. I wondered if Becky was heartbroken or more likely reeling from shock that Marcello was at the bar with a woman old enough to be her mother.

I told Marcello I had a 19-year-old son in college and asked him if he had kids.

"None that I know of, but then again…" He finished the sentence with a shrug. He told me he was 48 and had never been married.

What a rogue, I thought. But I couldn't help but like him. He was funny and charming. Conversation between us was easy and ran the gamut from politics to the qualities of a good margarita. Every so often, he'd casually take my hand in his.

At one point we were talking about his visits to Chicago and how much he liked that part of the U.S. I mentioned my parents had a vacation home in Wisconsin.

"Where in Wisconsin?" he asked.

"Oh, you wouldn't know it," I said. "It's a place called Door County."

"I've been to Door County," he said. He listed all the little towns he had visited on the peninsula: Ephraim, Sister Bay, Fish Creek. "I know it well." That really blew me away. I would later learn that he had visited there with his then-girlfriend, in August 1998. I had separated from my husband earlier that year and my son and I spent the month of August in Door County with my parents. It was possible Marcello and I had been standing on the same street corner at the same time. The degrees of separation between us were dwindling.

We left the pub and walked down Borgo Pinti, past La Giostra. I waited for him to say something like "I'm sorry about what happened that night." All he said was "I like La Giostra." I thought, wow, he's really good at bluffing or he has a terrible memory—or he can't possibly remember because standing up women is routine behavior.

As we turned down the street to my hotel, I felt nervous about the decision I needed to make. He took my hand in his. Our fingers intertwined easily and comfortably. I gave his hand a tiny squeeze.

When we got to the hotel entrance, I invited him in. I told him the history of the building—it had been a convent in the fifteenth century and later became the wardrobe facility for Florence's Teatro della Pergola as well as a studio for Federico Fellini's costume designers. The hotel had opened two years earlier after extensive renovations that included the addition of beautiful ceiling frescoes and decorative painting in all the rooms. I opened the door to my room, just off the lobby, to give him a peek at the artwork.

Marcello admired the room's vaulted ceiling, painted lapis blue and decorated with gold stars. "Very Florentine," he said. He also was impressed with the kitchenette hidden inside what looked to be an armoire.

"Do you have any wine?" he asked. There was enough left in the bottle the hotel had given me on my arrival for two small glasses.

I took Marcello's leather jacket and cleared the clutter from the room's only upholstered chair so he could sit down. I hadn't been expecting company.

I sat on the edge of the bed and took off my shoes and rubbed my sore foot.

"I remember how I felt at the end of the day when I was on crutches," he said empathetically.

Before too long, he came over to the bed and sat next to me. I pulled off my socks. Marcello saw my polished toenails. "Nice," he said.

"My California toes," I said, wiggling them.

"Why are they California toes?"

"Because we wear sandals year-round in California," I said. "It's nice to have colorful toenails."

I sensed there wasn't a square inch of me that Marcello was going to miss, starting with the painted toes.

I smiled at him and he kissed me.

"I want to see you naked," he whispered.

I was stunned by how quickly I gave in to that idea. I clearly was embracing my Italian adventure with *gusto*.

Marcello carefully helped me out of my clothes and ripped his off in a big hurry. He stood naked at the foot of the bed, looking at me like I was Titian's voluptuous Venus of Urbino.

"I've never been with a big, beautiful girl," Marcello said. At first I cringed, but then I realized he meant it as a compliment.

I was a sumptuous feast spread out before him, waiting for him to taste and devour. "You're so feminine," he murmured over and over. I surmised he had been with a long line of anorexic fashion models. Marcello is a connoisseur of the female body, and his appreciation of a woman's anatomy vaulted me somewhere beyond the vaulted ceiling's firmament of stars.

Later, as we lay in each other's arms, he rubbed his hand over my fleshy tummy. "I love a belly," he said. "I love hips." He gently squeezed the padding on mine.

"That's gelato, right there," I revealed.

He laughed. "Some men care only about a woman's body, not the face," he said. "Not me. The face is what attracts me." He slowly ran his finger along the ridge of my nose.

Before our clothes came off, Marcello had remarked how lovely my nose was. I told him it had been re-designed many years ago during surgery for a deviated septum. "My surgeon studied anatomy from an artist's perspective at the insistence of his father, who was a well-known sculptor," I said. Marcello studied my face. "He did a beautiful job."

There truly wasn't a thing about me that Marcello didn't admire. He loved my freckles, my curly hair.

"What color is your hair," he had asked between our first kisses. "In the light it looks blonde, in the shadow it looks red."

"It's more red than blonde," I said.

"I love red."

He loved everything.

I must confess there were times during our lovemaking that night when I was a bit distracted by our celestial surroundings. More than once as I soared above the stars on that vaulted ceiling, I braced myself for a collision with a flying nun.

Marcello was full of ideas for fun activities. But with nuns overhead, I had moments of hesitation.

"Let's do that on the second date," I replied demurely to one of his suggestions.

"Why not the first date?"

"My mother told me never to even kiss a guy on the first date."

He grinned. "We won't tell her. When can be the second date?"

I was loving this, wondering if I could work a leather jacket into the deal. "You'll have to check your calendar," I said, laughing.

There was a lot of laughter and chatter from my room at the convent that night.

At one point, Marcello asked, "How old are you?"

"You're not supposed to ask a woman her age."

"I think you are younger than I am."

"Maybe. Maybe not. I'll tell you on the tenth date."

"Okay," he said, kissing me. We made love again.

In the wee hours, I smiled as I watched him sort through the pile of clothes on the floor.

"This is mine. This is yours," he said. He pulled up the covers at the foot of the bed. "I'm not looking at your legs. I'm just looking for my underwear."

We found his briefs after a bit of a search. He retrieved his socks from the garment pile beside the bed.

"Don't take my bra."

It dangled from his finger. "I want it as a souvenir," he said with a devilish grin. He leaned over and kissed me. "Let me know if you sign the lease."

At that moment, I couldn't think of a single reason why I shouldn't.

3

The visa

The next evening, I signed a one-year lease for the apartment on Via Tavanti. I had butterflies in my stomach all day. Kathryn called to see how I was feeling.

"A little nervous," I said. "Not about the apartment, but mostly about the change that's coming."

"I know," she said. Her voice was soothing and motherly. "Don't forget to ask about window screens," she reminded me.

From the day I arrived, Kathryn had been standing at the gate of Florence, opening it wide for me, saying, *Come, you are meant to be here. Let me show you the way.*

I had been to her apartment several times, for lunch and dinner. We talked about life in Italy and a book she would like to write about a Tuscan hill near the village of Bagno a Ripoli, on the outskirts of Florence. Thirty years ago, Kathryn had lived in a villa on that hill when her husband had come to Florence on sabbatical.

Twice, she took me to the hillside: the first time to tell me the history; the second time for me to photograph the locations for a lecture she would be giving. We drove along the old Roman road, through the village, and up a rise to a lone cypress tree that had been planted by the Romans to mark a property boundary. We turned up a blind curve on a dirt road, toward the villa, and stopped at a church, where I stood mesmerized by the panoramic view. The Tuscan countryside below us was a pastoral tapestry of olive groves, bordered by cypress trees, umbrella pines, castle turrets and sprawling villas. In the distance, rising out of the misty spring air, was the Duomo and the steeples of Florence, looking so much like a painting, I could barely believe it was real.

Kathryn took me to a place, below the villa, where olive trees grow on a terraced slope. She told me the terraces had been dug in the twelfth century. Based on her research, she believed Dante used to come there.

Kathryn was struggling with how to structure the book. We brainstormed possible approaches. She was overwhelmed by the task at hand, but I suggested ways she could organize her research materials and map out the story.

One day, we were having coffee and she looked at me. "Where did you come from?" she asked. "I feel like you have dropped into my life to inspire me to write my book."

I smiled. "I feel like I'm floating under a parachute and you're guiding me to my landing spot."

The lease signing took nearly three hours. Sofie had written up the contract, which was only two pages, in English and Italian. It was the first time I had met Elena, an attorney in her mid-30s, who owned the apartment. My earlier meeting had been with her husband, Bernardo. Elena spoke excellent English, which made discussing the issues much easier.

The biggest issue was my visa. I had explained to Sofie, at the start, the problem I had encountered at the consulate. Sofie knew how to cut through the vortex of circular thinking. "I'll charge your apartment security deposit to your credit card and give you a lease signed by the apartment owner," she told me. "And if your visa isn't approved, I'll cancel the lease and return your deposit." In Sofie, I had met my Italian soul sister.

My phone rang as we were wrapping up. I didn't answer because we were close to finishing. I checked my phone on the cab ride back to the hotel, but didn't find a message.

Turns out the call was from Marcello. But I didn't learn that until the next night, my last night in Florence. I called to tell him I had signed the lease. He was happy to hear from me and even happier I would be returning to Florence.

"When are you coming back?" he asked.

"In June—if I get my visa."

"I wanted to see you last night," he said.

"I didn't see a message on my phone."

"We will get you a better phone when you come back to Florence," he said.

The next day I was on my way back to California. As fate would have it, Kathryn and I were on the same flight from Pisa to New York. A wink and a nod from the universe that what was meant to be was happening.

A week later, I returned to the Italian consulate in L.A. and as bad luck would have it, I got Snarky Bitch again.

She looked at me over the top of her glasses and said, "You were here before."

"Yes, I was," I said cheerfully. "In the meantime, I've been to Italy and found an apartment." I handed her the lease agreement. "The lease is in Italian and English, signed by the apartment owner, with a cover letter from the agent who drew up the contract."

Then I handed her a letter from my banker verifying my assets. I not only had the witch's broomstick but her bra and thong as well.

Snarky Bitch was speechless as she flipped through my documents. She looked at the visa application form. "You didn't sign this," she said, pushing the form across the counter.

"That's because the directions say I must sign it in your presence. Isn't that correct?" I asked.

"It is."

I was feeling a bit smug, recalling how she had accused me of not following directions on my previous visit.

"Did you sell your house?" she asked, scrutinizing my bank statement.

"Yes," I replied, though that was none of her business.

"Don't you have anywhere to live?"

"My current residence in Pasadena is at the bottom of the form, below where it says *address*." I knew she was going for broke now, with nothing in her hand.

"Do you have copies of these documents?"

I handed her a set of copies and she pushed them back at me. "You keep them," she said. "How are we going to mail your passport back to you?"

"In this self-addressed stamped envelope," I said. I stuck a few extra stamps on it for good luck and good measure.

"The fee for the visa is $94.30. Exact change," she said.

I gave her $100 and said, "Keep the change."

"I can't," she said brusquely.

I didn't mean she should pocket the change.

"Do you have thirty cents?" she asked.

I had just overpaid the fee by $5, but I opened my wallet and handed her thirty-five cents.

"Where's your appointment confirmation e-mail?" she asked.

"I gave it to him." I pointed to the man, sitting at the reception window, a few feet away from her.

Snarky Bitch retrieved the e-mail and handed it to me. "Write on the back these words," she said. "*I take full responsibility if my passport gets lost in the mail.*"

I was seething inside, as I wrote the words she dictated. But I wasn't going to let her get a rise out of me. When I looked up at her, I saw a flicker of approval in her eyes. I had successfully maneuvered through her labyrinth of trip-wires.

"Give me your phone number," she said. "I'll call you if I have any questions."

I gave her my number, though it was written in ten places on the documents.

"You'll hear back in three to four weeks, maybe sooner," she said.

I walked out of the building and stood on Wilshire Boulevard looking up at the sky. *If I'm meant to go to Italy,* I prayed to the universe, *you need to deal with Snarky Bitch.*

Three weeks later, my passport arrived with an Italian *visto.*

Marcello had been e-mailing me, asking how things were going. He was delighted to hear I had gotten my visa.

In five weeks, I packed up what little I had in my apartment and moved it back into storage. I gave most of my furniture to a consignment store, hoping to make enough to buy a leather sofa in Italy.

I packed and re-packed what I was taking with me to Florence at least ten times. I ended up shipping nine small boxes, books mostly. I stuffed an entire year's worth of clothes, coats and shoes into three big duffel bags. In my carry-on, I packed my laptop, iPod sound dock and camera gear.

My friends threw a surprise party for me two nights before my departure to celebrate my imminent adventure. They were hatching a plan to come visit me—all at once—to continue the party in Florence. They said good-bye with big hugs and good wishes.

One girlfriend said to me, with amazement and admiration, "Honey, you don't grab the bull by the horns. You grab him by the balls."

❧

I arrived in Florence on June 16, four months after I decided I should begin a new life in Italy. My son, Colin, drove me to the airport and blanched when he put the duffel bags on the scale at the check-in counter. Under his breath, he said to me, "Mom, what did you put in these bags?" He had been vigilantly weighing them all week to be sure they were under the weight limit. But the two female agents at the ticket counter were so impressed that I had packed a year's worth of clothes and accessories into three bags that they waived the overage charges. Colin was astounded. "We women stick together," I told him.

I gave him a big hug and a kiss. How our roles had reversed. He was waving good-bye to me this time, as I headed off to start a new chapter of my life.

My carry-on, with its electronic gear, drew attention in Frankfurt. Security pulled me and the bag out of line and took me to a room where they inspected the contents. The agent was friendly and asked what I would be doing in Florence. He was impressed that I was writing a book and knew that Florence would inspire me "like so many other writers," he said.

When I arrived in Florence that evening, Sofie and Elena were waiting at the apartment to greet me. Sofie had brought a young guy to help bring in my luggage and the boxes, which I had shipped to Sofie's office. Elena presented a ring with eight keys and took me on a whirlwind tour of the building to show me which locks they belonged to.

I got my first jolt of culture shock when Sofie explained the limits on my electricity consumption, pre-determined by the utility company for a single person. The apartment's only appliances were a dishwasher, a washing machine and a small fridge with a freezer big enough for a couple of gelato cartons and a few ice cube trays. I didn't have a microwave or a dryer—I had a rusted metal rack on the balcony for drying clothes, sheets and towels.

"If you run the dishwasher and your hair dryer at the same time, you'll lose all power," Sofie warned me.

"You're kidding."

"You can use only one appliance at a time," she said.

Elena showed me a circuit panel on the wall by the front door. "Sometimes you can fix it here."

"But if you use two big appliances at once that exceed your limit," Sofie cautioned, "you'll have to go to the main panel of the building and re-set the meter." The main panel was at street level and had its own special key on the ring.

"It doesn't happen often," Elena assured me.

When they left, I walked around the apartment, afraid to turn on the lights for fear I'd blow a fuse. I desperately needed sleep.

I woke up at about four in the morning. I had fallen asleep wearing ear plugs to block out the traffic noise. Via Tavanti was much busier than I remembered and, as I discovered that first night, is an ambulance corridor to a nearby hospital.

I went to the window of the second bedroom. I looked across the tiled rooftops toward the mountains. I thought I was looking at two church spires against the pre-dawn sky, but they turned out to be cypress trees. In a brief lull from the hum of motorcycles that raced by even at that hour, I heard songbirds chirping in the lone umbrella pine that seemed to grow out of the pavement of the street below. I thought of the grand deodar cedar tree that graced the front yard of the beautiful house that had been my home in Pasadena for twenty-two years. I felt a pang of loss. I had pared the essence of me down to nine small boxes, three duffel bags and a carry-on.

But this was not a day to mourn what I had left behind, I told myself. It was a day to celebrate everything new.

∽

The first e-mail I received was from Marcello: "*Welcome to Florence,*" he wrote. I called him to say I had arrived.

The moment he walked through my front door, we were back where we left off.

He looked me up and down. "I want to squeeze you," he said.

I smiled and pinched his sides as he embraced me. "I want to squeeze you, too."

I showed him around the apartment and we went out on the balcony. He couldn't take his eyes off me.

When we came back inside, I poured wine and we sat down on the sofa. I don't remember what we talked about exactly. I turned toward him at one point, with the sun in my face.

"Your eyes are so blue," he said.

He set his wine glass on the floor. It wasn't quite empty.

"Would you like more wine?" I asked.

"No. I want you."

We went into the bedroom. He helped me take off my top. Then he unfastened my skirt and slid it down over my hips.

I lay down on the bed and held out my hand to him. I'll never forget the look on his face—pure bliss.

4

Italy gone wrong

In the first six days after my arrival, Sofie managed to set up my bank and internet accounts and file the papers necessary for my *permesso di soggiorno*, which is like the Holy Grail in the nether world of Italian immigration. An amazing achievement, considering that great negative force-field known as Italian Bureaucracy.

On the seventh day, Sofie went on vacation. She was gone for only a week. But caca hit the fan. Big time.

Actually, it was more like toilet water, which began spewing from a ruptured pipe connected to one of my bidets. I'd never had a bidet in my life, but now I had two.

I came back from a walk one evening to discover my apartment had no water. I knocked on my neighbor's door. A young woman, who spoke English, answered. She checked her kitchen sink faucet, which was working fine, and then opened the panel in the hallway to the water shut-off valves to our apartments. Hers was on, but mine was off.

The water had been on before I left for my walk. I was a little creeped out that someone had turned it off and not even left a note.

At nine the next morning, all was revealed when my doorbell rang. An elderly woman was peering at my shut-off valve and looking very distressed. I was looking a little disheveled, still in my nightgown.

She didn't introduce herself, but much later I found out her name was Maria Pia. I couldn't understand a thing she said, but I quickly gathered she was my downstairs neighbor as she waved her hands at the heavens. I made the mistake of opening the door all the way, which she took as an invitation to come in and look for the leak. She quickly determined the problem was the bidet in my front bathroom. I tried to call Elena, but all I got was her voicemail. I handed the phone to Maria Pia so she could leave Elena a message. Maria Pia couldn't understand why Elena wasn't talking to her and kept shouting into my cell phone.

I called Marcello, who was still asleep, and apologetically asked him to speak with Maria Pia, who hadn't shut up for a minute since I opened the door. He was able to explain things to both of us, which helped a little. But in the end, Maria Pia threw up her hands, crying "*mamma mia,*" and left.

I ran into the bedroom to get dressed. But minutes later, Mamma Mia Maria Pia was back and she wasn't alone. She had roused her neighbor—a cute twentysomething guy who spoke a little English—from a sound sleep and dragged him to my door, which I had stupidly left ajar. Maria Pia had already entered my apartment and was coming toward my bedroom, where I was starkly naked. I quickly grabbed my robe.

"*Signora?*" she called out.

Her cute neighbor shuffled into my apartment in slippers, boxer shorts and a t-shirt with a serious case of pillow hair, looking like he thought the whole thing was a bad dream. Maria Pia led him into the bathroom and had him on his knees, with his face in the bidet bowl, turning off the valves.

It all ended on a friendly note, with us finally introducing ourselves and me cracking a joke about neighbors meeting in their pajamas. Elena called a little while later to say she had phoned Maria Pia to assure her that a plumber would come on Monday. Marcello called to congratulate me on terrorizing the building. Meanwhile, a water stain was growing on my living room wall just outside the bathroom. I put towels on the floor and moved valuables to higher ground.

The plumber didn't come on Monday, or Tuesday for that matter. He showed up almost an hour late on Wednesday. Elena was fuming, shouting at him on her cell phone. She clicked off and started ranting about how she hates it when people are late and that she could have stayed at the office and gotten more work done.

Elena has a stressful job and is the mother of a 2-year-old. Her husband Bernardo is darling, but according to Elena, he's a traditional Italian male who can't make himself a cup of coffee. And if she's not around to make him coffee, he goes to visit his mother, who will make it for him.

"Would you like a margarita?" I asked her.

"What is a margarita?"

"It's a drink made with ice and lime juice."

"I've never tasted a lime."

The kitchen sink was full of limes and green lemons that I had just squeezed. There's no such thing as limeade in Italy, I discovered to my dismay on my first day in Florence. But I was delighted to find in the liquor aisle that Jose Cuervo is no stranger here.

I cut Elena a thin slice of lime. "They're pretty sour."

She puckered up instantly and spit the lime in the sink.

"I add sugar," I assured her. "And tequila." I showed her the bottle of Jose Cuervo.

"Tekweela," she said phonetically. "What is this?"

"It's made from a plant that's grown in Mexico."

"I don't usually drink alcohol," she said.

"That's okay. I can make it without tequila."

She looked at me and back at Jose. "Why not. I'll try it."

It was the beginning of a wonderful friendship between Elena, Jose and me.

I pulled out my new blender, which I had bought along with an electric juicer and a printer for my computer. An odd combination of items, I admit. But I was learning to distill the needs of life down to the bare essentials.

Elena had never seen a blender. "This is so American!" When I told her its many uses, she started laughing. "No traditional Italian woman would make soup in this thing." She laughed harder when I showed the pictures of soups and dips on the blender box.

She watched intently as I cut a big slice from a frozen block of lime juice that I removed from a plastic bag (Italy doesn't have ziplocks either) stashed in my little freezer. I dumped it in the pitcher, along with ice cubes and a moderate splash of tequila. I ran a slice of lime around the rims of the glasses and then tipped the rims onto a plate of salt.

"Salt?"

"Oh yes. Wait till you taste this."

I made sure that all other appliances were off before I revved the blender, to avoid blowing out the Florence electric grid.

Icy vapors wafted out of the pitcher as I poured our drinks. I perched a slice of lime on the salty rim of Elena's glass.

She looked hesitant.

"*Cin-cin*," I said.

She smiled. "What do you say in English?"

"Cheers."

"Cheers," she said as we clinked glasses.

Elena's love for margaritas began with her very first sip. The taste of the salty-citrus-sweet elixir blew her away. Her eyes opened wide. She saw Jose coming toward her in a flowing poncho and sombrero. It was like a religious epiphany.

By the time Carlo, the plumber, arrived, Elena was in a much better mood. She slurped that margarita down so fast I was afraid to offer her another for fear she wouldn't be able to keep herself upright—or the scooter she rides.

After Carlo left, with a vague promise to return by Friday, Elena invited me for a traditional Italian dinner at her house the following week.

"What may I bring?" I asked.

"Nothing! I will cook Italian dishes for you."

"What about margaritas?"

She got that epiphany look again. "Yes! Margaritas!"

∽

I took a break from juicing limes and lemons and rented a car for a week. I really missed my wheels, L.A. girl that I am.

I was looking forward to taking a day trip out into the Tuscan countryside, but my first destination was IKEA. I had spent two hot afternoons wandering around the Florence train station, where, according to local lore, there was supposed to be a stop for an IKEA shuttle bus. On the second day, after waiting an hour in the blazing sun, I decided to rent a car and drive.

The folks who've designed IKEA's global business model may think they have a slick, efficient operation that can be adapted to any country or culture. But apparently, they didn't consider—or couldn't possibly imagine—what the Italians could do to screw it up.

As soon as I walked in the door, pushing a shopping cart I had picked up at the entrance, I was intercepted by a security guard. I was heading for the elevator to go up to the second floor. "No, no, *signora*. It is not possible," he said, taking the cart from me.

I got into the elevator, which was big enough for three shopping carts, and rode to the second floor, wondering what the big deal was about taking a cart in the elevator.

I discovered that there were no carts on the second floor—just big yellow bags with strap handles. I grabbed a bag and wandered into the sofa department. I sat down on about a dozen sofas, thinking how much I'd like something comfortable to sit on at the apartment. The futon sofa in the living room was low with no armrests and had a deep seat, requiring lots of pillows for back support.

But I had a clairvoyant moment in the IKEA sofa department. I heard a voice—and not in the Scando-babble that IKEA is known for. Nothing like PJÄTTERYD GRÖBY LJUSÅS YSBY FARTSKUN. No, the voice was clearly in English and whispering in my ear: *Don't get heavily invested here.*

I tore my shopping list in half and moved to the desk-and-chair department. Keep focused on the essentials, I told myself. The office furniture area was where I got a full-frontal assault of IKEA Italian-style.

I saw an empty cart. My big yellow bag, which already contained a few sets of sheets and pillowcases, was getting heavy, so I tossed the bag in the cart.

"Not possible," said a female IKEA clerk, shaking her head, undoubtedly thinking *americanos* are such idiots.

"Why it is not possible?" I asked. "It's a big store with big aisles. The IKEA store in Burbank allows carts on the second floor."

She looked at me blankly. She gave me a receipt for the desk and chair I purchased and told me I could collect them in the self-service aisles on the ground floor.

"Do they have carts there?"

Another blank look.

I wandered off with my yellow bag. Pretty soon I had two yellow bags, then three. At that point, I ditched the bags somewhere just before the kids department, which was near the coffee bar where I stopped for refreshments. About an hour later, I met an English couple who had ditched their bags, too. We were both re-tracing our steps through IKEA's trademark labyrinth, trying to find our stashed loot.

I collected my chair at self-service, but couldn't find the desk. I went to the register where I was informed that the desk was at the annex. At most of the IKEA stores I've been to in the U.S., you drive your car up to a loading area that's part of the main building. Not in Italy. You drive a quarter-mile to a warehouse, following signs no bigger than a Swedish meatball.

I parked at the annex and grabbed a dolly outside the entrance. Once again, I was intercepted by a guard.

"Let me guess," I said to him. "It is not possible." The guard smiled and took away the dolly.

I was catching on fast to the perversity of this culture. Nothing is possible. Everything is impossible and the sooner you accept that, the better.

I went to the register with three sheets of paper I had been given in the office furniture department to which two receipts had been stapled by the cashier who had sent me to the annex. (Generating paper is a favorite Italian pastime.)

The woman at the counter ignored me. I looked around for a ticket machine to get in the queue and saw the English couple roll-ing their eyes at me. There is no ticket to take. You wait for the kid who's in charge of the dollies to give you a number—a number he chooses at random and scribbles on a scrap of paper. I looked at the English couple and rolled my eyes.

In a little while, the kid came back with the top to my desk.

"Where are the legs?" I asked.

"Self-service," he said, pointing in the direction of the main store, a quarter-mile away.

"You're joking."

He smiled. "I no joke you."

I heard the Brits giggling.

I muscled the dolly out to the parking lot, threw the desk top into the back of the car and drove like a maniac to the main building. I marched into the store, ready to take hostages, and found the desk-leg aisle, which was roped off with a sign that said, loosely translated, "you will die of old age waiting for Luigi to help you."

There was a crowd gathered by the sign. No one seemed concerned that Luigi was nowhere around. They greeted each other with affectionate embraces. They probably hadn't seen each other since they walked in the store eight hours earlier. I looked at my watch. Five hours. I had been at IKEA for five flipping hours!

I went off to find Luigi, who was two aisles over, and gave him my papers. "I need the legs to my desk *now*," I told him.

If he sensed the urgency in my voice, he didn't show it. He shuffled halfway down the desk-leg aisle, then suddenly turned around and came back.

He pointed to my shopping cart. He didn't need to say anything. Of course, it was not possible for him to get the legs without my cart.

With the legs in the cart, I raced out the exit. Before I got to the curb, I heard a man yell, "*Signora!*"

I turned around. It was another security guard, who wanted to check my receipt. Apparently, the check-out girl, who had given me the receipts for the desk and legs, hadn't actually charged me for them. The guard, who escorted me back into the store, and the store manager, who rang up my final receipt, were sympathetic when I told them I thought I was having a nightmare and would one of them please wake me up.

I got lost on the way home. It was my first day driving in Florence. I quickly decided that the only way to navigate a traffic circle in Italy is to totally ignore scooters and motorcycles—they're on their own in my rules of the road.

When I finally pulled into the parking space in my apartment building's underground garage, I put my head on the steering wheel and prayed for mercy.

I made three trips, up the elevator, from the garage to my apartment, my purchases stacked precariously in a cart I had shanghaied from the supermarket next door.

I was just tucking in for the night when someone buzzed my apartment from the front entrance to the building. I had a high-tech TV screen that shows who's buzzing, but no one appeared on the screen—until just before the screen went dark. I briefly saw the profile of a young woman with dark hair.

I thought it was a little odd. But I was so exhausted, I quickly fell into bed.

At 11:15, my doorbell rang. I looked through the peephole and saw a young woman with dark hair. I opened the door a crack. I didn't recognize her at first, but I soon realized she was my neighbor whom I had met during the water-valve caper.

"Do you have a Volvo?" she asked in English. Apparently she had been downstairs buzzing everyone in the building to find out who belonged to my rented Volvo.

"Yes," I said.

"You're in my parking space."

"I don't think so," I replied. Sofie, the real estate agent, had shown me my assigned spot.

"It is my space, Rebecca." She was getting testy. "I have had that space for five years. I have papers to prove it." Italians have papers to prove everything.

"Can we figure this out tomorrow? I'm really tired. There are lots of empty spaces in the garage."

Her nostrils flared. "You must move your car, Rebecca. Now."

The conversation see-sawed for a few minutes, then she erupted into an Italian rant. When she finished, she said in English, "I give you five minutes. Then I call police." It was my first experience with an Italian on tilt.

I shut the door, turned off the lights and dove into bed. For the next thirty minutes, she stood at my door, pushing the buzzer almost non-stop, and screaming "Re-BEC-ca! Re-BEC-ca!" And when she wasn't pushing the buzzer, she was pounding her fists on the door.

Her tantrum finally ended about midnight.

The next morning, I called Elena and told her the whole story.

"Oh no, Rebecca," she said. "Your space is on level two, not level one."

Right space, wrong floor. *Shit, shit, shit.* I quickly got dressed and grabbed the car keys. I was relieved to see the Volvo hadn't been splattered with animal feces. I drove around the garage trying to find the ramp to the lower level. There were no arrows, no indication of a lower level. And when I found the ramp, hidden behind a dividing wall, it took me two tries to maneuver the car around the wall. The ramp was actually a one-lane blind curve. There were red lights in place to warn you that a head-on collision was imminent, but of course, the lights weren't working. As I've mentioned, Italians are stingy with electricity.

When I got back upstairs, I wrote The Screamer a note on a post-it sticker that said: *"I have moved my car. Sorry for the confusion. – Rebecca"* I thought about adding, *"P.S. You might consider enrolling in an anger management program."* But I restrained myself.

I tiptoed to her door, stuck the post-it and ran back into my apartment.

Of course, a story like this doesn't end there.

Marcello was over a few nights later. We were saying goodnight when he noticed the front door was ajar. "Look, the door is open." On his way to the elevator, he turned to me and said, "Make sure you close that tight." And I did.

The next morning, I came out of the bedroom and looked down the hallway. My front door was wide open, as far as it would go. I couldn't move for a minute, wondering if there was someone in the apartment. I walked toward the door, ready to run if I heard a noise. Nothing. No one.

That night was my Italian dinner at Elena and Bernardo's. He picked me up so that I could bring the blender and margarita fixings. We had a great evening and laughed a lot about the events of the past week. I wasn't laughing when Elena informed me that when she called the building manager about getting a plumber, his secretary had told her that a man from Palermo had called to complain that someone living in Elena's apartment had parked in his daughter's spot every night for a week.

"It was only one night," I said.

"That's what I told her." Elena had never met The Screamer, but she said, "I really want to talk to her about her behavior."

"I think we should leave her alone," I said. "I don't want to see you on the eleven o'clock news."

Elena thought that was funny.

I didn't tell Elena about the open door until the next day. She sent Bernardo over to look at the door latch, thinking it might be out of alignment. The latch was perfectly aligned.

I opened the door all the way. "This is how it was when I woke up."

"That's so strange," Bernardo said.

"Have you ever had trouble with this door before?"

"Never."

The writer-in-me concluded it was a message from Papa Palermo: *Don't mess with my daughter or her parking space.* She suddenly was inspired to write a treatment for *The Godfather: Part 4.*

I sent a mailing to my e-pals titled "Tales from Tavanti," about my ruptured bidet pipe and the maniacal Mafia princess living next door.

The response was incredible. The group consensus was that I should invite her over for a margarita, heavy on the tequila and whatever else I had in the liquor cabinet or under the kitchen sink. That scenario could end well—or not.

෧᧍

A few weeks after I arrived, I was at Piazza del Duomo, walking gingerly across the ancient cobblestones. Suddenly, the bells of the *campanile* began to chime. I took my eyes away from my feet for a split second, to look heavenward as church bells pealed, when my right foot twisted hard. How fair is *that*?

My ankle was sore and swollen for a few days. About a week later, as I was walking across my living room, my ankle buckled. The pain was so sharp I could barely breathe. I called my friend Susanna at the hotel where I had stayed, and she suggested that we go to the emergency room at Ospedale Santa Maria Nuova, a few blocks from the hotel. "I'll tell them you're a tourist," she said. "If you moan a lot, maybe you won't have to pay." Italians get free healthcare and apparently, so do moaning tourists.

I got to the hospital a few minutes before Susanna and read the plaque outside the ER entrance. The hospital was founded in 1288 by the father of Dante's beloved Beatrice. Her nursemaid is buried there, in The Cloister of the Bones. I felt like I was channeling J.K. Rowling.

Susanna arrived on her bike and escorted me down a long hallway. By the time we got to the reception desk, I knew we were time-traveling. They put me in a wheelchair—actually, an iron chair covered with blood-red leather—that looked like a sanitarium relic from the 1800s. An orderly wheeled me—on two wheels at the turns—to the X-ray chamber that I'm sure had once been a tomb. No bones there, but next door was the morgue where Leonardo da Vinci had performed dissections for his anatomy studies.

The X-ray equipment looked as antique as the chair I was told to sit on. The technician propped my left foot on a wooden box. She centered my ankle in the crosshairs of an "X" projected from the machine that hung from the ceiling. I was about to ask why she was bothering with my left ankle, but she disappeared into the control room. She soon re-emerged and cheerfully announced, "*Finito.*" I shook my head and pointed to my swollen right foot, as Leonardo rolled in his grave.

The medic-in-charge determined it was a bad sprain and sent me to the Mummy Wrapper. He was so adept at folding medicated gauze around the tender contours of my foot that I'm sure he had wrapped the bodies of pharaohs in another life.

I didn't moan or even whimper, so I had to pay for services rendered. I got a bill called a "ticket" for €60—about $90—that covered the gauze wrap and the X-ray (they didn't charge for the one of the wrong foot). The ER administrator apologized profusely for illuminating me unnecessarily; the medic-in-charge just shrugged her shoulders.

Susanna wheeled me to a cash machine where I inserted my ticket along with my cash payment. The machine spit out my receipt and change. And that is how medical billing works in Italy. In the morass of Italian bureaucracy, there is a system that is simple and efficient and dare I say, very enlightening.

༄

With my foot wrapped in gauze and hobbling on a cane, I ventured forth to the Ufficio Immigrazione on the appointed day of my *permesso* interview.

When the taxi pulled up outside the immigration office I knew I was screwed. It was only 9 a.m. and there were already dozens of people milling about in the street. The cab driver looked at me sympathetically and said, "It's Italy."

"Will you come back for me tonight?" I asked. He laughed.

Just past the front door, I gasped. But the air was so foul I quickly exhaled; the word "fuck" passed my lips.

If I were to write a modern-day version of Dante's *Inferno*, the fiery bowels of Hell would be in that airless cavernous hall. At least a thousand people, pressed together in lines and on benches, looked half-dead from the heat and the stench, which was a rancid mix of body odor and urine, probably from dirty diapers, though there were suspicious stains on the filthy floor.

I presented my papers to the official at the ticket machine. My appointment time was 9:11. Not 9:10 or 9:15. The official handed me my number. I looked up at the board. There were 361 people ahead of me.

Amazingly, standing nearby was a woman I knew—a 25-year-old American who worked for a Florence real estate agent and had shown me a few apartments during my spring visit. She was engaged to an Italian and had to get through five stages of this crap, within ninety days, before they could marry—and they were totally at the mercy of the bureaucracy. I told her to pay someone with connections to get it done.

"I know someone in Napoli who could do it," she said.

"Do it," I told her. "If that doesn't work out, I know a guy in Palermo."

I found an empty bench and some air in an adjoining room and sat down to wait my turn.

A few weeks earlier, I had waited in line for an hour-and-a-half at the post office just to get an appointment time for my *permesso* interview. After a half-hour my number was called. But when I got to the window, the female clerk shook her head and tore up my "P" ticket. She sent me back to the ticket machine to get an "A" or "C" ticket, I can't remember which. I waited another half-hour. When my new number was called, I was back at the same window, facing the same woman, who smiled at me sadistically. She didn't speak English and sent me down the row to a colleague who did.

He looked at my papers and said, "But you didn't copy all the pages of your passport."

"The only pages I didn't copy are the blank ones," I said politely.

"We need copies of the blank ones, too," he insisted.

I thought he was going to send me away, but instead he offered to copy the blank pages for me and told me to have a seat.

Twenty-five minutes later, undoubtedly after a cigarette and an espresso, he returned with copies of the blank pages of my passport.

But this level of Hell, at the Ufficio Immigrazione, was far worse. Although I was seated, I couldn't elevate my foot and my ankle was swelling like a puff pastry. Finally, at 11:42, my number was called. I hobbled to the window and slipped my papers under the glass partition. The clerk pushed them back at me, with another ticket—this time, an "H" ticket. H for Hell, of course. In English, he explained that the "A" ticket I was given at the door two-and-a-half hours earlier was for the first line. Now I must wait in another line. The number on my "H" ticket was in the 800s.

"I have been waiting almost three hours." I held up my cane and pointed to my bandaged foot. "I'm in pain. I don't know how much longer I can wait."

He told me to meet him at Window 16, at the other end of the hall. I threaded my way through the throng. Some stood motionless, like statues, clutching their papers. The benches were packed, people leaning on each other for support. The far end of the hall was very hot. Babies cried. Their tears were for all of us.

The clerk was waiting for me at Window 16. "The PC is dead," he said. "I don't know when will be working again. Sit down. I call you."

I glanced at my watch. It was noon. I looked at him, tempted to say, *"You're lying. You're going to lunch."* An Italian is never late for a meal.

The clerk disappeared and I walked back through the hall and out the front door.

"I hate this country," I said under my breath. At least a hundred people were in line outside the building, waiting to get a ticket for their ride into hell.

Fuck the *permesso,* I told myself. If they kick me out of the country, I'll gladly go.

∾

The next day, I girded myself for battle with an Italian cell-phone company. The sales clerk at the store where I had purchased the phone assured me that English instructions were in the box. It was a condition of the sale—I was buying a sophisticated phone and wanted to know how to use it. How demanding of me.

There wasn't time for me to open the box at the store because they were closing for lunch. Ten minutes later, in the lobby of my bank across the street, I opened the box and discovered the 177-page manual was in Italian only. The bank was also closing for lunch, so I was out on the street, once again swearing at the universe.

When I informed the store clerk that I would be returning the phone and canceling the contract because she had misinformed me, she said nothing could be done because I had already signed the contract. The phone used to come with English instructions, she said. She then informed me I would owe more than $500 in penalty fees if I canceled the contract.

I e-mailed my banker, Isabella, and told her the whole story. The phone company would be debiting monthly charges from my checking account and I wanted her to stop the payments. She suggested we meet at her office, across the street from the phone store.

"I can stop the payments as you request," Isabella told me. "But I'm afraid the phone company will make problems for you. In Italy, customers don't have many rights. You might need to get legal help, but that will be expensive—maybe more expensive than paying the penalty for canceling the contract."

I was determined to prevail. I once wrote a letter to the president of Pontiac after I was defrauded by a Pontiac dealership in New Jersey, and, as a result, the scumbag owner almost lost his franchise. I could easily take on a third-rate Italian cell phone company.

"Please stop the payments," I said with resolve. "I will send a letter of complaint to the CEO of the company."

Isabella's eyes widened. "What a good idea. Is that what customers do in America?"

I explained how consumer watchdogs run rabid in the U.S. and how credit card companies fight customer disputes with merchants all the time. "There's a saying in the U.S.—the customer is always right. Always."

Isabella was awed. "Come back and tell me everything that happens."

I crossed the street, steeled for combat. The clerk, named Lucia, apparently saw me coming and ignored me when I entered the store. She murmured something in Italian to her colleague, who was on his cell phone. He looked at me as if to say, "What do you want?"

"I'm returning this phone," I said, placing the phone box on his side of the counter, which was about a foot lower than the customer side of the counter.

Lucia murmured something else in Italian and he put the box up on my side of the counter.

"I am returning this phone," I said firmly, but calmly, and moved the box back to his side of the counter.

He returned the box to my side of the counter. This obviously was a battle of wills that eventually was going to wear the label off the box. Incidentally, the label was in English.

Lucia was becoming agitated, so I took a seat, with the box still on the counter, and waited for the fireworks to start. In the end, after much hand waving and paper throwing, I got my way— thanks largely to Sofie, who acted as translator and negotiator, by phone. Sofie had been with me at the shop when I bought the phone and was a key witness in my defense.

But the terms of the treaty weren't simple. First, I had to send a registered letter to the phone company asking permission to cancel the contract. Within fifteen days of receiving a letter of acknowledgment from the company, I then could return the phone. But if I waited more than fifteen days, the phone was mine.

"The conditions are very specific," Sofie told me as Lucia pounded her computer keyboard with a vengeance, loudly speaking every word she typed, shrilly trilling her R's.

"Sofie, my mother is unwell," I said. "I'm going back to the U.S. soon and won't be returning until September. I'm not going to stand in line at the post office for an hour to mail a registered letter or worry about returning a phone, which I'm trying to return today, within fifteen days of receiving a letter from the company giving me permission to cancel a contract that I am voiding because I was sold a product based on false information."

Sofie heard the hardness and exasperation in my voice. "I will take care of this, Rebecca. You must be with your family and not worry about this."

"You're an angel," I told her.

I hobbled out of the store, carrying that damn phone box, and went back to the bank, where Isabella was waiting for me.

"They will cancel the contract," I said.

She looked stunned. "Really?"

Isabella promised to keep an eye on my account to be sure the company didn't debit a penalty fee. I thanked her for her help and kindness.

I left the bank and noticed a church next door. The doors were wide open. I could see the flicker of candles inside. Maybe I should send up a prayer of thanks for this moral victory, I thought.

I was wearing a modestly cut sleeveless top. In Rome the previous year, on a boiling hot day, I had been barred from entering a Catholic church because my arms were bare. The guard had hissed at me, "Your body. Your body." As I was about to enter a church in San Gimignano (in a sleeveless top on another hot day), the guard at the door kindly had asked me to cover myself with an aqua blue diaphanous wrap. It could be tied at the neck to cover bare shoulders or at the waist, to hide bare legs. I secured the ties in a jaunty knot, but not quite tight enough. My flowing cape was seductively off-the-shoulder. I giggled at an American guy in shorts who was wearing two wraps—one as a skirt and the other as a sarong over his polo shirt.

But no one intercepted me as I stepped inside the church beside the bank. I saw a woman in a sleeveless blouse kneeling at the prayer rail with her dog. I quietly took a seat near the back of the sanctuary.

It was noon; the church bells chimed. I was thinking about a footnote I had read in my college copy of Dante's *Inferno* about why heathens who were born before Christ were condemned to purgatory because they worshipped false gods. One could argue in their defense that Christ hadn't been born yet, so what were they to do? The footnote said they were condemned because they couldn't *imagine* anything better.

So I was thinking how most of Italy will end up in purgatory in my Dante rewrite, for not imagining a better way of doing things, when I heard a cell phone ring behind me. I thought, how rude to come into a place of worship with your cell phone on. I turned around and who was standing behind me but a priest—a bald, elderly man in a long black robe with cape and hood. He was scrolling through text messages or stock quotes on his phone and said to me, "*chiuso*," and pointed to the door.

Of course. It was lunch time. The church was closed. Never mind that I hadn't finished my prayers. He didn't seem to care whether I had finished or not. He didn't care if I was sad or in pain. No, he kept scrolling on his phone as I collected my stuff—including my bag with the phone box—and hobbled out of the sanctuary on my cane.

He never even looked at me. When I stepped outside, I turned around and stared at him. But he never gave me a glance as he locked the door.

5

Marcello

In those early weeks of my growing despair, Marcello was my source of solace. He'd listen empathetically and tell me he understood my exasperation.

One night we were making margaritas. He was standing behind me, rubbing my bottom, as I revved the blender.

"You're such a good helper," I told him, turning to kiss his cheek.

"Don't get distracted," he teased. "I'm thirsty."

"We need to move this way," I said, pointing toward the fridge.

"Okay," he said, his hands firmly on my hips, as we shuffled sideways together.

I pulled a plastic bag of Italian-style ice cubes out of the freezer. "How do you get these out of the bag?" I asked. The bag had individual compartments for each cube.

"Like this." He started popping them out one at a time.

"No," I said in disbelief. "The package shows that you cut the corner and peel back the plastic. They should all fall out at once."

"Really?"

I was near the snapping point. "Marcello, why is life here so difficult?"

"You come from a culture where everything is easy and convenient. I understand your frustration," he said. "People hold to the old ways here."

I confessed to him that I wasn't sure I would unpack the boxes I had shipped from California. They were still stacked in the second bedroom, unopened. "Every day I talk myself out of going home."

He watched me salt the rims of the glasses. "You should be a bartender," he said.

I poured our drinks. We sat back on the sofa and clinked glasses. We sipped and then kissed.

"Put me out of my misery," I whispered to him.

And he did.

◌

Marcello helped me perfect my margarita recipe. I'd spoon-feed him samples from the blender pitcher as I gradually added sugar to the mix.

"I like my drinks sour," he informed me early on. "But I don't like sour women." Then he kissed me with his salty lips and said, "You're *very* sweet."

One night after we had made love, he asked, "Did you imagine that one day you'd be in bed with the man you met at the carousel?"

"No."

He smiled. "I never imagined you would enjoy sex so much."

"I enjoy sex when I feel passion."

"You're an artist," he said. "You need to feel passion."

We enjoyed each other so much one night, a side rail of the bed fell off. Marcello repaired it before he left and promised to come back with a drill to assemble the desk I bought at IKEA.

True to his word, he showed up a few days later with a drill. I had a pitcher of margaritas ready, but he didn't want to start drinking until the job was finished.

It was a hot summer's night and we were both drenched with sweat by the time the last screw was in place. The directions were so full of errors that he had to screw and un-screw the desk supports three times.

Getting the screws into the pre-drilled holes was a problem. I tried to be supportive, as he struggled with a particularly obstinate screw. "It's just like sex, darling. You just have to wiggle it into the hole."

"But there are so many holes here," he said, a bit overwhelmed.

He heroically finished the assembly, saying "fuck" only once.

I thought it was sweet of him not to head for the blender as soon as the desk was upright. He crawled under the desk to make sure the legs were even and at the right height.

"Do you want it higher?" he asked as I set my laptop on the desk.

I sat down and looked out the window at the sun setting over the mountains. I smiled at him. "It's absolutely perfect." It was the first moment since my arrival that I felt like I was back in my own skin.

"Good," he said, pleased. "Let's start drinking."

All that screwing had put us in the mood. There were moments of tenderness in our lovemaking that night that made me feel closer to him. After all, we had survived a 20-page IKEA manual with our friendship intact.

❧

One night, after the first pour from the pitcher, I regaled him with the tale of my ER visit.

"The receptionist asked me in English if I was still having periods," I told Marcello.

He looked puzzled.

"She wanted to know because of X-rays and pregnancy."

"X-rays cause pregnancy?" he asked incredulously.

Between spasms of laughter, I said, "They won't X-ray a woman if she thinks she might be pregnant."

"Of course not," he said, sipping his margarita.

"I told her I wasn't having periods anymore but was flattered she thought I might be young enough to get pregnant," I continued. "She looked at me closely and said, 'But your face is so young. You have no wrinkles.'"

Marcello nodded. "Your face is young. You look about 42." He stroked my arm. "You have beautiful skin."

"Good genes," I said. "My mother is almost 80 and has gorgeous skin."

Marcello pondered this for a moment, then asked, "So how old are you?"

"I said I'd tell you my age on the tenth date."

"We've had more than ten dates."

"Or did I say the 110th date?"

Marcello laughed.

"You're 48, right?" I asked.

"Yes."

"I'm older than you," I confessed.

"Really?"

I didn't want to reveal the extent of the gap. "I'll have to keep you away from my purse so you can't look at my driver's license."

He smiled, still stroking my arm.

Later when we were making love, he whispered, "So you're my older woman."

The first time we had sex, I asked if he had lost his virginity to an older woman.

"How did you know that?" he replied.

"I don't think it's that uncommon," I said.

He said he was 15 and she was in her 30s. "She was kissing me down there and I couldn't understand what she was doing," he told me.

"You just wanted to do it," I said.

"Exactly."

❧

We were folded in each other's arms one night, my head on his shoulder. His hand was resting on his chest and I slipped my fingers through his.

"Have you ever noticed how hands have a language of their own?" I said.

"It's true."

"That night as we walked back to the hotel, I can't remember what we were talking about, but I remember the conversation between our hands," I said.

Marcello smiled. "I do, too."

"I was nervous. I was thinking, we're not just going out for a drink, we're going back to my hotel."

"I wasn't nervous," he said with such sincerity in his voice. I looked at him wondering if he could be any more adorable.

"When you took my hand and our fingers did this…" I slid my fingers snugly into his. "I thought, this feels good. We're a good fit. And I squeezed your hand."

"I remember that," he said.

He held my hand to his chest for a long time.

❧

Our trysts continued for about six weeks. We never went out. We had sex and margaritas at my place.

We were in the habit of talking every few days. After the debacle with the cell-phone store, I had to change my phone number, which I had e-mailed to him. A week went by and I didn't hear from him. Maybe he hadn't received the message. So I sent him another e-mail, saying, *"You've been very quiet. Is everything ok?"*

I didn't get a reply, which I thought was strange, so later that day I called him. He said he hadn't been feeling well from the heat and had been working on the renovation of his apartment. I told him I would be traveling soon and he asked when I was leaving. "I'll call you one of these days," he said.

One of these days. It's okay to say, "One of these days, I want to visit the Grand Canyon." But when you're talking to a woman you've been having sex with and you haven't called her in a week, telling her you'll call her *one of these days* is bad form in my book. Marcello knows a lot of American slang, but he's not a native English speaker and maybe didn't realize the impact of that phrase. I was trying not to over-react.

Two days later, at 9:30 on a Saturday night, he called. It sounded like he was at a bar or a café. I could hear people talking in the background. I wasn't sure if he was waiting for an invite, but I didn't ask him to come over.

"Maybe we could get together tomorrow night," he said. "I'd really like a margarita."

Then he asked, "Is your last name Brickell? There was that singer in the early '90s named Edie Brickell. I think she married Paul Simon. She was really good. I just wondered if you were related."

We'd had sex at least ten times and he still didn't know my last name. I thought it odd that he was even thinking about my last name. I pictured him at a bar scrolling through his phone contacts.

He was on the B's. The night was yet young. "No," I said to Marcello. "My name is Bricker." And then I spelled it for him.

∽

Marcello showed up the next night a few minutes before eight. We kissed as he walked in the door. He was amorous and relaxed. But I could feel myself pulling back a little.

He had brought some movies to download on my laptop, which he did. At one point, he came over to the kitchen counter, where I was making margaritas. He stood close to me, with his hand on my bottom. I didn't respond and he went back to the sofa.

We talked for a while, then watched the beginning of a movie he had brought called *Un americano a Roma (An American in Rome)*, made in 1954 by Dino De Laurentis and Carlo Ponti, the Italian producer who famously married Sophia Loren. It's about a young Italian guy, living in Rome, who loves everything American. It's one of Marcello's favorite movies. It's very funny, at least what I saw of it.

About twenty minutes into the film, Marcello turned off the laptop. "You can see the rest later," he said, leaning over to kiss me. His hand was moving up under my skirt. The skirt was soon on the floor by the bed.

Our passion that night was raw and intense. As he brought me to a climax, Marcello whispered, "C'mon you fucking slut."

The room was dark, except for the flickering light of a few candles. I closed my eyes and turned my face away from him. As I lay there, my heart pounding, I could feel my eyes burn with tears. Don't cry, I told myself. But my heart hurt. I felt cut to the quick.

"Are you all right?" he asked.

"I can't believe what you just said to me."

"Come on," he said dismissively. "I like to talk dirty during sex. I've called you that before."

"I've never heard you call me that."

"I'm sorry. I won't say it again."

I thought, there isn't going to be an "again."

A war of emotions raged inside me. *You fucking slut* was ringing in my ears. Part of me wanted to rail at him and kick him out of my life. But, as had been true in the internal battles I had endured lately, the writer-in-me prevailed: *"If this is the last time you're going to see this man, you'd better ask him all the questions we want answers to."*

I took a deep breath to quell my anger and wrapped myself in the bed sheet.

Marcello reached for his margarita on the night table and settled back against the pillows. "Tell me the recipe again." He took a sip. "I want to make these for my mother."

His mother? I suddenly felt like I was in a really bad Italian movie.

Reciting the recipe had a strange calming effect on me. I began: "You need twenty-five fluid ounces of juice."

"I'll have to convert that on my calculator."

"If you buy a blender like mine, the pitcher is marked with milliliters and fluid ounces," I said.

"So it's twenty-two limes, right?"

"About. It depends on how big and juicy they are."

"And if I can't find that many limes, I use about six limes and the rest lemons," he said.

"That will work. The more limes the better."

"More limes the better, for the taste."

"Add three espresso cups of sugar. Not a regular cup measure. Use a little espresso cup." I didn't have measuring cups in my Italian kitchen, so I improvised with an espresso cup.

"What about the tequila. How much?" he asked.

"As much as you'd like. But maybe you should be careful with your mom." Marcello's mother is 85.

"You don't know my mom," he said. "She makes her own grappa and she's always complaining it's not strong enough. She makes her own limoncello, too."

"Mmm, limoncello," I said.

"I'll bring you some of her limoncello. She makes the best."

I think I would like Marcello's mother. From what I know of her, we have a lot in common. We both married late and had only one child, in our mid-30s, and we both like to sing, sew, socialize, grow roses and make stiff drinks. I was imagining the conversation I might have with her when I remembered there were a few pressing questions I wanted to ask her son. The writer-in-me was sitting on the edge of the bed, pen and pad poised.

Although Marcello sometimes mentioned past girlfriends, I didn't know much about his history with women. I wondered if he'd always avoided commitment or whether something had happened along the way that had turned him into a Casanova.

There was no way to ease into this conversation, so I took the direct approach. "Did you think, as a young man, you would ever marry?" I asked him, trying to sound nonchalant. "I mean, were you open to that or did you think you'd always be single?"

Marcello didn't seem surprised by the question or the odd timing of it. "I wasn't very successful with girls," he said. "I was shy and couldn't get girls to notice me." But eventually, he told me, he learned how to flirt and his luck changed. "I was 25 when I fell in love for the first time."

"What's the longest relationship you've ever had?"

"Two years." He looked at me a bit sheepishly. "That's it. Two years."

"Have you ever been engaged?"

"No," he said. "We don't have engagements like you do in America. We don't have the big proposal with the ring and the long engagement and the wedding planning. It's very different here. If you're in a relationship, you talk about living together or having a baby. You come to a decision about wanting a life together. I hear these American women talk about the marriage proposal like it's some big event."

I didn't want to get derailed into a discussion about the prenuptial customs of our cultures. I kept on topic.

"So was there ever a woman in your life that you thought about marrying?"

"There was one. She was pretty, the way I like. Very intelligent. I love intelligent women." He paused for a moment. "I regret…" He didn't finish the sentence.

I wouldn't have guessed Marcello had regrets about a woman who got away—or more likely, one he let go of.

"Have you ever lived with a woman?"

"Never."

"I've lived alone so long now that I wonder if I could ever live with someone again," I said. "I've lived with my son, but it's different when you're sharing space with a partner. The older we get…"

"The more damaged we are."

"And the more we're set in our ways," I said, intrigued that he had said "damaged."

"Little things annoy you," he added.

"There are no little things. "

"You're right. There are no little things," he said.

"They may seem little, but when you add them up at the end of the day, they're big."

And then I started telling Marcello about my affair with Loran. I don't know why I digressed. But we were having a moment of consensus and I wanted to reiterate my point with an example.

"Five years ago, I met a man in Paris and we started having an affair."

Marcello was instantly interested. "Were you divorced?" There was surprise in his voice, as if the possibility of me cheating on my husband went against what he knew to be true about me.

"Yes. I had been divorced for several years." I sat up for a moment and adjusted the sheet around me. "I learned a lesson about the dark side of travel romance."

Marcello smiled, as if he knew what I was about to say.

"You're in a different culture. You feel free, like you're a different person, with no constraints," I said.

"Yes, yes." He was relating, totally.

"But if you try to bring that relationship home, it's a disaster. Especially if you're from different cultures."

"He was French?"

"He was a French citizen. But actually he was Kurdish, born in Iraq."

"Was he Muslim?" More surprise.

"No, he wasn't religious. Yes, he grew up in a Muslim culture, but he wasn't Muslim," I said.

"Anyway, he came to visit me in Pasadena, about a year after we met. It was awful. Little things quickly became big things. We'd go to the grocery store: I'd put something in the cart and he'd take it out, saying, 'We don't need this.' We had so many control issues. I was relieved when he left. It was a nightmare. I should have seen it coming."

What Marcello said next has re-played in my mind over and over ever since: "You see what you want to see and you ignore what you don't want to see." Truer words were never spoken, certainly not by him.

I looked at Marcello in the candlelight. "It doesn't take long in a relationship before you see someone's true colors," I said. "You know in the first couple of months, even sooner."

"I don't think you can tell that soon."

Marcello got out of bed and put on his underwear. "I admit I'm chauvinistic. But compared with the Middle Eastern guys I know, I'm a feminist. I don't want you to take this the wrong way, but some women are really stupid. They don't see what's happening around them. Their boyfriends or husbands cheat on them. They don't want to see it. I was talking to the girlfriend of a friend of mine recently and she was telling me how she hates guys who cheat. I nudged the guy sitting next to me. When she left, I told him, 'I give her boyfriend the key to my apartment twice a week so he can screw other women.'"

Marcello was flying his colors high.

And then he said, "You know, sometimes I think women like men to abuse them. I don't mean physically abuse them." He put his hands to his chest. "But I think they like men to treat them badly."

Marcello went into the bathroom. I threw off the sheet and jumped out of bed. I pulled my bathrobe from the armoire and wrapped it around me as Marcello came back into the room.

"I have something I need to say to you," I said. My anger was rising.

"Okay."

"I don't like the way things are going here. You call me when you're horny, when you want sex and margaritas."

Marcello looked stunned.

"I don't do booty calls. And that's what this is feeling like to me." I took a really deep breath to keep my voice from shaking. "I have never been spoken to the way you spoke to me during sex tonight. Never. By anyone."

"I'm sorry. I didn't know it would upset you so much." He was tucking his shirt into his jeans. "You should hear things I've said to my best lover."

Best lover?

"Rebecca, I don't love you. I like you as a friend." He zipped up his pants. "I'm just being honest with you."

I could tell he had thrown that dart many times. It almost made me laugh. In the back of my reeling brain, I could hear Tina Turner singing *what's love got to do with it*? Love had nothing to do with this. This was all about R-E-S-P-E-C-T. Cue Aretha.

And then, as I walked out of the bedroom, Marcello said, "But you make great margaritas."

The writer-in-me dropped her pen.

I went directly to the front door of my apartment and opened it wide, waiting for Marcello to emerge from the living room, where apparently he was checking to make sure he hadn't left anything behind. Earlier in the evening, he had removed a crucifix necklace that he'd been wearing when we started undressing each other on the sofa. As I unbuttoned his shirt, I slid the cross around to the back of his neck and said, "I can't look at this when I'm undressing you."

I was at the front door, still waiting for him, when I realized the belt to my robe was still on the hanger in the armoire. I went back into the candlelit bedroom and grabbed the belt as Marcello approached the bedroom door.

"Where are you?" he asked.

"I'm in here," I said, cinching the belt tight.

He walked into the room and I walked past him into the hall-way. He followed me to the open front door. I stood aside to let him pass. He turned and kissed me on the cheek and said good-night. As soon as he crossed the threshold, I reached for the door knob. I caught a glimpse of him turning around to look at me. He had his hand on the pocket of his shirt, maybe to be sure the cru-cifix was there.

It was just a glimpse because I quickly shut the door.

6

Tom

After Marcello left that night, I called Nancy and told her everything. I e-mailed Tom a brief message before I went to bed: "Marcello came over…and it wasn't good."

Tom, Nancy and I shared the intimate details of our daily lives. Tom and Nancy have known each other for ten years. I met Tom when he came to visit Nancy during my stay with her in Berlin the previous fall. Although I had known him for less than a year, I felt like we'd been friends for a long time.

The next morning, Tom called early and wanted to know every detail. Tom is gay, funny and good looking—a lot like the guy, played so well by Rupert Everett, who's Julia Robert's devoted friend in *My Best Friend's Wedding*. He's her confidante, her shoulder to cry on, the dispenser of sound advice and sage wisdom, who at one point tells her: "It's amazing the clarity that comes with psychotic jealousy."

During my first months in Florence, Tom became my one-man Greek Chorus, except that he's New Jersey Italian. He totally gets Italian culture because he has lived it, breathed it, eaten it, rejected it, tolerated it, embraced it. Day in and out, he so patiently explained the world I felt so lost in.

Tom was quiet as I told him the story: "He was bringing me to a climax and he said, 'c'mon you…'" For a second, I couldn't finish the sentence. "He called me a fucking slut." I could feel the soreness inside my chest.

"I'm sorry." Tom has a big heart that wraps around you.

"Marcello has told me about his sex fantasies—they're basically whore fantasies," I said. "Maybe it's the sexual repression of the Catholic culture. Maybe it's what it takes for a 48-year-old man to rev his engine. Fantasies are your private world where you can imagine anything you want. But he crossed the line between fantasy and real life with me."

"He didn't really mean it. The male-dominant world Marcello lives in is fueled by fantasy." Then Tom asked, "You don't want to do the slut thing with him?"

"No way."

"Just asking."

Though Tom and I have become close friends in a short time, we still had these spot-check moments: No slut thing? Ok. Got it.

"I asked him last night if he remembered standing me up at La Giostra."

"What did he say?"

"The conversation started with him asking me how the book was coming along. He had noticed my journals, on the dining table. I told him I had been re-reading my diaries from my travels last fall. And I said, 'I need to ask you something that I've been wondering about for a long time.'"

Tom had never heard the whole story, so I spared no detail:

"What do you remember about meeting me last fall?" I asked Marcello.

"I remember you at the café by the carousel. You were writing in your journal. We talked. That was it. I think you were leaving the next day. I didn't see you again."

"That's all you remember?" I asked.

"That's it."

I was sitting next to him on the sofa and could plainly see his blank look.

"You asked me to have a drink with you that night. But when I got back to the hotel, I wasn't feeling well and I called you to ask if we could meet the next night," I told him. "You called the next day to see how I was feeling and we decided to meet for a drink that evening at La Giostra at 7:30. I waited outside the restaurant for you. After about fifteen minutes, I showed your business card to the hostess and told her you knew the owner—maybe you were in the back talking to him? She checked and said you weren't there."

"It's not like me not to have called," he said, sounding contrite.

"I sat down at the table. At 8:15, I ordered dinner. My phone rang at quarter of nine. I assumed it was you, and I didn't answer. Everyone was looking at me—the woman whose date had stood her up."

"How embarrassing for you."

"When I got back to the hotel, at about ten, my phone rang again. It was you, saying you had been detained at a meeting and you asked me if it was too late to go out for a drink. I was really angry. I had torn your card into pieces and thrown it in the trash. You said you hoped we could meet again if I was ever in Florence."

I took a sip of my margarita, then said, "You should read what I wrote in my journal."

Marcello chuckled.

"You don't remember any of this?" I asked.

"Nothing."

"When I was here in March, and we were leaving the Irish pub, we walked by La Giostra, remember?"

"Yes."

"I was waiting for you to say, 'I'm really sorry about what happened.' All you said was 'I like La Giostra.' That's it."

At this point, Tom jumped in, fired up. "'Oh, I forgot to meet her at the restaurant.' And now he's telling you he forgot he stood you up. Chauvinistic behavior is normal for Italian men. You're dealing with a local boy. He's going from one woman to the next. Marcello admits he's chauvinistic, but claims he's a feminist compared to his Middle Eastern drinking buddies. He's not telling you anything bad about himself. He's telling you the way it is. You have the grounds for a complex, complicated and difficult relationship with him. Is that what you want?"

Tom's question hung in the air for a moment.

"I've said from the beginning that I don't have high expectations with this man," I replied. "But I also feel he's in my life for a reason. Not because we're destined to be together, but maybe because he's meant to be a character in this book."

I thought for a moment of Marcello as the Italian Everyman—the chauvinistic, but charismatic Casanova who ignites the fire of passion in me and rocks my bed so hard that the side rails fall off. Sounds like a great romance novel to me. Put a sexy *italiano* in a torn shirt on the cover with a busty *prostituta* in his arms and I'm financially set for life.

I thought about the signs of destiny scrawled on my map of Florence. After I told Marcello the story of La Giostra, I picked up the map, which was on the table next to my journals.

"Have you heard the phrase—the hand of destiny?" I asked him.

"Yes," he replied.

"I want to show you the *handwriting* of destiny." I opened the map for him to see. "When I was here looking for an apartment this spring, I stopped by a leather shop and met Nadia."

Marcello smiled.

"Nadia used to work for you, right?"

"Yes."

"Well, Nadia got all excited about my apartment search and called someone she used to work with named Arman. He told her he had an apartment he could show me. Nadia took my map and said to me, 'You are here.' She drew an X and then said, 'You need to go here.'" I showed Marcello the dot Nadia had drawn on my map.

"My store," he said.

I nodded. "She told me I needed to go right away, Arman was waiting for me. So I went to your store, not knowing it was your store. As I walked in the door, I looked up at the sign and thought the name was familiar, but I didn't know why. Arman told me I needed to see his brother Kamil, who worked at a restaurant nearby. Arman wrote the name of the restaurant on my map." I pointed to Arman's scribbles.

"And that's where I saw you again," Marcello said. "At the restaurant."

"As I walked toward the restaurant, you looked at me and did a little double-take."

"I remembered your face."

"And I thought to myself, 'Oh shit, it's that guy. The one who stood me up.'"

Marcello laughed.

"We didn't exchange phone numbers that day. It was the next day, when I saw you at Piazza della Signoria," I said.

"That's right."

"Don't you think that's strange?" I asked him. "That we met two days in a row—the first time because of two people you know and the second time by accident?"

Marcello didn't have an answer to that.

⌒

I e-mailed Tom my 3,500-word take on my falling out with Marcello. Tom read it and called me right away.

His first comment was about the ending. "That is a crushing, biting-of-the-lip ending. You really feel the pain. You see the play-boy—the image of him standing in the hall, reaching for his shirt pocket, like he's going for a pack of cigarettes. He's back in his world. Becky, I had no idea how deeply hurt you were. When you told me the story on the phone, I knew you were upset. But I didn't realize how bad this was for you. I could feel you cinch the belt of your bathrobe. Your pain is well-depicted. The whole thing was like watching a man and woman, jockeys on their horses, seeing who's going to cross the finish line first."

"Who were you rooting for?" I asked.

"Neither one."

"Who do you think won?"

"They both lost," Tom replied. The writer-in-me was happy to hear that. Drama is conflict, the more the better.

"Was there a winner in this?"

"Life in Italy is winning—the oppression," Tom said. "Marcello has common views—sad, but common. His unfortunate views about mistreating women are common, wrong and bad. Women who get involved with men like this—it's painful. But there was one thing that made me think Marcello isn't as bad as I first thought—when he said that he thinks women like men to abuse them. Then he says, I don't mean physically."

"When he said that, he put his hands to his chest," I said. "There's so much subtext to this story that comes out in the body language. When he told me he didn't love me, he was zipping up his pants."

"He'll say to you over and over, 'I don't love you.'" Tom said.

"Marcello said something right after he zipped up his pants that I thought was really strange," I told Tom. "He said how attracted he is to intelligent women and to 'a woman who can drive.' I said, 'You mean drive a car?' And he said, yeah, a woman who can drive is a real turn-on for him."

"I wonder what he means by that." Tom was intrigued. "Does he mean Grace Kelly with her scarf blowing in the wind, listening to classical music on the radio? Or does he see Sophia Loren driving around Rome screaming at anyone who gets in her way. Can't you see it? Sophia Loren at the wheel—at her age now, as an older woman. She would be so great."

The screenwriter-in-me was shifting into third gear. "And she'd be coming up behind Marcello, honking her horn and giving him the finger when she passes him."

"Yeeeesssss!"

Tom and I shrieked with laughter.

Two days after my fateful evening with Marcello, there was a message on my phone saying he had called. I had gone back to using my unreliable, low-tech phone. There wasn't a date or time on the message, so I didn't know if it was new or old.

"Are you going to call him?" Tom asked.

"No. If he called, he'll call me back."

"What if he's waiting for you to call him and he thinks you're ignoring him."

"I don't want to call him."

"What are you worried about? That he'll say, 'No, I didn't call you.'"

"Yeah, and then what do I say?" I felt like I was back in junior high school.

"Just say what you told me. You didn't know if it was a new or old message and you didn't want him to think you were ignoring him."

"You said the part about ignoring him."

"So what if you call him and he tells you he didn't call you and tonight at the bar he tells his drinking buddies, 'You know that blonde from California? She called me to ask if I had called her. HA! We know that trick.' So what if he says that? You won't be around to hear it."

"Tom, when something upsetting like this happens to me, I just need to be still for a little while. I need things to settle."

"Okay, but he might be thinking you're ignoring him."

"Stop!"

After we hung up, I thought about what Tom had said. I'd feel more comfortable sending Marcello an e-mail, I decided. I could say that I had seen the message on my phone and whatever else I wanted to say, without having to hear him say whatever I was afraid he might say. I never imagined that at middle age, you could still feel like you were 14.

This is what I wrote:

> There was a message on my phone yesterday morning from you, with no date/time so I don't know if it's new or old. Anyway, if you called, I don't want you to think I'm ignoring you. I've thought a lot about what happened…we learned a lot about each other in one evening, which is not a bad thing. My hurt feelings were genuine, but so was your apology. Life goes on. I leave for L.A. next week, then on to Chicago…
> Ciao for now, Rebecca

I usually signed off with "kisses," so this was a significant departure. Marcello and I had talked about meeting in Chicago during my upcoming visit with my parents. He was thinking about going to Vancouver and returning to Italy via Chicago.

The me-side-of-me was having second thoughts about contacting him, but the writer-side-of-me clicked the SEND button, saying, *"He's a main character in the book. We need to stay in touch."*

I (she) sent that e-mail on Wednesday. By Sunday, we had no reply.

Tom, who had been sure Marcello would respond right away, was changing his spin. "I think you're going to hear from him, but he's probably re-grouping. You put him on notice that he can't fuck with you. You told him he can't come over for booty calls and talk to you like that. If he genuinely cares about you, he'll have heard what you said and be more sensitive. Marcello is a middle-aged Italian man. He's not going to change, but he can show some respectful restraint." Then Tom said, "I wonder if he'll call you before you leave. If he doesn't, he'll wonder what happened to you."

"I told him in the e-mail," I said. "I'm *not* calling him."

"Okay, okay."

7

Nadia

A week later, I was clearing off my desk and I found Nadia's card. I had been trying to reach her for weeks.

She answered and was happy to hear from me. "Oh Rebecca, I have been wondering what happened to you. I left messages for you. I keep saying to myself, I hope she calls me."

A month earlier, I was supposed to meet Nadia at the shop where she works. But after I sprained my ankle, I couldn't do much walking for a few weeks. I tried to call her, but I kept getting a message saying the number was either incorrect or unavailable.

"I want to see you," Nadia said. "I have so much I want to ask you." She was at the market, buying food for dinner. "Please come to my place tonight. We can have dinner and talk."

An hour later, Nadia was waiting for me at the shop with a friend named Tariq. She greeted me in Italian and started yelling at me when I answered her in English. "Why you don't speak Italian?" she asked in English.

Nadia is a dynamo, who struts down the street like she owns Florence. She greeted shopkeepers and waiters as we walked to her apartment. They all seemed to know her. She never stopped talking. Tariq turned to me and smiled, making his fingers move like the bill of a duck. At Nadia's insistence, he offered me his arm so that I wouldn't stumble on those ankle-twisting Roman pavers.

Nadia is from Morocco, where her parents still live. But her brothers and sisters now live in Italy. Fourteen years ago, when she was a 20-year-old student, Nadia was visiting one of her sisters who lived in Florence at the time. "I was just here for a visit," Nadia told me. "But my sister took away my passport and told me I must stay here."

Nadia says she loved life in Florence at first. "You get the disease of Florence after you have been here one year. You will see."

Tariq nodded in agreement. Like Nadia, Tariq is Moroccan and multi-lingual. He understands English, but is shy about speaking it. He lived in France for two years, so he and I would lapse into French if we couldn't communicate. Of course, Nadia would yell at him, "Why you don't speak Italian to her? She needs to learn Italian."

Tariq told me he has lived in many places—Germany, France, elsewhere in Italy. But he said there is something *magnetico* about Florence. He looked to Nadia to translate, but his meaning was clear.

"You feel a magnetic pull to this place," I said.

"Yes," he replied.

"Hmm." I thought about this for a moment. "I don't feel it yet. I love Florence for its history, its art, its beauty, but I don't feel at home here yet."

"You miss California," Nadia said.

"Yes, I miss my son, my friends. These first couple of months here have been difficult for me."

"Life here is difficult," Nadia agreed. "I want to get out of here. Find a place away from here where I can raise my son. I hate my fucking life here." Nadia is the single mother of a darling 3-year-old boy.

Tariq made a delicious dinner of pasta and lamb chops. As we raised our glasses, I said, "To Nadia's Place, the best restaurant in Florence." They laughed. I told them that I sometimes eat yogurt for dinner. They look surprised when I confessed, "I don't cook."

After dinner, Nadia went to the fridge and took out a bottle of red juice. "Would you like something refreshing, like flowers? I bring it from Morocco."

She took off the lid and held the bottle for me to smell. I inhaled and waited for the scent to register. Of course. I smiled at her. "It's roses."

She nodded and poured me a glass of floral nectar, arduously pressed from the petals of tiny red rosebuds. The juice was sweet, like drinking the fragrance of a rose. I swished the red liquid in my glass, thinking of the garden I used to have, filled with roses, many that I had propagated myself. Sometimes I think I miss that garden more than the house itself.

Nadia told me about her parents' house in Morocco, with its many rooms and beautiful gardens. I asked why she didn't go home, where life would be easier for her and her son. "I can't go back," she said. "I have the disease of Florence."

She showed me a stack of photos taken the previous summer in Morocco at the celebration of her son's circumcision. Nadia said she couldn't bear to be in the room for the actual cutting of the foreskin, but she has 5x7 close-ups of her son's penis after the snip. "My baby was screaming. I was outside screaming." She showed me another photo that really made me laugh. "My boy likes to fish so I brought him this present." In the photo, taken moments after the circumcision, Nadia is leaning over her distraught son who's clearly bewildered by the foot-long dead fish that his mother has given him.

Nadia looks stunning in the photos taken at the celebration later that day. She's in full makeup, her hands covered with henna designs, and wearing a gorgeous dress with a heavily beaded bodice that shows off her décolleté. In one photo, she's swirling her voluminous red skirt in front of her son who's next to her on the dance floor. He's adorable, in traditional Moroccan costume—with a long vest and little red fez. He looks up at her, mesmerized, as if to say, "Mommy? Is that you?"

She kissed every photo she showed me of her son. "My baby. My beautiful boy," she said over and over. He was with her parents in Morocco for a visit. "I miss him so much."

After a while, Tariq said good-night. Nadia waved good-bye to him. She closed the door and turned to me, lighting a cigarette.

"He is very nice—and a good cook," I said.

She exhaled. "He is nice. But we are just friends. I don't have a man in my life. I don't believe in love anymore."

"Nadia, that will change," I assured her. "There are many phases of your life to come that you can't imagine right now."

"I want to have another baby," she said urgently. "I want lots of children."

I understood her angst. "I wanted more children, too. But we are lucky that we have one child. There are some women…"

She finished my sentence. "Who want one and have none."

I smiled at the big photo of her son on the wall. "Every child is a blessing and a miracle."

"You are right, Rebecca."

Nadia talked about her fears of being alone after her son is grown. I could tell by the way she spoke of him that he was filling a huge void in her life.

"I want to sleep with him and hold him close to me," she said. "But my friends say it is time for him to sleep on his own."

"I know it's difficult to let go. Even now, with my 19-year-old son, it's difficult. But I want him to be independent of me and have his own life."

"I can't imagine not having my son with me."

"You don't want a *mammone* do you?" I had learned that word from Tom. A *mammone* is a mama's boy who never leaves home and is tied to his mother's apron strings. The declining birth rate in Italy is attributed, in part, to the strong bond between Italian mothers and their sons who can't separate.

Nadia laughs. "These men who are 40 and still living with their mothers! I know one day my son will leave me."

"But not for a long time."

"You are okay being alone?" she asked me.

"My husband and I separated when our son was 8. I've dated a few men since then. But it's difficult. As a mother you always put your child first. Some men can't understand that."

"What about now that your son is gone?"

"I'm enjoying my freedom. It's a new phase of my life."

All evening, Nadia talked about finding me a new apartment. She was upset that I didn't have air-conditioning and had to keep the windows open, which meant I had to use mosquito poison bottles that are common in Italy. They look like bottles of clear fingernail polish that attach to little electric vaporizers, which plug into the walls. The fumes, which slowly paralyze mosquitos, irritated my eyes and throat and gave me headaches.

Nadia told me about apartments she knows of around the city, cheaper than mine, with air-conditioning and nice views. She asked whether I had gotten to see the apartment that Arman was going to show me. I told her I went to the café to see Kamil, but the guy who had the key was in Arezzo.

"I waited for an hour, but he didn't show up," I said. "But while I was there I saw Marcello."

"You know Marcello?" she asked.

"I met him last fall when I was in Florence for a few days."

"I like Marcello. He has been good to me." She looked at me. "American women like him. Australian women, too. He's very *busy*."

The way she said "busy" made me laugh.

"You like him? Why not be with him. We must enjoy ourselves in this life, no?" Nadia said. "He never told me he knew you. I'm at his shop every day."

"When was the last time you saw Marcello?"

She shrugged. "Three days ago."

I imagined the conversation that might happen the next time Nadia saw him.

"You should ask Marcello to get you an apartment. He owns many places." Nadia was a spewing fountain of information.

I told Nadia I wanted to write a story called *The Dons of Florence's Leather Mafia*. She laughed about my encounter with amorous Antonio.

"I think Marcello moves quickly, too. No?" she asked.

I thought back to the spring night at the Irish pub when Marcello reached over and took my hand for the first time. He didn't pounce, not even when we got back to the hotel room. He sat down in the chair and waited before he came to sit next to me on the bed.

"Marcello is a gentleman," I said, though the writer-in-me was howling with laughter.

"Really?" Nadia seemed surprised.

I said good-night to Nadia and invited her to come to my apartment for dinner.

"I like yogurt," she said teasingly.

"I'll give you real food," I promised. "And I make great margaritas. Ask Marcello."

8

Home again

I packed a bag, with only the bare essentials for a three-week trip to Los Angeles, Chicago and Paris, and headed to the Florence airport. My plan was to spend ten days on home turf in Pasadena, a week in the Chicago suburbs with my parents and then five days in Paris to decompress from the week with my parents. And hopefully in my three weeks away, I could take a breather from life in Italy and come back with a fresh perspective.

The me-side-of-me wanted to pack up everything and go home to stay. But the writer side kept saying, *"Quit whining, you big baby. We're coming back to Italy. This is great material."*

On the long flight to L.A., I thought about an e-mail Tom had sent me during my first weeks in Florence:

> *You are in another world, sort of a time capsule, don't you think? Italy is so much in the past, and isn't this past so much of what we're attracted to?*
>
> *The Italians are circular, Becky. Not like us Americans, who are linear. We go from Point A to Point B, then on to Point C.*

Many Italians seem to go back to A after they get to B. And it is precisely this that preserves their past, which in turn justifies or explains their obstinacy. And pride.

How much do you know of Roman Catholicism? It has all the answers for the central and southern Italian lifestyle. Totally steeped in superstition and 'no answers' (that's what I say), promoting a lifelong dialogue wrapped around those superstitions.

AND dreams…lots of dreamy ideas of life and love and wealth. And bonds amongst ourselves in bondage to time and humanity. My Italian ancestors were all about the glint of the eye. That soul-deep connection with 'AHHHHHHH…you know what I mean' …we are what we are, we are who we are…it's all in God's hands.

Surrender…make love, eat, work hard and then do it all over again. Point A to Point B and back to Point A.

I confess I'm a recovering Type-A personality, adept at flying from Point A to C at warp speed. As has been said, I grab the bull by the balls.

I didn't realize how homesick I was until I arrived back in Pasadena. I love Pasadena. I love the mountains that the city nestles up to and the old Craftsman bungalows along its quiet streets, lined with camphor trees, spindly palms and California oaks.

For twenty-two years, my home in Pasadena was one of those bungalows, built in 1913. It had a big front porch, with a swing, and a great arroyo-stone chimney. I spent many hours on that porch swing—reading, daydreaming, singing to a baby boy I bounced on my knee. The house was shaded by a majestic, 80-foot deodar cedar. Deodars, native to the Himalayas, dot the landscape in Pasadena and its sister community to the north, Altadena. They have distinctly floppy tops with boughs that gracefully hang from the trunk like the arms of a woman holding the billowy skirt of her ball gown.

I had a garden behind my bungalow filled with roses. I loved sitting in that garden at sunset, watching the darkness chase the last light of day up the trunk of the deodar.

My then-husband and I bought that house two years after we married. We lovingly restored it and vowed we would grow old together there. We brought our newborn son home to that house. In the divorce settlement, the house came to me. I still dreamed about growing old in my lovely bungalow, but my more immediate goal, as I faced financial difficulties, was to hang on to it until Colin graduated from high school.

I got my wish, but just barely. When the mortgage crisis hit in the spring of 2008, I had already borrowed against the equity. Support payments would end when Colin left for college that fall. I had hoped to rent the house for a year or two and travel. But with so many houses on the brink of foreclosure, the market was flooded with rentals. I had no choice but to sell. So the week after Colin graduated from high school, I put the house on the market.

For two months there were no offers. House prices were tumbling; the inventory of houses-for-sale was ballooning. I finally had an offer on the table the day Colin left for college in mid-August. The car was packed. His dad and I waited at the curb as Colin went back into the house to say his last good-byes. He would never see his room again. My heart ached, standing there next to the man I had married and vowed to grow old with, while our son walked through the shards of our broken dream.

Escrow closed on September 11, 2008. Lehman Brothers failed four days later. Two days after that, I was on a plane to Rome. I had gotten out by the skin of my clenched teeth.

I wandered around Italy for five weeks: Rome, the Isle of Capri, the Amalfi Coast, Tuscany, Florence and Venice. I then flew to Portugal and spent a week on the Algarve with friends from Scotland. I hung out with Nancy for six weeks at her apartment in Berlin.

I liked the vagabond life. I traveled with only a carry-on suitcase. I loved my new freedom and the feeling of weightlessness.

I returned to Pasadena two weeks before Christmas. I rented an apartment online and moved in two days after my return. Once again, Point A to C at warp speed. Colin, my parents and I gathered at my new digs on Christmas Day. The apartment was nice, but it was hard not to think of Christmases past, with a big twinkling tree in the bungalow's bay window and logs crackling in the massive fireplace.

A few days before I moved to Florence, a crew from a Pasadena consignment shop took away most of my furniture, except for my bed, three dressers, an antique marble-top washstand, my desk and my desk chair. I couldn't justify keeping two storage units—at $250 a month each—so in a bold move, I decided to let almost everything go.

The crew carried away my Stickley sofa, my beautiful dining set from the 1940s, an antique oak china closet, a Morris chair, a walnut Victorian desk that belonged to my mother, an oak sewing cabinet that was my grandmother's. On the dolly, in the parking lot at the storage unit, sat four chairs that represented chapters of my life: the rocking chair my parents had rocked me to sleep in as a baby and where I had rocked my own son to sleep; the oak press-back chair I sat on as a young girl while doing my homework at the walnut desk; a bentwood Amish rocker that I purchased on a trip to Pennsylvania; and a French-made reclining patio chair where I used to relax in my garden. I took a cell-phone photo of the four chairs on the dolly. I walked over to the rocker from my childhood and gave it one last gentle push.

Let go, move on, I told myself.

The two-month consignment period ended just before I returned to Pasadena. Several of the antique pieces had sold immediately, for prices much less than I paid. But many of the items were still unsold. It was my option to reclaim them or donate them to the local hospital charity.

I walked into the store and there in the central display area was my gorgeous Stickley sofa. I sat down on its big roomy cushions and ran my fingers over the champagne-colored damask. A few feet away, I saw my dining set.

A volunteer who worked at the store came over to me. "May I help you?"

"I was just having a sit on my sofa," I said. "Actually, I've come in to close out my account here."

I gave her my name and she found my paperwork. "Is there anything you want to re-claim?" she asked.

"No," I said. But my answer wasn't emphatic. "There is one item. It's a rocking chair that has been in my family for a long time. Could I look around and see if it's still here?"

"Certainly," she said. "What does it look like?"

We searched the display areas, then went to a warehouse in back. The items there were packed in tight aisles. She looked at me sadly. "We have so much furniture. A lot of people have lost their homes in this economy."

I was indeed fortunate. I had some money in the bank and was living my dream. I wasn't out on the street selling everything I owned to make ends meet.

The rocker wasn't there. I thanked her for helping me look and she left me to wander. I saw my blue living room loveseat in the corner. As I passed one aisle, I caught a glimpse of the walnut desk. I was drawn to it. I opened the slant top and lowered it. I traced my finger around the B and the A—for Becky and Amy—that were finely etched there. My sister Amy, who was three years younger than I, had died the previous summer of undiagnosed heart disease. I quickly closed the desk top.

I was heading for the door and saw the back of my grandmother's sewing cabinet. I had forgotten to check the drawers before the crew took it from storage.

I walked around the cabinet and stopped short. The drawers were gone. There was a sold sign stuck to the cabinet. I took a closer look at the tag; the cabinet had been purchased just the day before.

I suddenly felt like I was in a very bad dream. I hurried out of the building and walked the long way around to the parking lot, not re-entering the main store, and got into my car. I closed my eyes. *Let go, let go, let go. Move on.*

෴

One of my favorite stores in Pasadena is a travel shop called Distant Lands. My travels to distant lands have been launched with books, maps, gear and staff recommendations I've gotten at that store. My favorite sales guy, Daniel, was stunned to see me walk in the door, only two months after I had left town.

"You're supposed to be in Italy," he said.

"I'm here on a little detour to Chicago, where I'm going to see my parents. My mom isn't well," I said. "And I wanted to see my son before he heads back to school."

"You're going back to Italy, right?" he asked, as if needing to be reassured that I wasn't abandoning the adventure he had been vicariously enjoying.

"Yeah."

"You don't sound sure."

"No. I mean yes, I'm going back. I left all my stuff there." I tried to muster some enthusiasm. "I like my apartment, my neighborhood is great. But living in Italy isn't as fun as visiting Italy. I didn't have an easy start."

He totally understood. He knows about the clash of travel fantasies and realities.

I told him I was scrapping the idea of writing an *Under the Tuscan Sun* fantasy-come-true and doing a modern-day rewrite of Dante's *Inferno* instead. "The levels of hell will be the post office, the immigration office and the Florence IKEA store."

He liked the concept and was ready to put in an advance order for the book. I nosed around the store and bought a Rick Steves clothesline and a few travel memoirs.

As I was leaving, he called after me, "Go back to Florence. Live your dream."

∽

My L.A. friends were happy to see me, but concerned that I was back so soon.

"Do you want a welcome-home party?" asked my friend Debbie, who had organized my festive send-off. Debbie loves throwing parties. "Really, it's no trouble. I'll call everyone. The last party was so much fun."

Of course, what I missed most about Pasadena were my friends. My return visit was full of lunches, dinners, coffees, movies. My dear friend Peg drove up from San Diego for the day. We had lunch at a little French bistro, lingered over frappuccinos at Starbucks and went to see the movie *Julie & Julia*, which we loved. I hung out one evening with my pool buddy Kevin, watching hummingbirds swarm the feeders in his garden at nightfall. I told him about Marcello and he told me about his summer fling in the Philippines. I had coffee with Phil, who had sent me a tough-love e-mail when I started whining about life in Italy: *"Hey, where is that lady I knew who wanted to taste the world raw and find new things to write about?"* But when I walked into the restaurant, he folded me in his big teddy-bear arms and said, "I've really missed you."

My girlfriends were very supportive, cheering me on, saying how "brave" I am. I don't think of myself as brave. Maybe I seem brave to them because their idea of a good time is not paddling solo in a canoe over the falls. Actually, I think they really admire my sense of adventure and would like to jump in the canoe with me, but perhaps avoiding the falls.

I had lunch with Helen and Emily—two of the three "muses" to whom I dedicated my first book. The third muse of the trio, Carole, died six months earlier of metastasized breast cancer. We leave an empty chair at the table for her now.

Emily's youngest child had left for college a few days earlier. Emily has been battling empty-nest anxiety for several years. She has a loving husband, a lovely home and financial security—no need to sell the nest and flee, like I did. But her sense of purpose in life has been largely about her children. Yet for all her years of fretting, she came to lunch with a cheerful face. She was pursuing new interests and enjoying her freedom.

Helen turned to me and said, "I'm worried about you and what you're going to be dealing with when you see your parents. This isn't going to be easy."

"I know." My mother, who has been in poor health for years, was in the grips of ferocious dementia. "Her eightieth birthday is next week. It will be nice to celebrate that with her. I don't know how much longer she will remember me."

Helen squeezed my arm.

"I had hoped Colin would come with me, but his classes start next week," I said. "I wonder if I should have insisted that he come. To say good-bye to her."

"No." Helen and Emily spoke in unison.

"Maybe it's better that he remembers her as she was, not like she is now," I said.

They both agreed. "How is your dad coping?" Emily asked.

"Not very well. He's understandably exhausted and exasperated," I said. "But he's not a caregiver. My mom cared for his needs all their married life. He wants me to help him weigh his options. He's made some appointments to visit assisted-living facilities. They both really need to get out of that house. It's too much for them to take care of."

"Don't go with an agenda," Emily advised.

"I won't. The only thing I'd like to do while I'm there is to get them set up on Skype so that we can be in touch. I think that would make them less anxious about me being so far away. But beyond that, there's not much else I can do really, except offer my opinion. My dad makes the decisions and writes the checks." I could feel the dread welling up inside of me.

One evening, I had dinner with my former neighbor John. Inspired by my "Tales from Tavanti" e-mail, he had sent me a film synopsis he'd written featuring me and my Mafia princess neighbor, along with this comforting note: *"Cara Rebecca, you fled safety, seeking the new in the Old World. That is the point. You are finding it. Perfetto. Va bene, va bene, you can be careful. Si. You could consider whether this is a matter for Madre Maria. She trumps Don Ombra ogni giorno nella settimana (every day of the week)."*

John was waiting outside the restaurant, smiling at me, as I walked toward him. We embraced and he said, "You look lovely." He wanted to know every detail of my misadventure and assured me that no matter how hard the boat rocks, no matter how big the waves, I am on the course I am meant to take.

Of course, the one person I wanted to see during my time in Pasadena was Colin, my son-gone-rogue. He had already moved himself into an apartment in Berkeley the week before I arrived and informed me, when he heard I was coming to visit, that he wasn't planning to come back to "SoCal" before school started. I, in turn, informed him he needed to return my car, which I had graciously given him for the year I was away. "I'm not renting a car while I'm in town when I already own one I could use," I e-mailed him. "And if you hang around long enough after you return it, I'll even take your sweet face to dinner." He showed his sweet face for one day, long enough for me to take him to dinner, a movie and to Office Depot to buy a desk chair and school supplies. Colin persuaded his dad to give me one of his two cars to drive for the duration of my visit and off he went, back to Berkeley, in my car.

On my last night in L.A., I had dinner with Teresa, my spiritual kid sister. She's twenty years younger than I, but we have a connection that transcends age difference. She has big dreams and is trying hard to make them happen. I had never been to her home, a rooftop apartment in Silver Lake, overlooking the city. I was blown away by the view. We sat on chaises on her deck watching the sun set on the facades of the skyscrapers downtown. She uncorked an amazing bottle of wine that she had been holding in reserve for a special occasion. As the night air cooled, we bundled ourselves in soft fleecy blankets and let the yearnings of our hearts take wing over the twinkling city below.

∽

My dad was waiting for me at baggage claim when I arrived in Chicago the next day and was so happy to see me.

On the day I left for Florence in June, I had called my parents to say good-bye. Before my mom got on the phone, my dad had said to me, "When are you coming back?"

"Dad, I haven't gotten there yet."

"I think you need to come back in July so we can talk about your mother."

I knew there was no use arguing or negotiating with him. "I can come anytime you need me."

"Good." I could hear the relief in his voice. He just needed to be reassured.

Mom couldn't make the trip to the airport, so Dad gave me his candid views of her condition on the ride home. He had been trying to get her to Mayo Clinic for a neurological evaluation for months. But every time they were due to go, she would be bedridden with vomiting and diarrhea, no doubt fueled by anxiety.

Earlier in the summer, they were driving to their vacation home in Door County and she said to him, "Where's my husband?"

"I'm your husband," he told her.

"No, you're not," she said. "He's in the back seat and he's not talking to me."

So I was prepared for what happened a few nights after I arrived. I was in my father's office, next to my old bedroom, when my mother came to the door and asked, "Have you seen Becky?"

"Mom, I'm Becky," I said.

"I know you're Becky," she said, easing herself off the hook. "But where is *our* Becky?"

"I'm right here, Mom."

She looked in my bedroom for a moment, then back at me. "Are you the only one staying in that room?" she asked.

"Yes, Mom."

She didn't say another word and walked down the hall. She went into her bedroom and closed the door.

The next day, she and I had a heated argument about her memory loss.

She railed at me for thinking it was a serious problem that needed to be evaluated. "How do you know? You're never here!" She was spewing venom at my dad as well. "You wouldn't have known I was having a problem if I hadn't mentioned it to you recently," she told him.

"Mom, the problem has been evident for a long time," I said.

"I only forget the little things," she said.

"Do you remember asking me last night if I had seen Becky?" I asked her.

She was red in the face, gripping the arms of her chair.

I looked at her sympathetically. "That's not a little thing."

At times she drifted into a dark place. She told me that she and Dad had just come back from a car trip to Texas. I knew this wasn't true. But she claimed he had left her in a motel where she met another man, who had the same name as my father and who knew my father's brothers. "He wasn't as good looking as your father," she said, "but he was very nice." My mother's fear of abandonment fueled many of her delusions.

For years, my parents' marriage had been stormy. Before her memory problems worsened, my mother told me that one of her close friends was urging her to get a divorce. Occasionally, she'd tell me about my father's outbursts toward her.

"You don't have to stay in this, Mom," I would say.

At first I thought she couldn't see a way out. But then I began to realize she didn't want to see a way out. She married him four days before she turned 21. She had never been on her own and I think the prospect of that terrified her.

As my mother wandered deeper into the fog of her dementia, she went through a period—perhaps in her distant past—where she was head-over-heels in love with him again. She'd tell me how wonderful he was and how she couldn't live without him. They seemed happy again, holding hands like young lovers.

But as the weight of my mother's care bore down on him, my father often lashed out at her in anger. He needed counseling as much as she needed professional care, but they were tangled in their own sticky web and in denial about the crisis that was looming.

We visited several assisted-living facilities during my visit, but I sensed it was my father's underlying wish for me to come back and take care of them. "I want to help you make good choices and get the care you need," I told them. But I wasn't willing to become their caregiver.

When I hugged my mom good-bye, I told her not to worry, that we would deal with whatever was to come. She stood in the kitchen, smiling at me as I walked out the door. I wondered if this would be the last time she'd recognize me.

At the airport, I called my mother's sister, Aileen, who wanted to know if my parents had made a decision about moving to assisted living. I told her that though they really liked one of the facilities we had visited, I didn't think they would make the move. "They're so resistant to change," I said.

In my mission to set up Skype on their computer, my dad balked when I told him he'd probably need to switch from dial-up to DSL, which might mean changing his e-mail address. I assured him I would take care of everything, but he wouldn't budge. "In my old age," he admitted, "I don't like change."

"I'm worried about your mother," Aileen said. "She seems to be getting worse."

I told her that, a few days earlier, Mom and Dad had watched the TV coverage of Ted Kennedy's funeral and burial. "We came back from dinner and there was a special on about Ted Kennedy's life. Mom asked, 'Is he still alive?' My dad looked at her in disbelief and said, 'Who do you think they've been carrying around in that box all day?'"

Aileen giggled. "Your dad said that?"

Then I giggled. "It is kind of funny."

Aileen had just finished writing a memoir of her own, which she had sent to my mother as a birthday gift. On the next to the last page, she mentions my mother's dementia.

"My mom has been reading your book and is really enjoying it," I told Aileen. "She has about ten pages to go. Don't be surprised if she calls you, hopping mad, when she gets to the end and reads the bit about her dementia."

My flight was boarding. I hurried down the jetway and took my seat. In eight hours I would be in Paris…far, far away.

9

Why I love Paris

When friends ask what I love most about Paris, I sigh and say, "The men." They're such flirtatious rascals. They blow kisses at you from open windows. They approach you on the street, wondering if you're lost or if you'd like to join them for a drink. They always ask the same two questions: Are you married? Are you alone? The answer to the first question doesn't matter. But if you say yes to the second question, the chase is on.

My most romantic encounter in Paris—the most romantic encounter of my entire life, in fact—happened in Montmartre in the summer of 2004. I was walking past the artists' stalls in Place du Tertre, having just bought a painting of vibrant summer flowers, when a handsome man stepped from behind his easel and smiled seductively at me. His dark eyes reeled me in.

"Are you American?" he asked in sexy French-accented English.

I nodded.

"Where in America?"

"California," I said.

"I knew it."

I just smiled, mesmerized by those dark eyes. I couldn't think of anything to say—so insanely, I walked away.

I walked directly to the taxi stand around the corner from Place du Tertre, where I had seen a line of cabs only twenty minutes earlier. To my surprise, there wasn't a cab in sight. I waited a few minutes and stepped out into the street to see if any were approaching. And when I turned around, there he was: the artist with the dark eyes and seductive smile, waiting for me at the taxi stand.

He asked me to have coffee with him.

"*No, merci*. I'm waiting for a taxi."

"What's the hurry?" He looked down the street and shrugged. "I see no taxis." He pointed to an empty café table next to the taxi sign. "Sit with me and we'll wait together."

Over coffee, he told me, "I could swim in your eyes."

That really made me laugh. "You're so good at this," I said.

"Good at what? I speak from my heart."

I laughed harder.

Holding my hand, he pleaded, "Have dinner with me tonight."

I made up a story that I had a girlfriend back at the hotel with a sprained knee, but he persisted. In a moment of weakness—I mean, why the hell not—I said yes.

I met him at his stall at seven that evening. True to a promise he had made over coffee, he gave me a tour of the back streets of Montmartre that tourists rarely see.

"It feels like we're in a village, far away from Paris, doesn't it?" he said.

We stopped walking, and I said, "It's so quiet here."

With his hand at the small of my back, he turned me toward him and kissed me. For several seconds, I was sure the earth had stopped spinning.

And so began my love affair with Loran that lasted, off and on, for five years.

A month after we met, I returned to Paris to see him. We spent most of our first two days together in bed, in a room with an incredible view of Sacré-Coeur. We went to Giverny, Monet's retreat outside of Paris, where I was researching an article about the American impressionist painters who had followed Monet to this tiny village on the Seine. We stayed in an ancient *moulin* and felt like we had stepped behind a curtain into another era. We were two lovers hidden from the real world for a few blissful days.

But there were major complications in this affair. Loran was married to a rich American woman. He bent the truth when we met, telling me their divorce was imminent. Not so. The divorce wasn't finalized until five years later.

When I realized that he wasn't soon to be a free man, I stopped fantasizing about a life with him. After his disastrous visit to Pasadena, we barely spoke for six months. But when I returned to Paris the following summer, we rekindled our romance.

In Paris or Provence, during my annual summer visits there, we would steal a few days together. I always said to him as we parted, "See you same time, next year."

I last saw Loran in December, on my way back to California from Berlin. I had two days in Paris and we arranged to meet at Place du Tertre. I arrived a few minutes early, just as it was getting dark, and walked around the square, empty of the café tables and awnings of the summer season. The square looked so small, under a few strands of Christmas lights, on a quiet wintry night.

I saw him before he saw me. I hung back in the shadows as he greeted his colleagues who were packing up their easels. I stepped into the light and caught his eye. He grinned. "Would you like me to get you a taxi?" he asked, pointing over his shoulder to the taxi stand where our romance started. He took me in his arms and we held each other for a long time.

He returned to the U.S. a couple of months later, for the next battle in his divorce war. We spoke by phone a few times. I told him I was hoping to move to Italy. I knew he was tired of Paris and wanted to start a new life in the U.S.; his one trophy from his marriage was a green card. In an ironic twist, we were trading places.

The first day I was in Paris, after my visit with my parents, I walked into Place du Tertre and held my breath for a moment, hoping I'd see Loran at his easel. He wasn't there, but the ghost of him was everywhere. I had a coffee at the café across from the taxi stand, remembering the photos we posed for over the years in front of that sign. I have them all in a photo book I brought with me to Florence.

Let go, move on, I told myself yet again. I'll always have Paris.

10

Return to Florence

When I opened the door of my apartment, the strangeness was gone. It wasn't quite home, but my books and photos were on the shelves, my pictures were on the walls.

My basil plant had died while I was away. My other plants looked a little wind-blown. I didn't have roses anymore, but I had a lovely little balcony garden of succulents and herbs overlooking Via Tavanti.

I leaned on the balcony railing and took in the night scene. Movie-goers were spilling out of the theater across the street. Bus brakes squealed, a motorcycle roared past. An ambulance siren wailed in the distance. A waxing moon was rising over the hills north of the city. In the cool night breeze, dry leaves rustled in the trees. The season was changing.

After three-and-a-half weeks away, I had only three pieces of mail waiting for me. That made me laugh. I would have had two big bins of mail and catalogs waiting for me back in Pasadena after a long trip.

My phone didn't ring for five days. I tried not to notice. I unpacked, did laundry, paid bills and immersed myself in my writing.

Then Marcello called. We had spoken briefly while I was in Paris. He had sent me a short e-mail while I was in Pasadena, in response to the message I had sent him two weeks earlier, after our last night together. *"Ciao Rebecca, sorry for delay,"* he wrote, *"but been very busy and when so hot I don't function very well. Ud be in US by now and I'm ready to go to Canada tomorrow for a little vacation. Talk to u when back."*

We had a long conversation. He wanted to know about my trip. I told him that when I got to California, I discovered I was more homesick than I realized. "Ohhh," he said tenderly. He told me about his trip to Canada, which took him to Montreal, Calgary and Banff. I asked if he made it to Seattle, which was on his initial itinerary.

"No. That part of the U.S. doesn't appeal to me," he said. "I don't like granola women."

"What did you say?" I asked incredulously.

"Granola women. You know, hippies."

"They're not your type," I said. Marcello is a writer's dream character. I reached for a pen.

"I like women from southern California," he said.

"Is that so?"

"Especially from Los Angeles."

He said his mother was in Florence for a few days, to visit his great-aunt, who was dying of cancer. "After my mom leaves, I'll call you. Maybe we can have a drink."

He didn't mention margaritas. A sign of respectful restraint? I e-mailed Tom.

I got a call from Elena, inviting me to dinner, and she mentioned margaritas. "Should I make ice?" she asked. She told me Bernardo would bring the car for me and my blender. She had e-mailed me a sweet welcome-home message: *"Dear Rebecca, how are things? Are you finally back? I've thought about you so much! How about your holidays and your parents? Please if you have any needing phone me or write me! You are not alone here!! Welcome again!"*

My second day back, I appeared at the neighborhood café, where I had become a regular on hot summer afternoons, soothing myself with gelato and their air-conditioning. As I walked in, Luan, my favorite barista, exclaimed, "Wow! You're back." He came out from around the bar and gave me a big hug. "Where have you been? We wondered what happened to you." *Ohhh.*

I stopped by the hair salon, on the ground floor of my apartment building, to make an appointment with Fabio, the stylist I had last time. He came to the front desk.

"Nice see to you!" he exclaimed, in his slightly jumbled English.

I smiled. "Nice to see you, too."

I called Guido, the osteopath who had been treating my ankle, to make an appointment. I had twisted the same ankle again, hauling a suitcase up the stairs at my parents' house.

In English, Guido said, "I can see you next Tuesday. Morning or afternoon?"

"Morning is fine," I replied.

"Morning is not possible," he said.

I couldn't stop laughing.

I was feeling a bit wistful the night I had dinner with Elena and Bernardo. Elena and I were in the kitchen: she was making bruschetta as I made margaritas. Her 2-year-old daughter, Giulia, was at the kitchen table playing with her food and the cuddly toy lamb I had brought her.

"Today is my son's twentieth birthday," I said.

"How does that feel?" Elena asked.

"I can't believe it has been twenty years," I said. "I remember the day he was born as though it were yesterday."

"You saw him when you were in California?" she asked.

"For one day."

"An Italian mother would not be happy about that," she said with a raised eyebrow.

"I know. But I feel I must let him go."

"Tell me how," Elena said. "I want to learn." She looked at me as if I knew the answer to a mystery of life.

"My son is just like me," I said. "When I was his age, I was very independent, eager to leave home and see the world. I understand how he feels."

"My friends couldn't understand how I was able to let Giulia spend the summer with my parents," Elena said. Elena had taken Giulia to her parents' home by the sea, away from the smoggy heat of Florence, and worked four-day weeks so that she could spend long weekends with her there.

"But it was a wonderful experience for your parents and for her," I said.

As we had dinner that night, adorable Giulia showed me her dolls and toys. I looked at her and thought what I wouldn't do to have just one more day with my son at that age. Just one day.

11

The list

A close friend of mine, also named Rebecca, died of breast cancer five years before I moved to Italy. A few months before her death, we had planned to take a trip together. But her cancer was spreading fast and her doctor didn't want her wandering too far from home.

At her memorial service, I cried so hard I could barely breathe. I remember trying to hold my sobs until the music played so that I wouldn't distract from the beautiful tributes given by her friends and family. I had kept my tears inside so long they were bursting through the dam.

Our two sons had been schoolmates and scouts together. Rebecca and I had shared many experiences, from decorating the art room for open house to presiding over raucous cub scout meetings as den mothers.

On the night she died, her husband had called me, an hour after she passed away. I went outside and looked at the sky. An amazing pink cloud was dancing around the moon and I knew she was there, among the stars.

When Rebecca received the news from her doctor that her breast cancer had metastasized, she made a list of things she wanted to do before she died. Most of the items were unfinished projects, including a quilt she had started for her sister. Quiltmaking had been a hobby of mine for years so I offered to help her. We were sitting at my dining room table, tying knots in the quilt, when she received a call from her husband that her oncologist needed to speak with her right away. Minutes later we were celebrating the news that the thirty tumors that had been in her liver had disappeared during the few months she'd been in a clinical trial for a new cancer drug.

She and I danced around the table. We finished the quilt in time for Christmas. But then Rebecca did something that surprised me. She threw out her to-do list. "I've been given a chance to live my life again," she told me. She wasn't dying anymore. She was *alive*.

A talented artist, she began giving art lessons to young people in her home studio. She camped out on her roof one night to watch a meteor shower. I slept through it, but she told me all about it the next day. She was living her life every day with joy and zeal.

The drug's cancer-quelling effect lasted about two years. Rebecca knew, as the results were coming in from other women who had started the trial before her, that her cancer would likely return. And it did, with a vengeance. She was too tired and weak to even think about making another list. Our hope to take a trip together was more wishful thinking than a plan.

After Rebecca died, I thought about making a list of my own. I felt blessed that I had my health and was inspired by Rebecca's example to celebrate life.

Ever since I was a young girl, I had yearned to see the world, which stemmed from growing up in small towns. I was 10 years old before I ever saw a photo in a book or a magazine of a place I had ever been. That momentous event happened on the first day of fifth grade when I opened my geography book. The photo was of the clock on the old Marshall Field building in downtown Chicago. (When I told Marcello this story, he said, "I know that clock—it's on State Street.")

I had traveled through Europe as a student, during a year abroad at the University of Edinburgh in Scotland. I had returned to the U.K. several times since, but I longed to see Italy again, and Paris…I made a list of places.

The summer after Rebecca died, I took myself to Paris and the lavender fields of Provence. I knew she was with me in spirit on that journey as "we" walked through the lavender rows, listening to the humming bees and the raspy mating song of the *cigales*.

By the time I moved to Florence, I had already visited seven of the ten places on my list: Paris, Provence, Tuscany, Rome, Florence, Venice and the Amalfi Coast. I planned to finish off my list during my time in Europe. But one day at the end of July, when my father e-mailed me news of my mother's deterioration, that little voice in my head said, *Don't wait too long*.

So just two weeks after I returned to Florence from my trip back to the States, I headed out the door again, to the remaining three destinations on my list: Lake Como in northern Italy, the French Riviera and the Greek island of Santorini.

As the train pulled out of the station in Florence, I wrote in my journal: "I love the feeling of imminent adventure."

In Milan, I boarded a shabby old passenger train that stopped at little towns on the east leg of Lake Como. My stop was Varenna. A sign at the station pointed down a winding road to the ferry dock. The road had a pedestrian lane, painted bright blue, for arriving tourists headed for the ferry. The foot traffic was light that day. High season was over.

It was a short ferry ride to Bellagio, situated at the point where the lake splits into an upside down "V." I sat on the ferry's top deck, watching picturesque Varenna slip away, dwarfed by the mountains that rise out of the lake. As we approached the shore at Bellagio, I spied my one-star hotel from the photo I had seen on Trip Advisor. Despite the one-star, the reviews had been reassuring. The hotel hadn't been refurbished in years. But my no-frills room had a million-dollar view, with a balcony overlooking the lake.

I spent hours gazing at the breathtaking scenery, understanding why Lake Como has inspired artists, writers and composers for centuries. These days most visitors to Lake Como enjoy gazing at George Clooney's villa, which sits prominently on the shore in the lakeside village of Laglio. The best way to see the villa is from the water. I knew we were getting close when the ferry listed to the right as passengers crowded the rail. "There it is!" one woman exclaimed. "It looks just like the picture on Google." We got our photos, but alas, there were no sightings of George. The mayor of Laglio has ruled that if more than three gawkers gather at the gates of George's villa, they will be fined. The ferry doesn't stop in Laglio.

My one-star hotel had a highly rated restaurant, where I dined every night. I had the same table, outside under the awning, where I could watch the sun set. One night, my favorite waiter approached my table with a woman who wanted to know if I was English.

"I'm American," I told her.

"Good. You speak English. Would you like a companion for dinner?" she asked in her Aussie accent. She was holding her wine glass; the waiter was carrying her salad plate.

"I'd love it," I said.

Sue, a stage and film producer from Melbourne, pulled up a chair and, three hours later, we were still at the table. She was on her way to London to meet with the producers of the West End production of *West Side Story*, which she was hoping to stage in Australia. She also would be having meetings about a book she had optioned for a film. Sue had turned over the project to a well-known Australian screenwriter-director team, but she was worried that the present version of the script was too slavish to the novel.

"Even the book author agrees with me," Sue said. "I'm thinking I should write the adaptation. How hard can it be?"

That made me laugh, having written ten film scripts myself. On average, I had rewritten *each* of those scripts a dozen times.

Sue had just been to the Amalfi Coast, where I had spent two weeks the previous fall. Her male partner back in Melbourne worried, needlessly, that she might get lonely traveling alone. "I love it!" she exclaimed. Sue and I were kindred spirits.

She told me later that she had walked past the restaurants on the waterfront looking for a woman alone she might dine with. I was flattered she had chosen me and admired her moxie. Sometimes I've been invited to join people dining next to me or have become part of their conversation, but I've never approached anyone with my wine glass and salad.

Sue asked the waiter to take a photo of us and promised to keep in touch.

I left early the next morning—back to Varenna by ferry, then up the hill (pulling a small wheeled bag, my only luggage) to the station. I stopped en route for a cappuccino and pastry at a little café, where at 7 a.m. on a Sunday, it was SRO at the coffee bar. I didn't know it then, but I would be traveling with several of the patrons there for the rest of the day.

I got on the old shabby train back to Milan and caught another train for a six-hour ride to Nice. I was in a compartment, with three seats facing each other, which is conducive to conversation. By the end of our journey together, my compartment mates and I were like the final contestants on *Survivor*. The train broke down at the

French border—mechanical problems, we were told. We gladly disembarked when a conductor mentioned there was something wrong with the brakes.

There must have been a hundred stranded passengers on the platform when an American man announced to the crowd, "I've got a cab driver who'll take four passengers to Nice—€20 a person. I need two more people." Thirty dollars for a ride to Nice. We had no idea when the next train would be arriving or whether there would be room for everybody. It was already late afternoon.

I raised my hand.

"Great," he said. "One more."

I stood with him looking at the faces in the crowd. Many were filled with anxiety and hesitation. One woman caught my eye. No way was she going to leave the herd. I wondered how many victims of wars and revolutions have missed opportunities to escape because they thought that following the pack was the best way.

I didn't have time to ruminate on this. I saw two people get on the train. The herd suddenly was pressing to get back on board.

I snagged the same conductor. "What's going on?" I asked.

"Train is fixed," he said.

"Does it have brakes?" I asked, a tad worried.

He shrugged his shoulders. I looked at the American guy who was throwing his bags back on board. I turned to the elderly Canadian couple who had been in my compartment all day. We hopped back on, without a minute to spare. The train was already rolling out of the station.

Everyone in our car was laughing and tossing their luggage helter-skelter in the corridor. The Australian couple who had been in our compartment didn't re-appear. We didn't even get to say good-bye. I hoped they hadn't been in the bathroom at the station when the train departed. There hadn't even been an announcement.

The train blew through the next station, which heightened my concern that we were on a runaway ride. But twenty minutes later, the brakes squealed and the train stopped in Nice—only an hour-and-a-half late. For years, since my student days, I had held tight to romanticized memories of my train travels on a Eurail pass. The romance was definitely over.

For the next week, I made myself at home at a B&B on a quiet street in Nice, two blocks from the beach. I loved the neighborhood. I had two small balconies, just big enough to stand on. I liked keeping the balcony doors open at night so I could listen to the man in the apartment across the street play the piano. One day he and I were out on our balconies at the same time. He waved. I pretended to play the piano on the railing and then gave him a thumbs-up.

"Thank you," he said.

"You're very good. I love listening to you."

"That was my son you heard this morning," he said.

"How old is he?"

"Nine."

The next day, I saw his son looking out the window at me, as I leaned over my balcony railing watching the street scene below— a habit I had picked up living in Italy. A few moments later, he was playing a jazzy piano piece for the entire street to enjoy. The hotel maid came out on the balcony next to mine. When the music stopped, we both applauded. The boy and his father appeared on their balcony.

"Bravo!" I exclaimed.

The boy took a bow.

A block from the hotel was a Mexican restaurant that served the best Mexican food I've ever tasted—and the margaritas weren't bad either. The second night I dined there, and before I even opened the menu, the owner served me a margarita, lightly salted.

"The way you like it," he said, smiling. I became a regular. On my last night, instead of just giving me a complimentary after-dinner shot of tequila, he put the whole bottle in front of me.

I had a great time in Nice. I went to the museums of Matisse and Chagall, two of my favorite artists. I've always wondered why people and animals float in Chagall's paintings. At the Chagall museum, I read this explanation from the artist himself: *"In the course of my life I have often had the feeling that I was someone other than myself, that I was born somewhere between heaven and earth, so to speak; the world has always struck me as being one vast desert where my soul wanders like a lighted torch."*

One day I rented a chaise called a "sun bed" on the beach and took a nap. I felt like I was in a Chagall painting, floating over the sea—on the French Riviera, at last.

I signed up for a couple of tours. The first was an all-day excursion to Monaco and Monte Carlo. We arrived in time to see the changing of the guard at the palace. It was pretty rinky-dink. The guards weren't in step and the band was off-key. I thought Disney should come in and do an extreme makeover of the palace and the ceremony.

A couple of days later, I joined another tour group that had spent the morning in Monaco, but were disappointed they had missed the guard ceremony.

"You didn't miss anything," I said. "It was so bad, I stood behind a tree giggling."

The driver looked at me in the rearview mirror and said gravely, "It was reported in the Monaco newspapers this morning that the head of the guard had a nervous breakdown because he heard a tourist laughing behind a tree."

Everyone in the van laughed, including the driver.

We had a great time the rest of the day on our tour of St. Paul de Vence, Antibes and Cannes. After I begged, the driver gave us a little extra time in Cannes. I walked along the famous promenade by the beach, called La Croisette, past the big hotels where celebrities hang out during the annual film festival. The walkway ends at the Festival Theater, where handprints of actors and directors are imbedded in concrete. I snapped a photo of Roman Polanski's handprint. I was tempted to draw a handcuff around his wrist with lipstick. He had been taken into Swiss custody only a few days earlier.

The funniest guy on the bus was from Quebec. He was in Nice to attend a fruit-juice convention. His specialty juices were cranberry and blueberry. Next time, we all decided, he should set up a bar in the back of the van and serve liquored fruit drinks. The driver said he'd take us anywhere we wanted to go.

The next day I was off to the final destination on my list—the island of Santorini, which is actually the rim of an ancient (though not extinct) volcano. My hotel was perched on a cliff in Oia, a village at the northern tip of the island. Much of Oia tumbled into the sea during an earthquake in 1956. The morning after my arrival, my bathroom sink fell off the wall. I was a little nervous about the rest of the room. I had a traditional Santorini "cave" room. The cliff dwellings in Oia are burrowed into soft lava rock.

An old house next to the hotel was the focus of much interest and attention during my stay. The house sits in the ruins of dwellings and stables that have crumbled away since the 1956 quake. Every morning, on the concrete slab in front of the house, an old woman dressed in black appeared. She re-appeared in the afternoon and would sit in her chair until well after sunset.

While photographing her one day, I was startled when she got up from her chair and moved to the edge of the concrete slab. I clicked off a few more photos and then enlarged them on my camera's viewing screen. I couldn't believe what I saw—I had photographed her pooping on her patio.

The old woman became the talk of the hotel guests. We all had different theories about her. My American neighbor Jo Ann was sure she was blind. I suggested she may have been blinded by the volcano that erupted on the island in 1650 B.C. (she looked *really* old). Olivia, from Australia, whose husband Jake watched the woman every day with binoculars, did a sketch of her. Olivia thought the woman sat there every day to be close to her dead husband.

When it became known to the group that I was a writer and a former *People* magazine reporter, it fell to me to find out the woman's story. Gertraud, the friendly German woman who served breakfast every morning, told me everything.

The woman's name was Yanula. She was 86 with failing sight (Jo Ann was right) and was no longer able to walk up the steep steps from the house to the road. She suffered from dementia, which was why we saw her going to the bathroom on the patio. A woman stayed with her at night, and as we all had seen on a Sunday afternoon, her family came to visit her.

Despite her meager existence, Yanula was rich in assets. She owned the swath of cliffside property from the road to the sea, a valuable piece of real estate given the development all around her. She also owned the windmill and the grocery store, run by her family, next to the hotel pool. The hotel guests, myself included, were frequent customers at the store.

As for Olivia's theory that Yanula was pining for her dead husband, Gertraud confirmed he died ten years earlier. But he was a worthless womanizer, according to Gertraud, leaving poor Yanula to work the farm and take care of the animals. She was probably pooping on a picture of his face, I told Olivia, who didn't take the news well.

Gertraud told me that an Italian film had been shot at the house and that Italian tourists often come to see the location. (Jake googled all the films that had been shot in Oia. I asked the hotel owners if they remembered the name of the film, but no one could recall.) According to Gertraud, one nosey tourist went down the steps to the house and nearly had a heart attack when Yanula appeared.

Jo Ann had gone home by the time I had tracked down the full story, which I e-mailed her from an internet café in the village. I signed it *"live from Oia, your intrepid reporter – Rebecca."*

Tom, who knows Santorini like a native, called one day to find out how things were going. He was concerned about my ankle and how I was faring on Santorini's steep slopes. The hotel's steps were treacherous, but otherwise I was doing well, I told him. I hadn't seen any of the sights he had recommended on Santorini, outside of Oia. I had been too busy finding out about Yanula.

"I need to talk to you," Tom said. He had been doing some reading online about the difference between a memoir and a diary and was concerned where I was going with my book. I thought he might be taking his role as my one-man New Jersey Italian Greek chorus a little too seriously and wondered if Sophocles and Euripides had had problems with mutinous choristers. But I listened carefully to what he had to say.

"What exactly are you doing in Santorini?" Tom asked pointedly.

"When I'm not sleeping in my cave, I'm gazing at the gorgeous view that looks like it's right out of a travel magazine," I said.

"But what's happening with you? I read online that unlike a diary, a memoir deals with the transformation of the author," he said. "Are you experiencing a transformation yet? A memoir must show a transformation."

"Yes, I know," I said meekly. I wasn't growing fangs or chest hair, but I did feel that internally I had grown a lot from my Italian culture shock and recent travels.

"What's going on with you *emotionally*?" he persisted. Tom was transforming into my New Jersey Italian Greek Chorus-turned-Analyst.

I told him I would have to get back to him. It was almost time for the sun to set over Oia, which is a religious experience in that village. People drop what they're doing and rush toward various cliffside viewing points. My viewing point was my very own terrace.

The next day, I sent Tom an e-mail saying I was in a very good place emotionally.

I remembered my dinner with my friend John, during my return visit to Pasadena. He had assured me that no matter how hard the boat rocked, no matter how big the waves, I was on the course I was meant to take. I had embarked on an excellent pre-destined misadventure. And like all good protagonists I would triumph over all obstacles. On the character arc, by which Hollywood scripts are measured, I was not quite at the top of the curve.

I had an e-mail from Sue, who was back in Australia. As promised, she sent the photo of us dining together at my hotel on Lake Como. She was despondent that she hadn't spotted George Clooney's villa on her lake cruise, even though I had given her a detailed description and told her to google a photo, which she had done. She told me she would send excerpts from e-mails a friend of hers had sent while she was writing a memoir about her life in a French village with her dog. Sue said her friend sold the book to Simon & Schuster, without an agent, and it has become a bestseller in Australia.

One afternoon at the hotel pool, I met another Australian woman named Susan, who was an artist from the outback of Australia. She lived in a rural town with her twin 14-year-old boys. She was divorced, but was still close to her ex, who was home with their sons as she traveled through Europe. I met her on the last day of her eight-week trip that had taken her to London, Paris, the French Riviera and on an extensive tour through Italy. She was already thinking about returning next year to Amalfi, where she had had a flirtation with a gorgeous young guy, a cab driver named Arturo.

We were having dinner together when she told me the story: For seven days, she and Arturo met at a café by his taxi stand. He wanted to take her to bed. She said no, but she really wanted to say yes.

One day, another cab driver, much older than Arturo, took her aside, "Do you like Arturo?" he asked her.

"Yes, very much," she replied.

"He likes you," he said. "Why don't you give him your pussy cat?"

A cat, sitting near our table meowed, and we burst out laughing.

Susan didn't give Arturo her "pussy cat" and she was now tormented by the "what ifs."

"I haven't been with a man in nine years," she said. "Not since my divorce."

"Oh, Susan," I said. "You need to go back to Amalfi *tomorrow*."

But she left the next day for home and left me with one of her sketches of Venice. We exchanged e-mail addresses. I was sorry to see her leave.

Soon it was my turn to return home. On the flights back to Florence, via Athens and Frankfurt, I thought about my list. I had checked off every destination. A great accomplishment, but I felt strangely empty. The yearning I had felt for so long was gone. If I really thought about it, I knew I could come up with other places I'd like to visit. But the wanderlust that had fueled my dreams had vanished.

A sign of transformation?

12

The hustler

The morning I left Santorini, I sent Marcello a short text saying I was on my way back to Florence and would call him the next day. We had exchanged e-mails while I was in Nice and he asked me to call him when I returned.

I was up early my first day back, eager to resume work on the book. While I was away, I had decided to do a major rewrite of the opening chapters. As I re-read my Florence journals, there were a few pieces of the story that just didn't seem to fit together and most of them had to do with Marcello.

Late in the afternoon, I took a break and went down the street to the neighborhood café. It was three-deep at the bar. Around five o'clock, everyone comes in for a quick hit of caffeine to wake up from their naps or a glass of wine to start the evening. It was Friday. There was a sigh of relief in the air.

That evening, I called Marcello. I got a phone company message that he was "unavailable" which meant he was on a call or his phone was switched off. Regardless, my number would appear in his message log.

I worked through the weekend on the book revisions, feeling strangely driven by a sense of urgency.

On Sunday, I called Nadia. I had promised to call her when I got back. She was glad to hear from me—she had something she wanted to talk to me about—so we arranged to meet the next afternoon.

"It's my day off tomorrow, but I'm doing some work for Marcello at the store," she said.

"I thought you didn't work for him anymore," I said, surprised.

"I don't. But he asked me to help them get ready for the trunk show they're taking to the U.S. soon," she said.

Nadia and I met at her apartment. She made a minty sweet tea and told me her news: she had fallen in love. But there were complications, which we discussed at length. She wanted me to tell her what to do. It had been almost a week since she had seen the guy. She'd sent him an e-mail, but he hadn't yet replied. So like Marcello, I thought, who had not called me since my return.

Nadia is strong and high-strung and isn't used to guys playing with her emotions. She likes to call the shots.

"This is the first time I've ever been rejected by a man," she said. She grabbed her cell phone. "Should I call him? What do I say? Tell me."

As I ad-libbed her script, she started dialing. She waited for him to answer. "Shit!" she said, clicking off. She got the canned message that he wasn't available. She re-dialed. No answer. "Why isn't he answering? What does he want with me?" She paced around the room, running her hands through her long hair. "I give him until midnight tonight. If he doesn't call, I delete him from my life."

"*Finito*," I said.

"*Brava*," she said. "You're finally speaking Italian."

"I know how you feel," I told her. "I've just gone through something very similar with someone."

"Here or in the U.S.?" she asked, eager for details.

"Here," I said. "You know him."

Her eyes widened. "Marcello?" She sat down next to me on the sofa. "Tell me. Are you in love with him?"

"No, I'm not in love," I said. "I like Marcello. He's smart and funny. We've had a good time together."

"What has happened between you and him?"

"We've been intimate," I said delicately. "We saw each other a lot this summer. But the last time we were together didn't end well. We've talked a few times on the phone since then and exchanged several e-mails, but I haven't seen him in more than two months."

Nadia looked at me for a moment. I knew what she was going to say.

"Rebecca, I don't want to hurt you," she began, weighing her words. "You know Marcello goes with a lot of women. He can be talking on the phone to you and the next minute be flirting with the woman at the table next to him. That's how he is. He can't stay with one woman. I ask him, Why you don't marry and have babies? He always says, No, not now."

"I know he's a Casanova," I said. "The last time I saw him, I asked him about his history with women—about whether, as a young man, he decided he would never marry. He told me he was shy. Girls didn't notice him until he learned how to flirt. He developed his playboy persona to attract women. But I think underneath there's still a lot of shyness and insecurity.

"I was surprised how open he was with me. He told me he fell in love for the first time when he was 25. He said he has never lived with a woman and has never been engaged. His longest relationship lasted two years. I asked if he had any regrets—he said there was one woman."

"Did he tell you her name?" Nadia asked.

"No, but he said she was very intelligent and pretty—'the way I like,' he said—whatever that means."

"She was from Australia," Nadia said. "She was really intelligent and beautiful and nice. But in the end, he dropped her like the others." Nadia shook her head.

"You know this is entirely your fault," I teased her. "You sent me to Marcello's store to talk to Arman about that apartment."

"And you saw Marcello at the restaurant. Because of me." Nadia laughed.

"And do you know what happened, the very next day? I was at Piazza della Signoria, lost and looking at my map, and who walks around the corner but Marcello. I've seen him all over Florence. What's with that?"

"I shouldn't tell you this, but I like you, Rebecca, and I want you to know the truth," Nadia said. "Marcello doesn't own the store."

Suddenly, the pieces of the story that didn't quite fit together were flying in the air.

"What are you saying, Nadia?"

"The Jordanian brothers own the store. Marcello works for them."

"On the card Marcello gave me, under his name, it says *owner*," I said.

"You can print anything you want on a card," she said.

The writer-in-me was jumping up and down, shouting, *"Oh my god!"* The me-side-of-me was speechless.

"Marcello wanders around the city all day looking for rich women, who are dressed well with expensive jewelry," Nadia continued. "He sits down next to them and talks to them. He gives them his card and invites them to come by the store. If they buy a coat, he gets a commission."

I remembered the day at the carousel. *"I'm not a designer," he said, "but I have something in mind for you. Come by the store and ask for me."*

He was hustling me. The pickin's must have been slim that day; I wasn't in designer clothes or wearing jewelry. But after all, it was the end of the season and he was hobbling around on crutches.

The pieces started falling into place likes chunks of concrete. Several times I had walked past the store during the summer and never saw Marcello inside. The first time I mentioned this to him, he said, "I don't spend much time there." The second time I mentioned it, he replied, "I told you, I'm not at the store that much."

"So when women come into the store wanting to see Marcello, the owner, what happens?" I asked Nadia.

"When I worked there, I would say that he wasn't there, but that I was his assistant and would be happy to help them. It was dishonest, I know, but that was my job," Nadia said.

"And now that you no longer work there, the brothers handle the sale?"

"They have a couple of sales people who do what I used to do." Nadia looked at me sadly. "Rebecca, I'm sorry to tell you all this."

"Don't be sorry. I'm so glad you told me."

"Do you feel hurt?" she asked.

"No, Nadia," I said. "I had a good time with Marcello. We enjoyed each other. I don't feel robbed. He didn't take anything from me."

"Good."

"And he didn't make any money off me."

"I thought you bought a jacket," Nadia said.

"No. He invited me to the store, but I didn't go. I didn't want a leather jacket."

Nadia burst out laughing. I couldn't help but laugh, too.

It was after six o'clock when I left Nadia's. She offered to call me a cab, but I wanted to walk, to let the concrete settle.

Nadia lives near the hotel where I had stayed, so I knew the neighborhood well. I walked to the arch at the end of Borgo Pinti.

I could still see Marcello smiling at me as he walked toward me that night in March. He was wearing a teal scarf and a black leather jacket. Later at the hotel as I hung up that jacket, I asked, "Is this one of yours?" He replied, "Yes."

At the carousel the day we met, Marcello said he and six cousins owned the biggest leather factory in Florence. According to Nadia, the factory that supplies the store isn't owned by Marcello or his so-called "cousins." I remember saying to Marcello one night shortly after I had moved to Florence that I'd like to go to the factory sometime. I was interested in seeing how leather garments are produced. He smiled at me, but said nothing. At the time, I wondered why he didn't say, "*Sure, I'll take you there next time I go.*"

The one consolation I took in all this was that, after our first meeting at the carousel, he never mentioned me going to the store to see the merchandise.

I continued walking, under the arch and past the Irish pub. My mind was spinning as I played back the reel of our conversations. I didn't feel sorry for myself. I truly felt I had lost nothing. I'd had a fun summer fling with a Romeo and a rogue. The writer-in-me was ecstatic: this was the twister of all twists.

I walked into the piazza at Santa Croce, the church where legends of the Renaissance are buried—Michelangelo, Galileo, Machiavelli. The façade glowed in the setting sun. I was living in Florence, walking on Roman pavers, in the footsteps of Dante. How incredible was that? I felt a rush of inspiration.

I walked to the taxi stand at the edge of the square and got in a cab. I couldn't wait to get home and call Nancy and Tom.

I called Nancy first. The story spilled out of me so fast that all she could say over and over was "oh no, I'm so sorry."

"I'm okay. Really. I'm not going to jump off my kitchen table," I assured her.

Then I called Tom, who was blown away. "I shouldn't be surprised," he said. "But surprise isn't the right word. It's shocking really. Don't you want to know if anything he has told you is true?"

"According to Nadia, he lied to me about his age," I said. "She says he's not 48. She thinks he's around 52."

"Don't you want to follow him and find out where he goes, where he lives?" Tom asked. "Maybe he's living with his mother."

Tom was so good at inciting riotous thoughts in me. "I think you should come to Florence and follow him," I said. "I'll get you a trench coat, but it won't be leather."

"I don't know what he looks like."

"We'll do a stake-out together." I could see us at Caffè Rivoire, one of Marcello's favorite haunts—Tom in his spy coat, hiding behind a newspaper, and me in dark glasses with a Grace Kelly scarf wrapped around my head. "No, no—I've got a better idea. You go to the store with Marcello's card and say you'd like to speak with him personally."

"I thought I was going to wear a trench coat and follow him."

"Forget the trench coat," I said. "You say that your wife met Marcello at a café and that you want to surprise her with a leather jacket for her birthday. You insist on speaking with Marcello directly. When he shows up at the store, you tell him you're going to call your wife and ask her to meet you at the store." I started giggling. "And you pull out a camera and take a picture of Marcello's face when I walk in the door."

The writer-in-me did cartwheels as Tom and I split our sides laughing.

13

Basta

The day of Nadia's revelation—just hours before, actually—Sofie, my real estate agent, stopped by my apartment with a fistful of papers.

A package of refill prescription medications that I had ordered from a mail-order pharmacy in the U.S. had been held up at Italian customs at the Milan airport. Everything was legit. But Italian Customs wanted copies of the prescriptions, my passport, the pharmacy invoice and the payment receipt. Additionally, I had to respond to four pages of questions. There was a box I had to check affirming that the medications had no ill side effects—like making me want to strangle the customs agent who had sent the letter.

Far worse things had happened to me during my first months in Florence. I don't know exactly what it was about that particular exercise-in-futility that set me off. But something in me said, *Basta!* In Italian that means ENOUGH.

I copied my passport and set it on the kitchen table, where Sofie was filling out the forms. This was not the first time Sofie had sat at that table, filling out papers on my behalf: the *permesso di soggiorno* documents, the letter to the cell-phone company and my application for a fiscal code number.

I opened my passport to the page with the Italian *visto* and thought how hard Sofie had worked to help me get it. I had already told her what had happened at the immigration office when I went for my *permesso* interview in late July. And I told her I would never return to that hellhole. I had given her a margarita before I broke that news.

Fingering the passport, I asked her, "I won't be able to renew this visa without a *permesso*, will I?"

"No," she said, shaking her head. "But I know people who have lived here five years on an expired visa."

"What's the worst thing that could happen if I'm caught with an expired visa—they'd just send me home, right?"

"That's it."

"No fines or jail time?"

"No, nothing like that," Sofie assured me.

I was talking to Nancy a few days later and told her how much I was missing California. The weather had turned wet and cold in Florence. I had complained when it was too hot and now I was unhappy about the dreariness. I had spent every day since my return from Santorini at my laptop, writing like a maniac, with little social contact—except for my afternoon with Nadia, which didn't exactly lift my spirits.

"I can't see you back in California right now," Nancy said. "Maybe Italy isn't the place where you're meant to stay, but it's good you're thinking about your options. You can always come to Berlin."

I remembered being blown across Alexanderplatz, near Nancy's apartment, in an autumn snowstorm. "I'll come visit again," I promised, but I couldn't see living there. Nancy loves winter. She's a November baby; I'm a May baby.

I had been reading a book set on the English Channel island of Guernsey called *The Guernsey Literary and Potato Peel Pie Society*, which I had bought, on my friend Peg's recommendation, at the venerable Galignani bookstore on Rue de Rivoli in Paris. I was transported by the descriptions of the sea and the light and the salt-kissed breezes. I had already decided I would never spend another summer in Florence, not after those broiling weeks in my mosquito gas chamber.

I couldn't sleep one night. I tossed and turned and couldn't get comfortable. My mind wasn't quiet.

I got up, turned on my laptop and googled "U.K. visa requirements." I read about the Tier 5 visa that allows "creative" types to work in the U.K. for twenty-four months, without having a real job. I filled out the survey that tallied my eligibility points. A message popped up saying, *"Congratuations. You are eligible."* I submitted my contact info, with a request for a visa consultant to call me. All very civilized, as one would expect with the Brits, I thought.

Later that same day, I received an e-mail from Fiona, a dear friend from Edinburgh whom I have known since my student days at the University there. She was just checking in. I called her and floated my idea of jumping ship and coming to the U.K. Of course, she was in favor and ready to toss me a life vest. "You can come here and figure out what you want to do," she said.

I then got a Skype call from a friend in L.A. who reported that temps were near 80. I went to bed listening to the rain, having second thoughts about running off to soggy Scotland.

The next morning, I went to a salon around the corner from my apartment and had a manicure and pedicure. My fingernails were a mess from so much typing and my toes needed attention after all the miles I had walked on my recent trek to France and Greece.

It was a beautiful warm autumn day. I'm such a sunflower at heart—I could feel my petals opening. I stood at a busy street

corner with my freshly polished pomegranate-red toenails spar-
kling in the sun. I stretched my arms above my head and filled
my lungs with air. A guy coming toward me in the crosswalk gave
me a sidelong glance and said "beautiful." I wasn't sure if he was
referring to my toenails or the rest of me, but it made me smile.

The writer-in-me whispered, *"We're staying."*

14

The anniversary

I was copying my book revisions to a backup memory stick and a pop-up message confirmed the "date modified" as October 26. I stared out the window at my view of Florence for a moment and did the math. It was the twenty-fourth anniversary of my wedding day.

I don't wake up on that day, remembering it as my anniversary anymore. Funny, after all these years, it's my laptop that reminds me.

Marcello and I were in bed one night, having one of our intimate conversations after sex, and he asked me, "Did you have a good marriage?"

"It was good until it turned bad," I said.

"Right," he said. "It's good until it isn't."

I told him the story of my marriage, which had followed a very long courtship—nine-and-a-half years, in fact. From the day we met to the day our divorce was finalized, the man I married and I had been a couple for almost twenty-four years.

During my conversations with Tom about chauvinistic men, I had a poignant realization. I told him, "The only man I've ever dated who was totally supportive of me—who never tried to hold me back or change me—was the man I married."

But in the last years of our marriage, my husband's personal problems got the better of him. I knew we were on the road to divorce and had become bold enough to tell him so. I don't think he believed I would ever break apart our family—our son was just a few years old then. But one dark day, our marriage ended, and I never looked back.

After the divorce, we remained partners in raising our son. My greatest regret in life is that I didn't marry a man I could grow old with and love more with each passing year. But the man I married and I had a child who is the joy of my life. And for that, I'm very grateful.

15

The lion and the gazelle

On the day of my wedding anniversary, I received e-mails from the two Australian women I had met on my recent trip.

The first one was from Sue, the producer from Melbourne. She told me she had been in touch with her friend who wrote the memoir about her life in a French village with her dog and that she would love to hear from me. Sue said I could probably get the book on Amazon or I could ask the author herself to send me excerpts. She gave me the woman's e-mail address.

Sue was flattered that I had included her in my chapter about my visit to Lake Como. I had told Sue I had been writing reams since I got back, partly the result of a major plot twist that had occurred since my return. She was intrigued. Sue mentioned her *West Side Story* auditions would begin in three weeks. I couldn't believe how quickly the ball was rolling. Sue was obviously a bull-by-the-balls kind of gal.

The second e-mail came from Susan, the artist from western Australia whom I met on Santorini. I had e-mailed her, asking if she was already planning her return trip to Amalfi.

She wrote:

Hi to you Rebecca, lovely to hear from you. Yes, I am planning another trip, probably to Venice, Rome and of course I have to go back to Amalfi, to see beautiful Arturo...can't stop thinking about him, even now. The old taxi driver was right, "you're gonna be thinkin' of Amalfi for a long time now." ...Remember what I told you darling, always have three men who you fancy, then you'll never get let down. Hope you are well and happy and I really enjoyed our dinner that night, thank you once again Rebecca.

Lots of love, Susan xxx

I laughed when I read the line *"always have three men you fancy."* That was her parting advice to me when we said good-bye that night. "Don't ever forget that," she told me.

Three men I fancied. A new list. I had my work cut out for me.

The next day I stopped by the leather shop where Nadia works. With her help, I chose a Perfect Travel Purse that would accommodate my boxy camera and a guidebook. She put me in charge of the store for five minutes while she ran upstairs to see if she had the bag in brown, which she thought was prettier than the black bag on display. No luck. She would try to special order one, she told me, promising to give me a girlfriend discount.

"All you want to do is come here and buy a handbag," Nadia teased me. "I have so much I want to talk to you about."

Nadia has two older sisters who live in Florence, but she doesn't feel close to them and she says it has been difficult for her to find female friends she can confide in. "I want a friend who's like a sister to me," Nadia said. "I've prayed to God about this and I think he brought you to me."

I could hardly speak when she said this, thinking about my own sister, Amy. She and I were not close and there had been a lot of friction between us over the years. Amy was three years younger and resented following in my shadow through school. I was a good student and involved in a lot of activities. Amy was a free spirit and a social butterfly who rarely cracked open a book. She got through life with a flirtatious wink and a smile. But she made a series of bad choices in her adult life that took her down a dark road.

What I liked about Nadia was her passion and fire. At the store, during a lull between customers, Nadia told me about an Italian proverb, which she translated for me:

> *Every morning the gazelle wakes up and starts to run.*
> *Every morning the lion wakes up and starts to run.*
> *It is not important to be the gazelle or the lion.*
> *The important thing is the running.*

"I can't understand people who want to go back in their lives," Nadia said. "We cannot go back. We must chase our dreams and run hard—like the lion and the gazelle."

She shared with me a journal she is writing that she will give to her son someday. Although her native language is Arabic, she writes in Italian, her son's native language. At the beginning of the story, she writes about her son's father, who left her early in her pregnancy, and whom her son has never known. Nadia wants him to know the story of his father. But mostly she writes about her desire to be a mother and her love for her child.

She opened the book to the first page. Leaning on the counter by the cash register, we read the lines together—first, she read the Italian and then helped me translate the words into English.

"You're a beautiful writer," I said, after she turned the first page.

"Really? You think I'm good?" she asked incredulously.

"Really," I said. "You're very poetic."

Nadia spun around, holding the journal to her chest. "That makes me so happy."

I imagined seeing her son as a man reading the pages of that little book. I smiled at her. "You're giving your son an extraordinary gift."

∽

After I left Nadia at the store that day, I wandered over to my favorite café by the carousel at Piazza della Repubblica. It was six o'clock and already dark. I sat under a heater at an outdoor table at the front of the café, with an unobstructed view of the carousel. A bright light shone down on the table. I took out my journal and started writing.

I thought about Marcello, whom I had met at that very spot, one year earlier, and all the drama he had inspired since. I knew I had met him and Nadia for good reason. The fact that I met them separately, at different times and in different parts of Florence, and that Nadia, in fact, had led me back to Marcello, confirmed my belief that destiny was at play in this story.

Nadia and I talked about my feelings for Marcello, now that I knew his little secret.

"Marcello got stuck in his own lie with me," I told her. "He should have just said at some point—look, this is how it works. But he didn't and the lie snowballed. I don't hate him for it. He was very open with me about so many things."

"He opened the doors of his life to you," Nadia said.

"And I did the same."

"Are you in love with him?" This was the second time in two weeks that Nadia had asked me that.

"No," I said. "I love the shy side of him. If I had met him when he was young and shy with girls, I probably would have fallen in love with him. I was always attracted to shy guys. I don't like the playboy, party-boy side of Marcello, not at all. But that's part of who he is and at this point in his life, that's not going to change."

I told her what Marcello himself had said to me that last night I saw him: "*You see what you want to see and ignore what you don't want to see.*"

"Yes, we had fun, great sex and wonderful conversations," I said to Nadia. "But I can't hang on to that and ignore the rest."

I wrote pages and pages at the café that evening. I had a hearty lasagna dinner and a glass of wine. But the chilly October night was giving me cold feet. I asked for the check—three times, in fact. Finally the waiter brought it to me. "I didn't want you to leave," he said. "You are good for business."

I laughed, but didn't understand what he meant until I was reading a Florence guidebook the next day. To my astonishment, the café by the carousel that had become my favorite place to write is a part of Florence's great literary heritage. The café, Giubbe Rosse, has been a gathering place for writers and artists since the early 1900s. Without knowing its history, I had experienced its magnetic pull.

When I got home that night, I e-mailed Marcello. Despite my initial intention to sit back and wait, I wanted to hear his side of Nadia's story sooner than later.

My message was short. I told him I was back from my travels and busy working on the book. I suggested we meet for a drink to catch up.

Two hours later, shortly after midnight, he e-mailed back: "*Ciao Rebecca, think I don't have your last phone number. Give me a call so can have it.*"

I thought about e-mailing him the number. But the next day, I called him and he answered.

"So you've deleted my number?" I teased him.

"No, I still have your old number in my phone," he said. He recited the old number, which I couldn't even remember.

We talked for a bit and he asked if I'd like to meet for a drink over the weekend. I told him that friends from Britain would be visiting. "Let's get together after they leave next week," I said.

When we hung up, I felt extremely mature.

16

The harvest

I received an e-mail from Kathryn, saying she was back in Florence. I called her cell. The phone rang and rang. Finally she answered.

"Hello, my dear," she said when she heard my voice. She was out in the olive grove she owns near Florence, assessing the year's crop.

"It's awful," she lamented. "There are hardly any olives. We probably can pick them all in a weekend."

Her two young cousins from Portland were coming to Florence in a few days to help with the harvest as were my British friends, Clare and Gavin.

"I don't know if I'll have enough olives for one pressing," she said.

This sounded disastrous though I had no idea how many bottles of olive oil one pressing would yield. And at that moment, she didn't either.

The picking began a few days later. Kathryn called that morning to tell me how to get to the grove.

"Take the No. 36 bus to end of the line, where it turns around, just past the church," she said. "Call me when you get there and I'll come get you. We'll have a picnic lunch and you can help us pick in the afternoon." Then she said, "I hope your friends know this is serious work."

"They brought gloves. They're ready to pick," I said. Clare and Gavin had been eagerly awaiting this experience for months.

"Good," she said. "What about you? I don't suppose you can go up a ladder with your ankle."

"No, I can't go up a ladder," I said. "But I'm glad to help in other ways. I can take photographs for you."

"Fine," she said. "It will be wonderful to see you."

I called Kathryn from the bus to let her know where we were, as we passed Porta Romana, one of the grand gates of ancient Florence on the south side of the Arno.

"Tell the driver to let you off at Magori," she said. At least that's what I thought she said.

About twenty minutes later, the bus pulled into a turn-around area. I asked the driver where Magori was. He shrugged and shook his head, telling me in Italian that he didn't understand me. If, at that moment, I had just glanced out the bus window and seen the sign at the bus stop, I might have saved us all a lot of aggravation. The sign said "Le Gore." The Italian pronunciation of "gore" is "goray." With all the noise on the bus, I didn't realize Kathryn had said Le Gore, not Magori.

When we reached the end of the line, the driver turned off the engine. We were in the middle of nowhere. I called Kathryn, who had no idea where we were. I handed my phone to the bus driver and he and Kathryn had a long conversation in Italian. Clare, Gavin and I crossed the road to look at the timetable posted for the return bus.

The driver handed me my phone. Kathryn told me to take the bus to the main square in Galuzzo. I told her I would call her when we got there.

When I called her from Galuzzo, I could tell she was irritated. "Have you eaten yet?" she asked me.

"No," I said. I didn't remind her that she had invited us to join their picnic.

"I don't know if I have enough food to feed all of you," she said. "There's a bar across from the square. Go get yourselves some *panini* and whatever else you'd like to eat."

She was exasperated that I couldn't see the bar from the bus stop. There was a farmer's market in the square, so I didn't have a clear view of the shops around the piazza. I had never been to Galuzzo.

Finally I said, "Look, Kathryn. I'm sorry about all this. I think we'll just have lunch here and take the bus back to Florence. We tried, but it's just not working out."

"No," she insisted. "I'm getting in the car now and I'll be there in seven minutes."

Having heard my side of the conversation, Clare put a sympathetic arm around my shoulder. She could see and hear my stress. This was supposed to be a fun day in the olive grove.

We found the bar and bought ourselves sandwiches and dessert pastries. Gavin ran across the street to get some fruit from the farmer's market.

I was standing in front of the bar talking to Clare when I saw Kathryn walking along the sidewalk toward us.

"Kathryn!" I put out my arms and gave her a big hug. I had so been looking forward to seeing her again.

She was pleased to meet Clare and Gavin, who came running from the square with his bag of fresh fruit. We piled in Kathryn's little rental car.

I had never been to the grove, which sits on top of a hill with a sweeping view of Florence, to the north. The dome of the Duomo rises above a ridge in the middle distance. And directly below the grove is the grand monastery of Certosa.

The olive pickers had made good progress that morning. Soon after we arrived, Kathryn called us to lunch in the *capanna*, a wooden shelter where she had laid out a Tuscan feast. The table was a veritable groaning board, with roasted herb chicken and potatoes, Tuscan bread, a wheel of Pecorino cheese and freshly picked grapes. Kathryn passed the chicken, but I let it go by me. I took my ham-and-cheese *panini* from the bag. As Clare had predicted while we were waiting in the village for Kathryn to arrive, "You know in the end, she'll realize there's plenty of food for everyone."

There was plenty for everyone, which Kathryn eventually acknowledged. I couldn't help but feel the irony in this. Wasn't the Tuscan lifestyle all about breaking and sharing bread, no matter how small the loaf. And wouldn't it have been more gracious to say, in the face of a possible food shortage, "Rebecca, why don't you pick up some sandwiches just in case I don't have enough."

Kathryn clearly was not in good form. But it went beyond that. At one point during the conversation at the table, I asked Kathryn to translate something that had been said.

"I see you haven't been learning Italian," she said.

I bit my tongue, remembering her telling me how long she had struggled to learn the language.

The cheese wheel had dwindled down to a wedge. As it was passed around the table, everyone had scraped a slice across the core of the wedge, like scooping soft fruit from its skin.

Kathryn picked up the gutted wedge and looked around the table. "Who cut the cheese?" she asked.

I started to giggle, thinking of the slang meaning of the phrase. I knew Kathryn wasn't asking if someone had farted. One of Kathryn's cousins meekly raised her hand.

Kathryn scolded her. "You take the best part for yourself and leave this for the others?"

As she upbraided her cousin for her bad manners, I wanted to say to Kathryn, "And *your* manners are appalling."

After lunch, Kathryn announced she was going to go get a friend of hers, a 78-year-old Italian woman who was an expert olive picker. I offered to come with her.

In spite of Kathryn's bad temper, I wanted to feel the rapport that had forged our friendship. As we drove through the Tuscan countryside in its autumn splendor, I said to her, "We've seen Tuscany together in the spring and now the fall." She smiled at me.

I had told Kathryn on the phone a few days earlier that I was thinking about leaving Italy before my visa expired the following summer. She knew I'd had a rough start in Florence and she had been empathetic—to a point.

On the ride up to the olive grove, she had told Clare, Gavin and me how the summer drought was to blame for the scant olive crop. When I commented about the blistering summer heat, Kathryn retorted, "I don't want to hear about it. You could have had a comfortable place to live." Yes, the apartment below hers would have been very comfortable. It had screens and air-conditioning, but the rent was €1,500—about $2,250 a month, excluding utilities, which would have been sky-high with an air conditioner running.

The apartment I chose had no screens, no air conditioning and certainly no Old World charm, but it was well within my budget. When I had told Kathryn about the building's elevators and the supermarket next door, she said dismissively, "You are not living the life of an Italian." I was amused, thinking of all the Italians who lived in my building, including the Mafia princess.

By the end of our day in the olive grove, I'd had enough of Kathryn's attitude and arrogance. As we stood side by side stripping olives off her trees, Kathryn said to me, "When you go back home, Rebecca, find something to do with your life that will be good for the world."

"How do you know that I'm not already doing something good for the world, Kathryn?" I said, tossing the olives in my hand down onto the net under the tree.

"That's true, I don't know you that well," she said.

"What you don't know about me, Kathryn," I said, "is that I have a great wellspring of joy inside of me that enables me to embrace life wherever I am, no matter what difficulties I'm faced with. I came to Florence to write a book and that's what I'm doing. And it will be a candid account of my experience here. I hope people who read it will be inspired by my story."

Kathryn even took a swipe at that. "I could never, ever do that," she said. "I could never write a book about myself. I have to write about the *other person*."

"There are many ways to tell a story, Kathryn," I said. "What matters in the end is that you tell the story well."

I went for a walk through Kathryn's grove, photographing the last light of day as it turned the gray-green leaves to silver. I found Gavin sitting on a slope, painting a view of the monastery. Gavin is an accomplished watercolorist whose sketchbooks are filled with images of his travels around the world.

I photographed everyone gathering the olive nets and emptying the fruit of their labors into red plastic baskets. The day's harvest was stored in a shed on the side of the hill. I took a group photo of the tired, but smiling pickers.

We said our good-byes to Kathryn and her cousins. I promised to e-mail my photos. Pietro, the caretaker of the grove, gave Clare, Gavin and me a ride into the village. But on the way, he stopped at his house—which, ironically, was across the street from the Le Gore bus stop. He motioned for us to follow him inside the garden gate. He took us up onto his patio and plucked clusters of plump grapes off his arbor for each of us—the sweetest grapes I've ever tasted.

He told us that this was the house he had lived in since birth, with his mother and father, and later with his wife and their own children. He was alone now, he said. He shrugged, as if to say, that's life. I knew he was enjoying our company as much as we were enjoying his.

He led us inside the house and up the stairs to his living area. He pulled back a curtain at the front window to show us the view of the village and of the monastery tower, illuminated by a spotlight on the hill above his home. He proudly showed us his garage, where I noticed a shelf lined with bottles of homemade tomato sauce and jars of pickled capers and peppers. He offered us samples. We passed the jars among us, tasting the salt and the fire of the Tuscan earth.

Pietro drove us into the village to a bus stop near a bar. We asked him to join us for a glass of wine. He held up three fingers, saying he had already had his limit of "*tre*" glasses for the day. He embraced each one of us as we said *arrivederci*.

As I watched him walk away, I thought, *this* is why I came to Italy.

17

Giubbe Rosse

Early one morning during Gavin and Clare's visit, I found him, with his sketchbook and watercolors, painting the view from my apartment balcony. Deep in thought, he didn't hear me step outside. When I said *buongiorno,* his brush nearly flew off the pad.

"Sorry to sneak up on you," I said, anxiously peering at the sketch. "Did I do any damage?"

Gavin laughed. "Only to my heart."

At the end of each day, I loved looking at Gavin's sketchbook. It was a pictorial diary of our wanderings around Florence. Every sketch had a story. But one story was extraordinary.

I had asked Gavin if he would do a watercolor of my favorite spot in Florence—the carousel in Piazza della Repubblica, with Giubbe Rosse in the background. He beautifully captured the scene—the blur of the carousel's bright colors and the crowd at the café, including the waiters in red jackets. ("Giubbe rosse" means red jackets. Ever since the café opened in 1896, its waiters have been known for their attire.) Clare and I ended up as little splashes of paint, sitting at a front table under the café's canopy.

Gavin eventually joined us, and while he filled in the finishing touches of his sketch, I went across the piazza to a cash machine. When I returned, Clare and Gavin were wide-eyed.

"Becky, you won't believe this," Clare whispered.

"The waiter has gone to get his boss," Gavin said. "He wants him to see the painting."

"Are you going to sell it to him?" I asked. I had hoped Gavin would give me first dibs. "I can go back to the machine and get another €40." Gavin laughed.

The waiter returned with a handsome, elegantly dressed man who wore a knee-length black coat over jeans, with a taupe colored silk scarf stylishly tied around his neck. He had soulful eyes and a beautiful smile. His name was Claudio. Clare and I were instantly swept away. Gavin snapped a photo of us, capturing our rapture.

Claudio admired Gavin's painting and asked if we had seen the art exhibition in the cavernous room at the back of the café. He talked about the artists who show their work at the café and the possibility that Gavin himself might want to exhibit his paintings there. Claudio gave Gavin his card.

Clare said to Claudio, "We also have a writer at the table. And she's going to be a famous writer when she finishes the book she's writing."

Claudio wanted to know all about my book.

"The story begins here, at this café," I said.

"Really?" he said.

"This is my favorite place to write," I said. "But I didn't know, until a few days ago, about its literary history."

Claudio told us the story of the café, which he explained was "the birthplace of Futurism." In the early 1900s, artists and writers gathered at Giubbe Rosse to ponder what the future may hold, not only in the world of art and literature, but in all aspects of life, including cuisine—and cocktails. Present-day futurists had recently had a meeting at the café, where they enjoyed a drink dreamed up by futurists from the turn of the twentieth century.

"I will go ask the bartender to make it for you," Claudio said. A few minutes later, Claudio returned with a large bowl-shaped stemmed goblet with what looked to be red wine and shavings of some hard dark substance floating on the surface. Perched on the glass rim was a long stick, with three cubes of Pecorino cheese.

"What is this called?" I asked.

"*Giostra d'alcool*," Claudio said. "Do you know the word *giostra*?"

"Yes," I replied. "It means carousel."

"Yes and there's another word in English, which I can't remember at the moment," he said.

"Merry-go-round."

"Yes, merry-go-round," he said. "The drink makes you feel like you're on a merry-go-round."

Claudio excused himself. "Enjoy."

Clare, Gavin and I looked at each other, bewildered. I went first. I dipped a cheese cube into the drink and swirled it around. The alcoholic merry-go-round began to spin.

I peered at the shavings, which looked a bit like tree bark. "I think this is chocolate," I said hopefully.

With the shavings clinging to the cube, I popped it into my mouth. The shavings were chocolate and the icy brew tasted like mulled fruity wine. I was ready to become a disciple of *Futurismo*.

We were feeling mulled and mystified by the drink's flavors when Claudio returned. He wrote down the recipe for me: equal parts of Barbera red wine, a sweet citrus drink called Cedrata, and Campari.

Claudio brought a book to our table about the literary cafés of Florence. Giubbe Rosse was on the cover. He showed us a photo of the piazza after the demolition of the ghetto that had been there in the late 1800s. The piazza's reconstruction was part of a grand renewal plan that would have destroyed many of Florence's ancient buildings. An outcry from foreigners, mostly the British, forced the city to abandon the plan.

Claudio and I talked about the impact history and tradition have on a culture. "When you have a history, it is sometimes difficult to see a new way of doing things," he said. "In the U.S., for example, it is easier to come up with solutions to economic problems than it is in Italy because in your culture you are open to new ideas."

Futurists passionately rejected political and artistic tradition. They embraced everything new—technology, speed, youth, industrialization. It was no accident, I realized, that I had been drawn to this place, not only for its literary legacy, but for the rebellion that had occurred here against Italy's old way of life.

"In Italy, it is the tradition of having lunch together on Christmas Day," Claudio said. "Even if you have not seen the person all year or have no feeling for him, you must sit at the table with him. But why, I ask. Because that is the way it has always been."

The Christmas season was approaching and I surmised that Claudio was in the midst of some family squabble about the Christmas-lunch invitation list.

Claudio and I exchanged cards and he said he hoped to see me again, writing my book at the café.

"When it is published," Claudio said, "we will have your book presentation here."

෨

Two days later, I was walking across the piazza on my way to meet Clare and Gavin at the Uffizi. I was early and decided to stop at Giubbe Rosse for coffee.

I saw Claudio immediately, at the back of the café. He saw me, too, and walked toward me, smiling. "Rebecca! So nice to see you. What brings you here?"

"A place to write and a cappuccino," I said.

"Would you prefer a table near the front?" he asked.

"If there's one available," I said.

"Anything for you."

Claudio spoke in Italian to a man with a gray goatee, who was at the table next to mine. Claudio turned to me and said, "Rebecca, this is the head of our artists' group."

The man stood up and introduced himself. "I am Massimo Mori."

What a great name, I thought. "I'm so pleased to meet you," I said, shaking his hand.

Massimo's English was very good. He asked me about the book I was writing and said, "Many writers have written their books at Giubbe Rosse. There is no place like this."

Massimo told me he had just finished writing a detailed history of the café. "There are five seasons of the history of Giubbe Rosse, starting with the Futurists," he explained. He pulled a brochure, printed on heavy cardstock, out of his backpack. "We would like to publish this in English. Would you be interested in writing the translation?" he asked.

"I don't know Italian," I said. "But I could ask my friends here if they could help me."

"That would be wonderful." Massimo gave me his phone number and e-mail address. "I look forward to hearing from you." I knew it wouldn't be just a matter of translating the text; Massimo wanted me to polish the English version of his prose.

I phoned Clare and Gavin, who had just staggered out of the Uffizi.

"Meet me at our favorite café right away," I said. "I have the most incredible news."

18

A penny drops

On Clare and Gavin's first day in Florence, I gave them a tour of the city's grand piazzas. Our first stop was Piazza del Duomo. The cathedral was open, so we went inside. I sat down on a bench at the side of the sanctuary and took out my journal. Gavin sat down on the floor next to a pillar and took out his sketchpad. Within minutes, he was on the bench next to me, saying a guard had told him he couldn't sit on the floor and sketch.

We decided to move on to Piazza della Repubblica.

I already had learned two things about sightseeing with Gavin: he walks fast and stops often to look at his map. He was a half block ahead of Clare and me, reading his map, when I realized what was about to happen. Of all the stores in all of Florence, Gavin had stopped directly in front of Marcello's—or more precisely, the store that isn't Marcello's.

Gavin still had his nose in the map when Clare and I caught up with him. I held my breath for a second and looked through the front door of the shop. There at the counter was Marcello. Nadia had told me the Jordanian brothers were doing a trunk show in

New York, so apparently Marcello was minding the store in their absence.

Marcello was looking at a computer monitor. We could have slipped away without being seen. But Gavin was deeply into his map.

Feeling mature and emboldened, I stepped in the doorway. I addressed Marcello by his last name, preceded by *"Signor,"* with an Italian lilt in my voice.

He looked up from the monitor. There was no telltale emotion in his eyes as he walked toward me. It was the first time we had seen each other in three months. He looked like he had just stepped from the pages of *GQ*. He was wearing a beautifully cut dark suit, jacket buttoned, with a blue shirt and no tie.

Marcello didn't greet me by name, but he was cordial, asking if my friends had arrived.

"They're right here, in fact," I said. "I'd like you to meet them."

We stepped out onto the street to where Clare and Gavin were standing. I introduced him as "my friend Marcello." He was relaxed and amiable, asking where they were from.

I told Marcello about our experience at the Duomo. He wasn't surprised. "It's a national museum. They don't like people sitting on the floor."

We chatted for a few minutes. If Marcello was at all uneasy, he didn't show it. As we said our good-byes, he turned to me and said how nice it was to see me again—and then shook my hand.

We were barely around the corner, when Clare said, "Okay—who was that?"

"He's a main character in the book," I said, giggling. "I may have to change his name. But only if he's nice to me." Clare wanted to know more, but my lips were zipped. "I don't want to spoil the book for you," I told her.

On the last day of their visit, after we met at Giubbe Rosse to discuss the day's developments with Massimo, Gavin wandered off to do a sketch and Clare went off in search of souvenirs. We agreed to meet back at the carousel in an hour.

I walked toward the Fabriano paper shop, where I had bought a journal a few days earlier. I was about to cross the street and saw Marcello standing in front of "his" store, talking to a guy. I walked toward him, checking out his outfit—a bit over-styled for my taste. A silvery gray suit, with a pink striped shirt and a pink pocket hankie. He was wearing ear phones and fiddling with his MP3 player.

He showed no flicker of recognition as I approached. The guy he was talking to glanced at me and walked away.

"Where are your friends?" he asked.

"Gavin's painting and Clare's shopping," I said.

I told him the story of my entrée into the inner circle of Florence's preeminent literary café. Marcello did not know Claudio. "We can go there next week for a drink," he said, "and you can introduce me to him."

I thought that was a little strange. But I didn't have much time to think about it before Marcello said, "Okay, ciao, ciao." He shook my hand and went back into the shop.

As I walked away, I wondered if Marcello had been uncomfortable talking to me in front of the shop—the second time in five days. I felt uneasy myself at the prospect of introducing him to Claudio, especially if Marcello was going to misrepresent himself as the owner of the store.

The next day, shortly after Clare and Gavin left for the airport, Marcello called and asked if I was free for a drink that night.

"Okay. Where would you like to meet?" I asked, thinking he might suggest Giubbe Rosse.

"What about your apartment," he said.

I considered this for a moment. "I suppose you'd really like a margarita."

Marcello laughed.

Torrential rain fell that day. He called back and asked for a rain check. We rescheduled for two nights later, at my place.

He showed up that night about 7:30. He kissed me on the cheek. I kissed him on one cheek, then the other, as is the custom in Italy.

"You like two kisses, yes?" I said.

He smiled.

I took his coat—a parka-style jacket (not leather)—and hung it in the closet of my second bedroom.

I had decided about ten minutes before he arrived to make a simple dinner. We had never made dinner together. This would give us a little project, I thought, and some transition time to get comfortable with each other again.

But first, I made a pitcher of margaritas. After his first sip, Marcello said, "Ah, this is so good."

We were back in our zone. Marcello was alarmed when I told him there were no more limes in the market and that I had only one more bag of lime juice in the freezer.

I had already set the table. I put a pot of water on the stove and pulled a package of ravioli and a bag of lettuce from the fridge. Marcello said he'd had a late lunch and wasn't hungry. I knew he didn't normally eat his evening meal until after nine.

"I'm hungry," I said. "All I've eaten today is cereal and yogurt."

"I'll sit with you and have some salad," he said.

While we were waiting for the water to boil, we sat on the sofa with our margaritas. It wasn't long before he reached over to adjust my watch bracelet, noticing a red mark on my wrist.

"Is it too tight like this?" he asked. "What is this redness?"

"A mosquito bite," I said. "I know it's November, but they're still after me."

As always, we had much to talk about. He told me about two U.S. major league baseball players who recently had come into the store. They must have spent a lot because Marcello said he took them to La Giostra for dinner. He was appalled when one of the guys smothered his pasta with parmesan cheese, masking the flavor of the white truffle sauce. "He put so much cheese on the pasta, he couldn't even taste the truffles," Marcello said. "I don't understand how people with so much money can't appreciate the fine things in life."

Italian white truffles are akin to Provençal black truffles—both are scarce and expensive. The Italian varieties look like small warty potatoes and grow in the soil near the roots of oak, poplar, linden and willow trees. Truffles are prized as culinary delicacies because of their pungent, earthy scent and flavor.

We talked about the methods of hunting for truffles.

"They use dogs," Marcello said.

"They also use pigs," I said. "But the problem with pigs is that they like to eat the truffles. I stayed at a B&B in Provence where a pack of wild boars tore up the lawn around the pool, scavenging for truffles."

"What is lawn?" Marcello asked.

"A grassy area," I replied. He nodded. Marcello speaks English well, but occasionally I use a word that he'll ask me to explain.

"Pigs can be vicious," he said. "The Mafia uses them."

I sat up straight.

"There are three ways the Mafia can kill you," he began. "They pour your body into concrete and you end up in the support of a bridge. Or they dump you into acid and you dissolve. Or if they really don't like you, they feed you to hungry pigs."

I reminded him of the Mafia princess in the apartment next door. "So you're saying if I hear a pig squealing outside my door, I should just throw myself over the balcony if I want a pretty corpse," I said. He laughed. I patted his knee. "Thanks for the tip, Marcello."

We moved to the stove, where Marcello took charge of making the ravioli.

"You cook?" I asked, surprised.

"Sure."

"I don't," I stated for the record. "What do you make?"

"Pasta, meat." He looked at the pot. "Did you put salt in the water?" he asked.

"I thought we had enough salt on the margarita glasses," I said.

"You put salt in the water for flavor," he said.

"Salt also raises the boiling point so the pasta cooks faster," I said.

He looked puzzled.

"Salt raises the boiling point of water and lowers the freezing point," I said.

"Really?"

"When they throw salt on the icy streets of Chicago, what are they doing?" I asked.

"Melting the ice," he said.

"That's the end result," I said. "But they're actually lowering the freezing point."

He shook his head, clearly mystified. One summer's night, during one of our after-sex conversations, I had told him that my eighth-grade science project was a hurricane machine that won first prize in the Illinois State Science Fair. He was fascinated when I told him that hurricanes, like water going down a drain, spin counterclockwise in the northern hemisphere and clockwise in the southern hemisphere. The reason for this discussion was because one of the male judges who awarded me the prize told me I'd make a great TV weather girl. In reply, I told the judge politely, "I'd really like to be a meteorologist." Marcello had liked that answer. "How old were you?" he asked me. "Fourteen," I said.

Marcello sprinkled some salt into the pot and stirred the simmering water.

"Do you remember what I told you about how hurricanes spin?" I asked. I was in Science Girl mode.

"Yes," he said. "Because of the tilt of the earth."

I wanted to be supportive even though his answer was incorrect. "Good. There will be a quiz on all this later," I said, making a mental note to explain the Coriolis Force to him before the quiz. (It's the eastward *rotation* of the earth that causes storms to spin in opposite directions on either side of the equator.)

The ravioli I had purchased contained *ortica*. "Do you know *ortica*?" he said.

"Is it cheese?" I asked.

"No. In English it's called…" He checked the translation program on his phone. "It's called nettle."

"Nettle? How do they get rid of all the prickles?" I asked.

"They cook it a long time."

I set the timer on my phone for two minutes as Marcello gently lowered the ravioli into the boiling water. In the two ensuing minutes, I prepared a salad.

"We need oil and parmesan cheese," he said, lifting the ravioli with a slotted spoon onto the platter I was holding.

"I have both."

Marcello sat down at the table. "Now you can make a good meal that's easy," he said. I felt encouraged.

I took a bag of grated parmesan from the fridge. "Sorry to spoon this right out of the bag," I said.

"What are you doing?" he asked.

I held the spoonful of cheese in mid-air.

"You're just like my mother," he said. I was relieved to hear I was in good company, but I wasn't sure what I had done.

"You put the oil on first, then the cheese," he said. "I argue with my mother about this all the time."

I was loving this. The *americana* who can't cook, getting lessons from an Italian guy whose *mamma* needs lessons, too.

For dessert, we ate dried figs. The Italian word for fig is *fico*, but its female cousin *fica* means "a woman's pussy," Marcello informed me.

"It's a very erotic fruit," I said in total agreement. The perfect segue to the next course, which took us to the bedroom.

It was nothing short of a miracle that the bed's side rails did not fall off. Our passion hadn't waned, that was clear.

On his best behavior, Marcello hardly said a word during our lovemaking—until the end.

"I felt like a prisoner," he said, climbing over me to get on his side of the bed.

I laughed, though I wasn't sure whether he was referring to being tangled in the sheets or to his suppressed loquaciousness. "My next book will be titled *Marcello's English Phrasebook*," I told him.

During our repose, he said, "I thought of you traveling and imagined you with French and Greek men."

"I was as good as a nun," I said.

"Sure," he said.

"It's true."

"Greek men." Marcello let out a sigh filled with envy.

From there, our conversation wandered from an Italian politician in the news who had been caught with a transvestite, to prostitution. Though brothels and pimping are banned in Italy, prostitution is legal and very much a part of the culture. At least one in seven Italian men has had sex with a prostitute, according to statistics—and apparently sometimes with a spouse's permission. I had read an account of an Italian woman, who didn't enjoy sex that much, telling her husband that if he wanted to experience things she wouldn't allow, it was okay with her if he did them with a hooker.

I told Marcello about my first apartment-hunting trip with Sofie. She drove me out to the Chianti countryside to see renovated farmhouses. We passed two black women sitting at the side of the road. Several miles later, there were two more black women standing on a bridge. I asked Sofie about them.

"They're prostitutes," she said.

"Out here, in the middle of nowhere?" I asked.

Sofie told me they had been chased out of the city. Now their clients come to them in the country.

I remembered my tour of Pompeii the previous fall and our visit to the city's brothel. Inside, murals on the walls showed available services and sexual positions. Patrons even had choices regarding partners, whether for heterosexual or same-sex encounters.

After our group was back outside, the guide asked us, "Which way to the brothel?" We pointed behind us. "In Pompeian times, you wouldn't have to ask or point," the guide said. She looked down at a paving stone in the street. There, chiseled in stone, were two testicles and a penis that pointed the way. In 79 A.D., prostitution had its own road sign.

I was tempted to ask Marcello if he had ever been with a prostitute. I was intrigued by the effect religious sexual repression has on the libido—for example, to what extent does Catholic guilt heighten wanton sexual desire? But I decided to table that conversation topic for another time.

It was about ten o'clock when Marcello got out of bed.

"Where are you going?"

"Home," he said, yawning.

I thought it was early for him to be leaving, knowing what a night owl he is. "Do you have a date?" I asked. We were both fishing for reassurance.

"No."

He got dressed. I put on a robe and followed him to the dining table where he had left his phone. He checked his message screen.

"I have some advice for you," he said.

I thought he was going to tell me about a new phone plan.

Instead, he said, "Be careful what you tell Nadia. She has a big mouth."

He put on his suit jacket and tugged at the cuffs of his shirt. "I know you and Nadia are friends," he said. "She came into the store one day and said to me, 'So you fucked my friend.' I was talking to some guys I know and she said that to me, in front of them."

Marcello and I were standing on opposite sides of the dining table, our eyes locked on each other.

"How do you know she was talking about me?" I asked.

"Because right before that, she asked if I knew you were in Greece," he replied.

I had asked Nadia the week before if she had said anything to Marcello about me. She said she told him what a nice person I was and mentioned to him that I was in Greece. "That's all I've ever said," she said, assuring me she would never tell Marcello about our private conversations.

Marcello walked into the second bedroom. I took a deep breath and followed him.

I stood in the doorway as he put on his coat. "Nadia didn't know that I knew you until August," I began. "She invited me to have dinner at her house with a friend of hers. It was a hot night, and she was upset with me for taking an apartment without air conditioning. She asked what happened with the apartment Arman had told her about. I told her that Arman sent me to the restaurant to see his brother to get the key."

Marcello nodded, remembering that day.

"I told Nadia that the guy who had the key never showed up, but that I saw a man at the restaurant I knew. When I told her it was you, she said, 'You know Marcello? He never told me he knew you.' And I asked her, 'Does Marcello tell you about all the women he goes out with?'"

That made Marcello smile.

"She told me, 'American women really like Marcello. He's very busy.' And I said to her, 'I'm sure he is.'"

Marcello didn't say anything to that.

He looked at the framed photo of my son on the bookshelf above my IKEA desk that he had assembled. Although Marcello had been in that room before, he had never noticed the picture.

"Is that your son?" he said.

I nodded. Colin has my auburn coloring and a gorgeous smile.

"He looks so Irish," Marcello said.

Marcello had his coat on and was ready to leave. No doubt, he had been waiting until the end of the evening, thinking he'd let the penny drop, as the saying goes, and make a run for the door.

But I also had a penny burning a hole in my pocket. I decided to keep it there for another day.

As we walked to the door, he said, "I like Nadia. I've known her a long time."

"She told me you've been good to her."

"I have," Marcello said, turning toward me.

If this incident happened the way Marcello described, I was at a loss to explain Nadia's motive. She betrayed a confidence with me and embarrassed a man who had been a friend to her for many years.

I kissed Marcello, once on each cheek.

"What can I bring you from New York?" he asked, smiling. "A little Statue of Liberty?"

I thought for a second. "What about a can of limeade?"

"What is limeade?" he asked.

I smiled at him. "It's frozen lime juice. We're going to need some if you want margaritas this winter."

19

Truth and lies

When Marcello told me he was going to New York for a week, as we were preparing our ravioli dinner, I casually asked what was taking him there. He said he was meeting a friend who had been in Chicago and who was going on from there to New York.

I knew from Nadia that the Jordanian brothers were doing trunk shows in the U.S. She told me that Marcello had to pay his own expenses if he wanted to go with them.

"The airfare is only €300," he told me.

"That's great," I replied. "Where do you fly?"

"Florence to Rome to New York," he said.

"Central Park will be beautiful, with all the fall colors."

"It's supposed to rain next week," he said.

Later, when we were in bed, he told me, "I don't like New York. It's a young person's city. At my age…" His voice trailed off. Maybe he was just feeling tired from our romp, but I felt at that moment I probably could have asked him his true age and gotten an honest answer.

While we were making dinner, I explained why I had come by the shop that day with Clare and Gavin. "Gavin had stopped to read his map just outside the store," I said. "I didn't think you'd be there. I've never seen you at the store." I was holding the door wide open for him, wishing he'd tell me the truth.

Looking at the floor, he said, "I'm not usually there." This wasn't the same Marcello who, a year earlier, had told me that he and his six cousins own the biggest leather factory in Florence.

The next day, Tom and I talked about this.

"I'm very concerned," Tom said. I could hear that brotherly love in his voice.

"About how he'll react if I tell him what Nadia told me?"

"Yes. What if he gets really angry?" He was quiet for a moment. "I might need to come to Florence."

"And do what? Play bodyguard?" I envisioned having the leather dons of Florence and the Mafia pigs after me. It might be good having Tom watch my back.

On the day Marcello left for New York, I stopped by the shop where Nadia works to see the Perfect Travel Purse she had ordered for me in brown. I liked the black one better. The owner walked into the store and Nadia asked him if she could lower the discounted price she already had offered me. They spoke in Italian. I walked toward the front of the store to give them some privacy. After the owner disappeared upstairs, she apologized that she couldn't do better. "He wasn't happy about the price I gave you," she said. "He told me I was giving away the store."

I thanked her. But I couldn't help but wonder what he really had said. I now had good reason to doubt Nadia.

She wanted me to come with her to pick up her son from school. I told her I needed to go. Up until that point, neither of us had mentioned Marcello.

But as I turned to leave, she said, "Why don't you call Marcello and ask him to join you for coffee?"

I was so tempted to say, "Girl, your middle name is Trouble."

∽

After I left Nadia, I walked over to Piazza della Repubblica. I had my choice of tables at Giubbe Rosse. I ordered a cappuccino and a chocolate gelato and opened my journal.

I was lost in thought, scribbling away, when I heard a man say, "I was thinking about you today." I looked up to see Claudio, standing by the table, smiling.

He told me he had been thinking of me at the print shop (so writerly, I thought), wondering if I would translate something for him into English.

"I'm not bi-lingual," I said to him. "But I have a friend who is. He may be able to help me. He's in New York right now, but he'll be back next week." Marcello had said he would help me translate Massimo's history of the café. "Once I have the English translation, I can polish it for you—like marble."

Claudio grinned. "I want to print up special cards in English for our customers about the café and our exhibits. I will give you the first one."

A short while later, I was still scribbling away when I heard a woman say, "There you are!" It was a Canadian woman I had met at Nadia's shop a few hours earlier. I had given her and her husband my Top Five list of things to do and see in Florence and had recommended Giubbe Rosse as a good place for a cappuccino.

I joined them for my second cappuccino and, at one point, as they were telling me about their travels, I glanced at the entrance to the café. Claudio was standing in the doorway, looking at me. When I went inside to use the restroom, I saw him near the bar and told him that I had recommended the café to the couple I was having coffee with. "She's a travel agent," I told him. "I really *am* good for business."

"I'm going to need to pay you," he said.

"I'll give you a bill," I said, kiddingly, which made him laugh.

I had become a cappuccino hustler. The irony of this didn't escape me.

As Marcello once told me: If you walk with someone who limps, you limp, too.

20

More tales from Tavanti

On a gloomy Sunday in November, I decided to write another of my group e-mails. It had been a few months since my last one and I had been getting messages from friends asking if everything was okay and wanting an update on my Excellent Misadventure in Italy. One inquiry as to my health and whereabouts asked pointedly: *ARE YOU STILL ALIVE?*

Under the subject heading of "More Tales from Tavanti," I assured everyone that all was well and that Papa Palermo had not poured me into a bridge footing. I thanked everyone who had sent suggestions about how to appease the princess. I reported that the consensus was to make her a pitcher of margaritas, but noted that the suggestions had been evenly divided as to whether the mix should include whatever I found under the kitchen sink.

Once again, the response was heartwarming. One friend wrote: *"Great to hear your tales of life as a Florentine. Just keep an eye out for fish wrapped in bullet-proof vests or a few random horse heads lying around."*

My reply: *"No sightings of dead fish or horse heads yet. I always pull down the covers before I jump into bed, though, just in case."*

Clearly, the pitch for the film version of this book should be: *Under the Tuscan Sun* meets *The Godfather*.

There were many questions about my plans for the holidays. American Thanksgiving isn't on the calendar here, I replied. One friend was confident I'd find someone to have a turkey dinner with. I hadn't seen signs of a turkey anywhere. In the market downstairs, the featured item in the freezer section was octopus.

My plans for Christmas were still vague. Nancy and I had spoken briefly about me coming to Berlin, though I knew her plans could change. Her mother, too, was slipping into dementia.

This would be my first Christmas since my son was born that I would be without him. I was being very brave about the prospect of spending Christmas alone. For many years, I suffered through the stress of Christmas—the shopping, the entertaining, the exhaustion of holiday merrymaking. One year, however, I bought a honey-baked ham with all the side dishes and spent the day helping Colin assemble a Playmobil castle instead of spending the afternoon in the kitchen. I loved that Christmas. But too many Christmases for me had been a blur of hyper-planning, frayed nerves and burnt pie shells.

Maybe this was the year that I was meant to take a walk in the snowy woods on Christmas Day.

The snowy woods got me thinking. I had packed a few of my favorite children's books in the boxes I shipped to Florence. One of them, titled *A Carol for Christmas*, is the story of the pastor of a small church in Oberndorf, Austria, who, on Christmas Eve of 1818, struggled to write a song that he could play on his guitar at services that night because the organ was not working. The poem he wrote, set to music by Franz Guber, was *Silent Night*.

I googled Oberndorf and went to the Trip Advisor link. They get A LOT of snow in Oberndorf. Serious snow. Forget walking in the woods. I'd need a horse-drawn sleigh. Or at least some skis. Forget the skis. I once fell off a chair lift in the French Alps. Luckily, I fell into a chute, built to catch dropped poles and hats, that was filled with snow. For a few minutes, everyone thought I was dead. I was in a pile of snow at the end of the chute and couldn't move because I had so much snow in my pants. They really freaked out when the snow corpse sat up and began shrieking with laughter.

Maybe I should go for a walk on a beach on Christmas day. Oh, yeah.

21

Silentium

One November day, I set off by bus to photograph the skyline of Florence from a church on the hill above the Arno, south of the city. I took the No. 20 bus from Via Tavanti to Piazza San Marco, hoping to catch a No. 23 bus across the river.

Florence's bus routes wholly embrace circular thinking. They make grand loops around the city, which means that if you get off the bus on the loop, you have to get back on and finish the loop, and sometimes the loop includes a ten-minute cigarette break for the driver. When I'd go to see Guido, my osteopath, the round-trip ride, including cigarette break, would take about an hour and ten minutes—fifty minutes on the outbound (including cigarette break) and twenty minutes for the return.

Apparently I was on the loop portion of the route because the only No. 23 buses that stopped at San Marco weren't going across the river. The Italian word for bus stop is *fermata*. In music, a fermata is a prolongation of a note, hold or rest beyond its given time value and is indicated with an upside down smile over a dot. After a half hour, my patience had been prolonged to the snapping point and my smile had turned upside down. So I reverted to linear thinking and hailed a cab.

Ten minutes and eleven euros later, I was at Piazzale Michelangelo, which is actually a big hillside parking lot, on the south side of the Arno, with a statue of David (one of the replicas around town) and a panoramic view of Florence and the northern mountains beyond. In the autumn sunlight, the cityscape was saturated with splashes of color: the red tiles of the rooftops and the Duomo's dome, building facades of rich ocher and burnt sienna, and the golden umber of turning leaves.

I walked up Viale Galileo Galilei, the road leading to San Miniato al Monte, which is often described as the most beautiful church in Florence. According to legend, Minias, the church's patron saint, was decapitated by Roman soldiers on the banks of the Arno in 250 A.D. and afterward managed to climb up the hill, carrying his head. I was having a hard enough time getting up the hill and the stairs to the church with my head firmly screwed on. I thought back to the days of summer, when I was limping around with my wrapped ankle and a cane, and decided my recovery had been pretty miraculous as well.

The 1,000-year-old basilica is home to Benedictine monks. A large sign on the basilica door reads: SILENTIUM. The church brochure asks visitors to be respectful of the *"necessary aura of silence."* Apparently Benedictines don't make a vow of silence, but they have strict hours of silence and, generally speaking (bad pun), don't engage in idle chit-chat.

When Clare and Gavin visited the basilica a few weeks earlier, she told me they heard the Gregorian chanting of the monks from the concealed monastic choir on the upper level of the church. I was hoping for a similarly inspiring experience. But mine took another form.

I was photographing the beautifully restored frescoes when I heard some commotion behind me near the bottom of one of the marble staircases that led to the upper level. A guy in street clothes and a monk in a gray robe were carrying a hand truck loaded with boxes up the staircase. They had the hand truck on its back. The monk was on the high end, bent double, holding on to the wheels. He was anything but silent. I don't know if he was speaking Italian or Latin, but I expected lightning bolts to start dancing around the sanctuary any minute. I giggled and ducked behind a pillar. (I felt like I was back in Monaco at the changing of the palace guard.)

They disappeared into the shadows of the upper level and I went over to look at the remaining stacks of boxes at the bottom of the stairs. According to the labels, they contained brochures in English, French and Spanish.

I took a seat in the front pew. This was the best show in town. Back they came for the next load and the next. By the third trip, the monk was rubbing his sore back. Every time they went up the stairs, I sensed imminent calamity. This was like watching Laurel and Hardy move a piano. God only knows what the monk was saying. He became more verbose with each trip up the staircase.

Suddenly the lights went on upstairs, revealing a glimmering Byzantine mosaic above the apse. Other visitors were going up the steps, so I followed. The illumination was short-lived, however. I saw a coin box at the top of the staircase. Apparently someone had dropped a euro in the slot to get the lights on. I was already doing a rewrite of Genesis: *And God said, "Let there be light. And for a euro, I'll give you ten extra minutes."*

After the lights went out again, I made my way into the sacristy, where the frescoes of Spinello Aretino tell the story of the life of San Benedetto. As I sat in a choir stall, reading my brochure, there was a crash at the door. In came Laurel and Hardy with another truckload of brochures.

There was no place for me to hide this time, so I just burst out laughing. The monk gave me a look. I wanted to say, "Could we have a little SILENTIUM here!" I gave up on my hope for a quiet moment and put my camera in video mode to record this divine comedy.

I wandered outside and walked through the cemetery behind the church. I felt like I had stepped onto the set of a horror movie. The plaque at the gate said the author of *Pinocchio* was buried there. I looked for a little puppet with a long nose pointing the way. Pretty soon the tombstones gave way to pathways lined with enormous crypts that looked like temples. One was a replica of a Russian Orthodox Church with onion domes. The sun was setting. The hollow eyes of the statues became darker; the bestial gargoyles, more menacing. I freaked out when I saw the tombstone of a young girl reaching out to her dead self or maybe her dead sister, who was sheathed with a funereal veil. Forget Pinocchio. This place was molto creepy. I hurried toward the gate.

The church gift shop was open, so I ducked inside. The shelves were stacked with a wide range of merchandise: decorative religious items, hand-painted ceramics, soaps, notecards, journals, coffee-table books, postcards, jars of flavored honey (made at the monastery), bottles of olive oil and homemade biscotti.

I bought some biscotti and a book, and who was at the register but the same monk. This guy was putting in a full day. He silently put my purchases in a bag.

It was almost 5:30, time for vespers, when a group of about twenty students boisterously appeared on the church steps. Turns out they were from Penn State.

We all went inside the church and down the stairs into the crypt, where the remains of St. Minias are entombed in an altar behind an iron gate. The altar is lit, but otherwise, the crypt is dark—except for a wrought-iron stand of votives in the shape of a Christmas tree. And it's very cold.

As I went down the stairs, a monk who apparently had lost track of time, came flying down the steps carrying a tray of communion wafers. Late for mass again. He'll have penance to pay, I thought. Poor guy. He looked to be about 40, balding with a rim of red hair.

The chanting began before everyone was seated. The monks stood against the wall behind the altar, their voices reverberating off the low ceiling's vaults. They wore cream-colored hooded robes that looked a lot warmer than the sweatshirts and light jackets the rest of us were wearing.

The sound was truly heavenly. I felt transported to the Middle Ages, sitting in a cold, dark crypt on a night in late autumn.

The monk leading the chanting stepped forward. It was Laurel, the monk-of-all-trades. He not only schleps boxes and works the register, but he's the lead chanter. And what's more, he has perfect pitch. He often sang the first measure of each chant to make sure his small choir of brothers stayed in the same key.

I watched the monk with the red hair helping an older monk next to him who often was on the wrong page. The red-headed monk would motion with his index finger for him to turn the page and sometimes two pages. An act of fraternal love.

After about thirty minutes, my feet were starting to feel like ice. Quietly, of course, I left the crypt and slipped out of the church into the night. It was much warmer outside than in the crypt. I went down the steps to the massive front gate only to discover it was chained with a heavy padlock. The only way out was to walk past the cemetery and follow a dark and winding road down the hill.

I went back to the crypt. Stay with the group, I told myself.

The chanting went on for another half hour, followed by communion. By the time it was all over, no one had any feeling left in their feet. We stormed the gift shop, hoping to get warm. An

American woman from Arizona and I were stomping our feet in the corner. I noticed bottles of wine and grappa on a shelf.

"Look, they sell grappa," I said to her.

"They've got to keep warm somehow," she murmured. I stifled a giggle.

Laurel-the-Monk was back at the register.

"*Bellissimo*," I said to him. "You have a beautiful voice."

He smiled.

"Do you have perfect pitch?" I asked.

He looked puzzled.

"*Perfetto…*" I didn't know how to say pitch in Italian, so I hummed in a Gregorian way.

He nodded. Then he pointed to his neck as if to say he had a sore throat. I had seen him wiping his nose during vespers and thought maybe he had a cold. Or maybe he was pointing at his throat to tell me he couldn't talk.

I was feeling parched with all this non-talking about sore throats, so I motioned to the monk that I'd like a bottle of water from the fridge behind the counter.

And lo, he spoke. "Gas?" he asked.

That giggle I had suppressed was bubbling to the surface. "Gas" is a slang word often used in Italy for "carbonated."

"*Si*, gas," I replied.

Suddenly the red-headed monk appeared out of nowhere and asked me in English, "Where are you from?"

"California," I said.

He looked around at the shivering students in gift shop. "Are they with you?" he asked me.

"No, they're from Penn State," I replied.

He nodded and grinned, as if he were a fan of U.S. college football. Then he waved good-bye.

Laurel-the-Monk was helping the next customer as I unscrewed the top of my gassy bottle and took a swig.

I turned to the American woman from Arizona and whispered, "I thought they were a silent order."

She looked at me over the top of her glasses and said, "Apparently not."

22

A man bearing gifts

Marcello e-mailed me the night he returned from New York. I e-mailed him back: *"Ciao bello. Glad you're safely back. Did you bring limeade?"*

He called the next day and seemed eager to see me. He arrived at my apartment the next evening with a bottle of Mr. and Mrs. T's margarita mix. He couldn't find limeade in New York. Later, in bed, he said he had bought me a tube of KY Jelly (not available in Italy), but it was confiscated by a female security agent at Newark airport.

You know you're dancin' near the end of the high dive when a man's gifts to you are margarita mix and KY Jelly.

I teased him, "I'm surprised the agent didn't take you into a cubicle for a private screening." I told him to stand his ground next time that happens. According to TSA's web site, liquids and gels that are exempt from the carry-on allowance include baby formula, liquid medications and KY Jelly.

We had a fun evening. I made him *Giostra l'alcool* from Claudio's recipe. Marcello loved that I was in the *Futurismo* club and drinkin' the Kool-Aid. He liked the Kool-Aid, too.

He entertained me with his imitation of a New Yorker. "*You got it*," he said in his best Brooklyn accent. "Everywhere I went, whether I was ordering a drink or picking up tickets to a show, that's what I heard—*you got it*."

I didn't give that penny in my pocket a moment's thought. We fell into bed, happy lovers, truly enjoying each other.

Later, during a quiet interlude, he actually fell asleep. His jet lag was catching up with him. He stirred for a minute and asked me, "How long have I been sleeping?"

"Ten minutes," I said.

I pulled up the covers. He pulled me close and whispered, "Let's take a nap."

∾

Our conversations that evening covered a wide range of topics. We discussed the tenets of *Futurismo* and its impact on Italian architecture. Marcello hailed the form and function of the futuristic Florence train station, built in 1932, as a brilliant design that still works today, while deriding urban development that's now taking place in Italy.

The retail-residential complex where I live is a prime example of contemporary design devoid of aesthetics (not to mention decent plumbing). My apartment building has a penthouse that resembles a watchtower. The park that's adjacent to the building and the supermarket is sterile and uninviting, with hard edges and surfaces (concrete benches built into retaining walls), few plants and absolutely no shade. On a hot day, the pavement and bricks shimmer with heat. The grassy areas are brown all summer. Few people actually sit in the park. There's no play area for children or a place to socialize. It may have been a visually pleasing concept on the drawing board, but in reality, it's a joyless, uncomfortable space.

"Italy has produced some of the greatest thinkers who've ever lived," Marcello said. "But sometimes we get in the way of ourselves."

To me, the blight of Florence is the graffiti that covers almost every wall and building. "Why do the young people of this city have no respect or appreciation for its great architecture and history?" I asked Marcello.

"They think they're artists," he said.

"But how can they think it's okay to use the wall of a Medieval church as their canvas?" I was stunned to see, on one of my recent bus rides, a tagger's scrawl on an old stone church. The city's ancient landmarks—the Duomo, Campanile, Baptistry, the Palazzo Vecchio—seem to have escaped the spray can, but, in time, who knows. When a culture loses a sense of its history, nothing is sacred.

For centuries, Italy has been a hotbed of feuding tribes and warring political and religious factions. Italy didn't become a unified country until 1861. Through the twentieth century, the Republic survived many crises, most notably the rise of fascism between two world wars.

Marcello credits the Marshall Plan after World War II with keeping Italy from slipping behind the Iron Curtain. "Americans were very smart after the War," he said. "They fed people who were hungry. When people are hungry, they turn to those who have the food."

After all these months, I felt I was still getting to know Marcello. His worldliness enabled him to defend the merits of his culture while acknowledging its shortcomings because he appreciated other ways of life and points of view. In my Dante re-write, he wouldn't be a soul condemned to purgatory. He could *imagine* a better way of doing things—the margarita mix and KY Jelly were evidence of that.

When I told him about my encounter with the monks at the St. Miniato gift shop, Marcello smiled and said, "Sometimes I wonder if there isn't something to be said for the life of a monk." The thought of Marcello as a monk of course made me laugh.

After we said good-night, I closed and bolted the door—my nightly lockdown procedure. From the hallway, I heard Marcello say, "Bolting the door, are you?"

I released the bolts and opened the door a crack. "Did I hear a pig oinking out here?"

He laughed. I blew him a kiss as he got in the elevator.

23

The ghost of Thanksgiving Past

The day before Thanksgiving back in the U.S., I was feeling very homesick. I had been getting e-mails from friends about their Thanksgiving plans and preparations. I felt like I wasn't at the party.

Later in the day, I received an e-mail from my dear friend Carol, whom I've known for thirty years. There isn't a Thanksgiving that I don't think of her, with fond memories of the celebrations I've shared with her wonderful family.

I met Carol through her mother, Mimi, an opera singer who had been my voice teacher when I was a teenager. Mimi had a profound influence on me, not only as a young singer, but as a young woman on the threshold of adulthood. "Be true to yourself," she would always tell me. At 14, I wasn't sure what she meant exactly, but in time, in moments of doubt or indecision, her words lit my path.

When Mimi came to live with Carol during the last years of her life, I was in my mid-20s and had just moved to northeastern New

Jersey, not far from where Carol lived. I visited Mimi frequently and soon felt part of Carol's family. As a teenager, I had heard Mimi's stories about Carol and her children, who were my age. So when I finally met them all, I felt like I had known them for a long time.

Every year, I was included in Carol's Thanksgiving celebration. It was always a happy affair. The table grew leaf by leaf over the years. When I moved to California in the mid-1980s, I missed having a seat at that table on Thanksgiving Day.

When my son Colin was 15, he and I went to Carol's for Thanksgiving. By then, Carol's eight grandchildren were in high school and college, so Colin felt right at home. It was such a tight squeeze around the table that year that Carol broke with her family's tradition of leaving an empty chair at the table—for missing friends and loved ones. Colin nearly had a meltdown setting the table as Carol kept adding place settings. He was already exhibiting the traits of an engineer, precisely positioning each knife and fork. But as we gathered round the table that night, elbow to elbow, I couldn't imagine a better way to celebrate the day.

It was Carol's last Thanksgiving in that house, which she sold the next summer. She moved to an independent-living facility for seniors in the same town. But her holiday traditions continued. At 85, Carol is the proud matriarch of a fun-loving family that collects her at 6 a.m. on Thanksgiving morning and takes her into New York to see Macy's parade before sitting down to yet another sumptuous feast at the family table.

As I read Carol's e-mail, Tom called. I told him the story of Carol and Thanksgivings past and said, "If I could get on a plane today, I would go."

"Well," he said, knowing I hadn't yet made plans for Christmas. "I do have a buddy pass."

I could hear him typing on his computer keyboard. "The flights to Newark on December 16 and 17 are wide open in business class," he said.

Wouldn't that be perfect, I thought. Carol's birthday is December 18.

Colin was planning to spend Christmas with his dad at Lake Tahoe. I felt a twinge of guilt, thinking about my parents. Would I need to tell them I was spending Christmas with Carol?

No.

For all the years I had done my holiday duty as a mother, a wife, a daughter and a daughter-in-law, I gave myself permission to say no.

I truly love Christmas. I love the lights, the music, the cards, the tree—especially the tree. Colin had turned into a teen humbug about Christmas and would grumble on that day in December when I'd cheerfully announce it was time to get a tree. One year I said to him, "Do you not realize—or care—that this is *my* favorite part of Christmas?" He looked contrite and followed me out the door.

The last Christmas we spent in our beautiful bungalow, I sat by the tree every night, in the dark living room with the tree lights twinkling, listening to carols as logs crackled and sparked in the fireplace.

Carol loves Christmas, too. For years, she made the rounds on St. Nicholas Eve, filling the wooden shoes (she's of Dutch descent) that her grandchildren had left on their doorsteps. In early December, she sets up a beautiful crèche and during the days of Advent, the Wise Men slowly make their way through the house to the stable in "Bethlehem," perched on top of the grand piano in her living room. Carol's Wise Men have a habit of not showing up on time—they get way-laid by the cat or a mischievous grandchild or get lost in the commotion of holiday festivities.

I couldn't imagine a better way to celebrate my favorite holiday than with a like-minded spirit. After I got off the phone with Tom, I e-mailed Carol and floated the idea. Her response was swift and ecstatic: *"Becky! No question about it!! Come!! We'll figure out details later!!! There is always space for you. What exciting news!! Love you!! Hugs and more."*

24

The love and wisdom of a friend

When I have my heart set on something, especially when it comes to travel, it's difficult for me to take "no" for an answer, particularly from an airline. I'm good at finding ways around high fares and long layovers. But, of course, that's a challenge during the holiday season.

Tom's offer of a buddy pass presented an array of complications because I had to get myself to Rome, Frankfurt or Paris before the pass kicked in—the airline Tom works for doesn't have service to Florence. In addition to the employee price for the fare, I would have the added expense of getting to Rome, Frankfurt or Paris as well as cab fare to New Jersey if I flew into New York.

A further complication to all this was that Tom and I have very different views about travel. My approach to travel is similar to my approach to life: A-to-B-to-C, the fastest way possible. Tom doesn't care if he has a five-hour layover somewhere as long as he gets to fly business class. As an added wrinkle, the pass doesn't guarantee a seat in business class. And if the entire flight is full, you wait in the stand-by queue for the next flight.

Tom suggested a variety of options that included me taking the train to Rome and staying overnight there in order to catch a morning flight the next day to Newark, which didn't appeal to me because of the expense of a night in a hotel.

Then brusquely he said, "Look, I can't spend a lot of time on this. I'm not your travel agent. Figure out what you want to do. If you want a buddy pass, it's yours."

About a half-hour later, he e-mailed me from work and asked *"r u there?"* It was just after midnight my time. I replied, *"Si."* I waited a few minutes, then sent a second message that said *"heading to bed."* I was tired and didn't want to continue the conversation. I hadn't asked him to figure out my travel plans.

When I got up the next morning, there was a message from him saying he was sorry he had been short with me. He had lost track of time, he said, and suddenly realized he had to leave for work.

I went online and found round-trip flights from Florence to Newark, with short connections, for $1,100. I'd be flying coach, but I didn't care. I sent him an e-mail, telling him that, yes, I had been stung by his abruptness and that I had found a better solution. I sent Carol an e-mail, asking if the dates for the $1,100 flight worked for her. In the time it took me to make a cup of coffee, the fare jumped $100. I sent her another e-mail, saying I was having second thoughts—$1,200 had tipped the scale.

A few hours later, she e-mailed back, saying how dismayed she was at the cost and that she loved me for trying to make it happen. And she worried that potential weather problems may make it a "foolhardy" trip. She suggested I wait until I was traveling again to Chicago to see my parents and plan a stopover to see her on the return trip, to "decompress."

Sitting at my desk, I started to cry. The tears of five months of frustration and loneliness had reached the lip of the cistern.

I saw on my computer screen that I had a Skype message. It was from Tom, suggesting that I rent a car and drive to the Rome airport.

I knew he was probably feeling guilty and was trying to be helpful, but I didn't want to discuss another convoluted scheme to get me to New Jersey. I wrote him a short message, telling him what Carol had written. I wrote, "*I'm feeling pretty low...I'm going for a walk. I can't stop crying.*"

I was stunned when Tom sent me this reply: "*Oh no, this is regrettable. Time to go hit Franciso at the customs office over the head and get your meds.*"

Tom knew about my ongoing battle with Italian Customs, which still hadn't released the package containing my prescription medications. One of the meds was a sleep aid that I sorely missed on nights when ambulance sirens kept me awake. But I wasn't coming unhinged because of the occasional restless night.

A month earlier, Tom had called Nancy and me and had tearfully told us about an encounter he had with a woman in a fabric store who was making quilts for people in dire need. He had felt so inspired by her—and so full of remorse that he wasn't doing charitable deeds—that he, too, couldn't stop crying.

I pounded out this message: "*Wow – when you were crying a few weeks ago after meeting the woman in the fabric store, did Nancy or I ask if you were on/off or needed meds?! What kind of remark is that? Even after what you said to me in haste (and arrogance) last night, I got a good night's sleep. My tears have everything to do with feeling alone in a strange place, feeling far away from the people I love and knowing I can do nothing to help my parents whose lives are swirling around the drain. If you know of a med that can make that pain go away, please advise. Otherwise, take a moment and remove your foot from your mouth, Mr. NJ Italian-Greek Chorus!*"

He wrote back: "*Cool it, Becky. Wow indeed. Where's your sense of humor? Don't add me to your list of concerns. I was just trying to be a friend.*" And sticking his finger deeper into the wound he said he wouldn't offer me a buddy pass again.

The writer-in-me was already thinking of dramatic ways to silence this chorister-gone-rogue. Something very Italian—like choking on a hot *peperoncino*. No, no—we'd need a Mafia pig for this scene.

Moments later, another e-mail arrived from Carol, who knew about the difficulty I was having with my parents. By the time I finished reading her message, I was sobbing. She wrote:

My dear, dear Becky,

How my heart aches for you, but you are going to have to let go. Your mom and dad have had their problems for many, many years and it is not new. They must have enjoyed their misery to some degree. It is only relatively new to you. However, what and where they are in their relationship is not your problem but it does become somewhat of a responsibility to see that they are fed, clothed and sheltered, if only to give you some peace of mind. If they are as bad as they sound, something is going to happen that will give you the legal right to see that they are taken care of. In the meantime, there isn't anything you can do. So shed that guilt and get on with your life.

It's a bit like mourning. Mourning for what was long ago. For what never was, what could have been. Anger for what it is and eventually acceptance for what it is.

To know that you did such a terrific job with Colin, that he can stand alone and is a gift to the human race—responsible and sensitive, happy and productive—is a bonus for you. You can be proud of yourself and take great comfort in that.

I love you dearly and am so proud of you. I do believe that God does guide us and protect us. On one of your walks, stop in at a church in Florence. (There must be houses of worship in that city even if it is the headquarters of the mafia! ;) or because it is!!) Just go in, sit down and empty that active head of yours. Let some peace come in.

Go to a market and buy some glitzy ribbon and whatever else strikes your fancy. Trim that apartment for all it's worth for Christmas. Shop for a folk art crèche or look for a figure for one you already may have.

I know where you are. I've been there. But as soon as you reach the top of this mountain, start enjoying the slide down the other side. It's a different view.

As the saying goes, "This, too, shall pass." And do you know!!??? It does.

Love you, love you.
Big, big hugs—Carol

25

Linens, candles and ribbons

A few weeks before Christmas, I stopped in at a shop near the Duomo that sells beautiful linens from the Umbrian village of Montefalco. I had discovered these linens during my travels through Italy the previous year and had become adept at identifying them at a glance. They take many forms—from hand towels to table runners to napkins and placemats. They're made of cotton, linen or a blend of both. The patterns range from floral garlands and intricate mosaic designs to griffins among palmettos.

An older gentleman, who later introduced himself as Francesco, appeared from the back of the shop, and greeted me, in English. I noticed that the tags on the linens had only the name of the shop, with no mention of where they were made.

"These are from Montefalco," I said.

He smiled at me. "Most Italians don't even know that."

"Oh, but they should," I said.

Francesco was impressed that I knew that the factory had been in business since 1949 and that the patterns of the linens were taken from ancient Umbrian designs. He opened a cabinet under the display and took out a box.

"This is already sold," he said. "I bought it."

He opened the lid and I gasped. It was a Montefalco linen table-cloth with matching napkins, in a pattern I had not seen before. The exquisitely woven border motif was of a woman plucking a harp. Francesco removed the napkins and unfolded the tablecloth.

"This is extraordinary," I whispered, as I carefully ran my fingers over the fabric. "Are you going to use it as a tablecloth?"

"Absolutely," he said. "It's meant to be on the table."

"What if someone spills red wine on it?" I asked.

"It will wash out," he said confidently. "Though my wife won't like washing and ironing it. That's the only problem." He laughed.

Francesco's wife and daughter appeared a short while later. Francesco, who turned out to be the owner, had come into the shop only because an employee had called in sick.

"I'm never here," he told me.

"Then I consider this my lucky day," I said.

I mentioned to Francesco that I was thinking about spending Christmas in Montefalco. He said that the linen mill was just a few kilometers away, in a village called Bastardo.

"It's a funny name. It means 'bastard' in Italian, like in English," he said. "The owner is Signor Pardi. I will call him and tell him you are coming. Maybe he can arrange for you to have a tour of the mill, if they are not closed for the holidays." Francesco looked at his watch. "He is not in his office now. He owns a winery, where he spends his afternoons. His wine is famous."

Francesco jotted down the name of Signor Pardi's wine (Sagrantino) and the places I should visit in the area, including the village of Bevagna. We exchanged e-mail addresses. I bought a custom-made cloth, designed to go under a table centerpiece, which Francesco's daughter—also named Rebecca—carefully wrapped for me.

After I left Francesco's shop, I wandered over to Piazza Santa Croce, where a German Christmas market had opened that day. I thought it was curious that Italians don't do their own Christmas market. In fact, most of the Christmas decorations I had seen in Florence's shops were "Made in PRC" (People's Republic of China).

At the German market, I found a vendor selling Christmas windmills, powered by small candles. In my Pasadena storage unit, I have a large nativity windmill, with angels, Wise Men and shepherds on the pyramidal tiers. It's my favorite Christmas decoration and was the centerpiece of our dining table every holiday season for many years. For my table in Florence, I chose a small windmill—with a snowman, a boy on a sled and a girl on skis, spinning on a single wooden disc. It was well-made—authentically German. I liked that it had a little birdfeeder, hanging from an arch, with specks of birdseed and a tiny bird inside.

My new windmill was on the table that night, lit and spinning, as visiting friends from Chicago and I dined on *ortica* ravioli (oil first, then the cheese). For dessert, I served a *panforte al cioccolato*—a chewy brownie-like cake filled with dried fruit and almonds—that is a traditional holiday confection from Siena.

By candle glow, my apartment looked very festive. The day before, I had bought a huge poinsettia at the market and had hung two long swags of red-and-gold ribbon from the living room curtain rod, which I thought would be a nice way to display Christmas cards. I wasn't sure I would get many cards, living in a distant land. But to my delight, on the day I hung the ribbons, the first card arrived.

26

Fa la la

My plan to spend Christmas in Umbria sprang from a Google search of holiday happenings in Italy. One link led to another and I ended up on the website for an inn in Montefalco. It looked lovely and appeared to be in a wooded area, with incredible panoramic views. I could take my walk in the woods on Christmas Day, without trudging through drifts of snow. There was a restaurant on the premises where Christmas lunch was included in a three-day holiday package. I would be alone on Christmas—something I had never experienced. But in my solo wanderings, I've always found great camaraderie among travelers.

The inn had been the retreat of Italian poet and playwright Gabriele D'Annunzio, a Fascist who was the political forerunner and rival of Benito Mussolini. In 1919, D'Annunzio was outraged that Italy had given up the port city of Fiume at the post-war Paris Peace Conference and led a band of two thousand Italian nationalists in a siege of the city that forced the withdrawal of the occupying Allied Forces. D'Annunzio declared Fiume an independent state, appointed himself as "Duce" and declared war on

Italy. D'Annunzio and his followers controlled Fiume for more than a year before the Italian Navy bombarded the port and forced him to surrender.

D'Annunzio lived in Florence for a year and likely had more than a few espressos at Giubbe Rosse. Known for his modern tragedies laced with political allusions and his decadent lifestyle, D'Annunzio got himself in trouble with the Vatican, which placed all of his works on the Index of Forbidden Books. D'Annunzio collaborated on operas and musical plays (including one with French composer Claude Debussy). He wrote a modern Greek-style tragedy for stage legend Sarah Bernhardt and had a tempestuous affair with actress Eleonora Duse. His sexual exploits were legendary and according to Italian lore, he broke a rib trying to give himself a blow job. (In another version of that legend, he had a rib removed so that he could give himself a blow job.)

If nothing else, I decided, the ghosts of this inn-in-the-woods should be interesting. I had a rush of anticipatory pleasure as I clicked "Book Now."

⌒〜⌒

I went online one evening to read more about the history of Montefalco linens and found a website that had a "random selection" of travelers' "favorite shops" in Italy. Just below the listing for a linen shop in Montefalco, a recommendation for a leather store in Florence caught my eye. The review was written by an American woman named Jessica. When I got to Marcello's name, I was sure I had entered the twilight zone. Jessica raves about Marcello's quality merchandise, made at his own factory, and his expert fashion sense. She urges shoppers to visit the store and ask only for him.

The writer-in-me was dancing on the ceiling. The rest of me was staring at the laptop screen, calculating the implausible odds that a random internet search for linens had led me to a random selection of Italian stores with a random review by one of Marcello's customers. I wondered if Jessica had bought Marcello's story about owning the factory, along with everything in the store, or whether she and Marcello were in cahoots.

A week later, Marcello came over for one of our evenings of sex and margaritas. I told him about my idea of spending Christmas in Montefalco, in search of linens and D'Annunzio's ghost. Marcello hadn't heard of Montefalco linens, so I showed him my collection, which I spread out on the bed. He was impressed with the patterns and the exceptional weaving.

He was sitting on the edge of the bed, taking off his shoes, as I tucked the linens back in the dresser drawer. "I was reading an article online about travelers' favorite shops in Italy," I said casually. "It talked about where to buy linens and leather."

I walked over to the bed and stood next to him. "I read a great review about you by someone named Jessica."

He chuckled. "A lot of people have seen that article," he said. He looked up at me, with a sly grin. "Jessica was one of my clients. She was doing a little advertising for me."

He lay back on the bed. I unbuckled his belt. "You're somethin' else," I said.

I don't know whether Marcello was feeling a little heat, but our conversation topic, of his choosing, later that evening was global warming.

⁊

Two weeks before Christmas, I decided to postpone my rendez-vous with D'Annunzio's ghost when I was invited to spend the holidays with friends in Edinburgh. The kind woman at the

Umbrian inn, who had been e-mailing me details about the Christmas festivities there, sent this message: *"We are very sad for your decision, but really hope to have you here soon. Merry Christmas and Happy New Year."* I assured her I would re-schedule my visit.

I found cheap non-stop flights from Pisa to Edinburgh. On a chilly December afternoon, I dashed around Florence, shopping for Christmas prezzies for the Scottish clan. I went to my favorite woolen shop and bought a lovely pashmina for Fiona. I purchased beautiful Italian notecards for Clare, her mother and Fiona's sister, Liz. For Gavin, I bought a set of cards, made by Fabriano, with renderings of Italian villas and gardens. (Gavin and I are big fans of Fabriano, which has been producing paper since 1268. I love their journals and Gavin loves their watercolor sketch pads.) I stopped by Nadia's store and chose leather pouches for Fiona's and Liz's grown daughters and, with Nadia's help, a silk tie for Fiona's husband, James, who is Clare's brother. (Perhaps I should include a map of the clan in an appendix to this book.)

Nadia asked me if I had heard from Marcello. I just shrugged my shoulders, as if to say "nothing." I intended to keep my vow of *silentium*.

Marcello came over the day after his birthday, in mid-December. With two lit candles in his margarita, I turned off the lights and sang "Happy Birthday" to him.

As I made a simple supper of spinach-and-egg *tagliatelle*, I asked him, "So how old are you?"

"I'm 48," he replied.

"You just had a birthday yesterday," I reminded him.

"Then I'm 49," he said.

"Are you sure?"

"Do you think I look older?" he asked.

"Well, you told me you've had work done."

"I don't look that much different," he said. "I can show you some pictures. I just had my eyes done because I was dating a woman who was into plastic surgery."

"I will never have plastic surgery," I declared.

Marcello smiled at me. "You've never told me how old you are."

I said, "Let's put our driver's licenses on the table. You first."

He laughed. The timer went off for the pasta. We were both saved by the bell.

ॐ

Exactly one week before Christmas, snow fell on Florence—not a common occurrence. In fact, it was only the second snowfall in Florence in twenty-five years.

That night from my window, next to my toasty radiator, I watched kids throw snowballs on the sidewalk below. Flurries swirled around the street lights as the tops of cars and the seats of motorcycles disappeared under a blanket of white. The snow clung to the boughs and long needles of the umbrella pine, under my balcony. It was the perfect Christmas tree.

The next morning, a Saturday, I went down to the neighbor-hood café, which is known for its pastries. My favorite barista, Luan, was setting out freshly baked *panettone*, a Christmas treat in Italy. The loaves look like giant muffins, with puffy tops. The bread is laced with sultanas or sometimes chocolate bits. I bought a large chocolate one for Elena and Bernardo, who had invited me for dinner that evening. Luan packaged it in a festive basket of sweets, along with a bottle of champagne, and presented it to me with great flourish. Baskets of sweets, pastas, condiments, nuts and wine are popular Italian Christmas gifts.

Elena, who loves to cook, made a delicious dinner of Tuscan-style roast beef, seared and rare, with roasted potatoes and a side dish of marinated orange and yellow *peperoni* (peppers) with olives.

"I've heard the Americans put *peperoni* on pizza," she said to me.

"Pepperoni pizzas are really popular in the U.S., but pepperoni, to us, is salami," I explained. "We do put peppers, like these, on pizza, too." I didn't tell her that Americans also like barbequed chicken, pineapple and guacamole on pizza.

Little Giulia entertained us by babbling, in an apparent imitation of me. Though she's only two, she knows I speak a language different from hers—and perhaps a language that's uniquely mine. After my last visit, she told Elena (in Italian), "Rebecca says hello, which means ciao." Giulia's Anglo-gibberish that evening was occasionally punctuated with "Rebecca." Despite my alien status, she liked sitting on my lap and even showed me her room. She literally took me in hand, which I found very touching.

As we were saying good-night, Elena gave me a gift basket containing a package of Tuscan biscotti, called *cantucci*, and a bottle of *vin santo*, a sweet dessert wine into which the *cantucci* is meant to be dipped. Elena told me that Giulia's babysitter, who works at a local bakery, made the *cantucci* herself.

"It's a wonderful Italian bakery," Elena said. "And the funny thing is, it's owned by an American."

27

Hogmanay in Edinburgh

For all the time I've spent in Edinburgh, both as a student and a visitor, I had never been there for Christmas or for the Scottish New Year celebration called Hogmanay.

Scots ring in the new year with pagan gusto. For four hundred years, Scottish Protestants banned the celebration of Christmas in Scotland, regarding it as a Catholic observance. (In fact, as late as the 1950s, Christmas was a work day for many Scots.) So the big year-end blowout in Scotland has traditionally been New Year's. In days of old, revelers dressed in cattle hides and ran around villages lighting bonfires, tossing torches, rolling blazing tar barrels down hillsides and beating each other with sticks. All to ward off evil spirits on the darkest days of the year. In Edinburgh, the shortest day has only seven hours of light.

The origin of the word Hogmanay is much debated, with ties to the Vikings, the Saxons, the Celts, the French and the drunken sots who immortalized it as their party cry. Hogmanay festivities begin with the custom of "first footing." To ensure good luck, the first foot across the threshold after "the bells" of midnight should be that of a dark-haired man (those blond Vikings were trouble), bringing gifts of coal, shortbread, salt, black bun (fruitcake) and, of course, whisky. The party continues all night, as friends and neighbors meet, greet and make merry. In modern-day Scotland, January second is a national holiday to give everyone a chance to recover from the debauchery of the previous twenty-four hours.

On the afternoon of Hogmanay eve, I was sitting at a Starbucks, sipping a tall "skinny" latte (in Scottish Starbucks parlance) while noting the brisk business of the wine shop across the street, in an area of Edinburgh called Stockbridge. Stockbridge was actually a small village—named for a bridge that spans a stream called the Water of Leith—that became part of Edinburgh in the early 1800s. Though it's only a ten-minute walk up and over the hill to the center of Edinburgh, Stockbridge retains its village feeling. Its winding main street, with original cobblestones still evident in places, bustles with commerce. The shops are trendy bohemian with a conscience—charity thrift shops and an Oxfam bookstore and record shop—alongside coffee shops, galleries, pubs, delis, artisan boutiques, restaurants, and some of the best butchers, bakers and fishmongers in town.

Before leaving Florence, I had checked a few websites for Edinburgh apartment rentals and had found a flat in the heart of Stockbridge, at Glanville Place, just a hammer's throw from the Starbucks where I was sipping my latte and Stockbridge's famous pub, The Bailie. Perfect locale, I thought—a pub and a Starbucks within ten paces of home.

James and Fiona had driven me by the apartment building a few days earlier.

"There it is," James said, reading off the street number.

"It has a blue door," I said, pleasantly surprised. I looked at Fiona. "Remember the blue door at Robertson House?" During our university days, Fiona and I had lived in a student house on Marchmont Road, with a blue front door.

With latte in hand, I walked along Glanville Place to survey the neighborhood. I noticed a set of keys in the lock of the blue door. I lingered, waiting for the owner of the keys to return, which he did within minutes. He was about 30, with dark hair (a good first-footer), and had been in the shop next door, apparently stocking up on provisions for the night's festivities.

"Would you mind if I followed you in?" I asked him. "I'm thinking of renting a flat in the building."

"No problem," he said. He held the door open and I stepped into the entry hall. "Just close the door behind you when you leave." He disappeared up a spiral stone staircase at the back of the hallway.

For a moment, I was transported to a September night in 1974, as I opened the blue door on Marchmont Road for the first time. I was with a friend named Steve, who was in the same study-abroad program. We were the only students in the program attending universities in Scotland; Steve was on his way to St. Andrews. We had been traveling all day by train from London and had arrived at Edinburgh's Waverly Station after dark. As our taxi pulled away from the station, we caught our first glimpse of Edinburgh Castle, towering above us on an enormous volcanic rock called the Mound. Steve and I looked at each other in disbelief.

Standing at the threshold of a nineteenth-century tenement on Marchmont Road that night, Steve and I were not especially eager time travelers. The entry hall wasn't exactly inviting. The lights were dim, the walls gray and grimy. I remember a bicycle propped near the door. At the end of the hall was an enormous rectangular staircase.

I looked at Steve for reassurance.

"You go first," he said.

I was on my own this time, taking the stairs at Glanville Place. I held on to the curved wooden railing as I rounded the stone steps to the second-floor landing. On the door was the number "3" and a shiny brass knocker—the face of a woman with a wreath of leaves in her tousled hair. I was tempted to knock, but didn't. I had tried to make an appointment to see the flat, but the owner told me she didn't want to impose on the tenant, which I thought was odd. I stood there for a minute, imagining the rooms beyond. In the flat across the hall, where the dark-haired man had delivered provisions, a Hogmanay party was in progress.

At midnight, Fiona, James and I watched the spectacular fireworks display over the Castle, from their lovely home on a hill overlooking Edinburgh. A perfect welcome to the new year. The next day, fifteen people—grandparents, cousins, aunts and uncles—gathered at the house for dinner. Though I wasn't related to anyone at the table, I felt very much a part of the family.

On my last day in Edinburgh, I had lunch with James and Fiona at The Bailie. It's a classic pub, with a big island bar of polished brass and wood and a loyal clientele. The place was festively decorated for the holidays. A fire crackled in the hearth. The Bailie is known for its tasty, hearty fare, which didn't disappoint. We toasted the new year and my idea of moving my tent to Edinburgh.

That night, as I flew back to Florence, I read *The Unbearable Lightness of Scones*, a novel set in Edinburgh, by Alexander McCall Smith, widely known for his No. 1 Ladies' Detective Agency series.

James and Fiona used to live near Mr. Smith, in an area of Edinburgh known for its writers-in-residence, including Harry Potter's J.K. Rowling. (Mr. Smith used to come to James and Fiona's house at Christmastime, playing carols on his saxophone.) *The Unbearable Lightness of Scones*, which was serialized in *The Scotsman* newspaper before it was published as a book, is an affectionate portrait of Edinburgh that locals-in-the-know would appreciate most.

I had a good laugh when I got to a scene set at The Bailie. I seem to be drawn to bars frequented by fellow scribes. Whether in Florence or Edinburgh, I realized, I sit in good company.

28

The new year

Marcello came to see me the night after I returned from Edinburgh. He had spent Christmas with his parents at their home in southern Italy and brought me a bag filled with beautiful oranges grown in that region along with a bottle of Sicilian red wine.

He loved my photos of snowy Edinburgh. When I mentioned I was thinking about moving there, he laughed. He knew my tolerance for winter weather is between zilch and none.

"I could see myself in Edinburgh for a year," I said.

"Maybe a year," he said. "But you're going back to L.A." And then he said, "I could see living in L.A. for six months of the year. But I'd have to be somewhere in the winter where there was snow."

Sometimes I wondered if he might be pondering the possibilities of something more between us. But then I'd remind myself: *You're dealing with the Casanova of Florence.*

Marcello and I had become good friends who had great sex. After our falling out and subsequent three months apart, we had come back to each other. This wasn't a love affair. But the affection and passion we shared probably was the next best thing.

On our first night together of the new year, our pillow talk was about our favorite holiday memories.

In Italy, on the eve of January 6, a witch named La Befana (which means "epiphany" in Italian) flies on her magic broomstick, delivering presents to children who have been good and coal to those who've had behavioral issues. She goes up and down the chimney with her broom and is known to sweep the floors of houses she visits. That may depend, however, on whether the family leaves her a glass of wine and some nibbles.

Marcello confessed that one year, Befana brought him coal.

"Were you naughty?" I asked.

"No," he said with an angelic smile. "The best present I ever got was a toy Winchester rifle with bullets. There was a compartment where you could put the bullets. You could really shoot it. It had those caps that made a big popping sound."

As he described the snowy day when he took his new gun out to play, I clearly could see the boy in the man.

౿

A few days after my return to Florence, the owner of the Glanville flat e-mailed me to say that the present occupant had decided to stay on. She was apologetic, but I suspected she had used me to pressure her tenant to renew the lease. I sent out a flurry of e-mails to Edinburgh property agents, asking if they had vacancies coming up in the spring.

I e-mailed a friend who has written women's travel guides that have great chapter titles like "best places to kiss in Paris." I knew she would understand the feeling I was having about Edinburgh: *"It's not only a familiar place, where I have a long history and many friends, but I've always felt like I've come home when I'm there. Must be my Scottish heritage. I know you'll get this—while I was in Edinburgh over the holidays, I had this strange feeling that someone is there, waiting for me. I'm intrigued."*

The weather in Florence was chilly, grey and wet. I began taking brisk walks around the neighborhood, to boost endorphin flow and thwart mid-winter malaise. I was really missing L.A.

I never encountered a single street in Florence named after something simple, like a number, a letter, a bird, a flower or a tree. A walk around the block in a typical Florence neighborhood is an Italian Who's Who lesson. The streets are named after famous and not-so-famous Italians whose life stories and accomplishments are known mostly to historians and Wikipedia nerds. And their names don't exactly slip off the tongue—at least, not mine.

On one stroll around my neighborhood, for example, I crossed Via Angiolo Tavanti to Via Gian Romagnosi. I took a right on Via Vittorio Emanuele II and then another right onto Via Giovanni Fabroni. I turned left at Via Gianfracesco Pagnini, past Via Gaspero Barbera and Via Raffaello Lumbruschini, and turned right onto Via Cesare Guasti, which led me to Piazza Pietro Leopoldo, and back up Via Angiolo Tavanti.

A veritable MapQuest Directions nightmare.

To make my walks more interesting, I did a Google search of the streets' namesakes. All of them were men, I noted, starting with Mr. Tavanti, who was an eighteenth-century jurist and politician, buried in the Basilica of Santa Croce. Mr. Romangnosi is thought to be the uncredited discoverer of electromagnetism. Vittorio Emanuele II was the king of Italy from 1861-1878. (Marcello once sat next to his great-grandson at a Florence bar.) Google contends Mr. Giovanni Fabroni is a fashion designer, but I'm sure Florence's street namers had someone else in mind. Mr. Pagnini published a book, in 1766, called *Della Decima* about Florence's financial history. Mr. Barbera wrote a book in the nineteenth century entitled *Memoirs of an Editor*. Mr. Lumbruschini was a nineteenth-century politician and educator who published a newspaper on educational topics. Mr. Guasti was a nineteenth-century writer, editor and publisher, who published Mr. Barbera's book. And Mr. Leopoldo was the Grand Duke of Tuscany who brought Florence into the Age of Enlightenment in the eighteenth century.

The ghosts of Florence are not only on every street corner, they're in the middle of traffic circles as well. On the ride to my osteopath's office, the No. 8 bus goes past what's known as the English Cemetery, smack in the center of a busy round-about. The graves are crammed onto a hillock, contained by a wall and a wrought iron fence. Hardly a serene resting place for the likes of English poet Elizabeth Barrett Browning, who had lived in Florence with her husband Robert. He designed her marble crypt that sits atop the round-about.

I started exploring the backstreets of Florence and discovered hidden gems: a book bindery, a leather workshop, a seventeenth-century apothecary, an art supply store that displays paintbrushes used by Renaissance masters, and a silk factory whose eighteenth-century looms produce damasks, brocades and taffetas depicted in Italian paintings of that era.

I shared my research and discoveries with a new friend, Gaya, whom I met one day at the neighborhood café as she was struggling to get a stroller up the steps and in the door. Her baby was just three weeks old. We became fast friends and met every other day or so. Some afternoons we would walk together, to pick up her 4-year-old daughter from school, with a stop afterward for pastries. If the weather was bad, I would go to her apartment, just a few blocks from mine. We'd talk at her kitchen table, over cups of tea, as she nursed the baby.

Gaya, 37, is Sri Lankan and has had an interesting life, filled with travel. She and her Swiss husband, both lawyers, met when they were living in Brussels. They had moved to Florence a year-and-a-half earlier. Multi-lingual, Gaya learned Italian quickly. Raised on British English, she loved my American slang—as well as my stories about Marcello. He became known in our conversations as "the Romeo and the rogue."

ॐ

On those winter days, my frequent destination was the Odeon, a grand old theater in Florence that shows movies in English a few days a week. The schedule featured that year's Golden Globe and Oscar nominees: *Avatar, Up in the Air, Invictus, Sherlock Holmes, Nine, The Hurt Locker.*

The Odeon is housed in Palazzo Strozzino, built in 1462. Redesigned in the 1920s, the Art Nouveau-style cinema-theater looks like a mini opera house, with tiered balconies, an enormous stained-glass cupola and plush velvety seats. There's a bar that serves hard liquor and espresso, along with popcorn and candy.

There's no fanfare preceding movies at the Odeon. No previews, no announcements to turn off phones and refrain from talking. The lights go out and—boom—the film begins. I was in the ladies' room next to the stage when *Sherlock Holmes* started. By the time I got myself zipped up and presentable, I had already missed the first lines of dialogue.

The Italians hold fast to the tradition of an intermission—*intervallo*—but they don't allow enough time to go to the bar *and* the bathroom, which meant that I missed a few hundred frames of *Avatar* (again, I was in the ladies). Not that it mattered. In the moments before and after intermission, the film flaps around the projector spool so that everything is blurry and garbled anyway.

It became my routine to see one or two films a week at the Odeon. Afterward, I'd pop in for a cappuccino at Giubbe Rosse, just a block from the theater. I'd sit at a table inside where the regulars hang out. The tourists sit outside under the tent, huddled around heaters, and pay €5.50 for a cappuccino. The regulars sit inside where it's cozy and warm and pay €1.60 for a cappuccino.

I liked to sit in Giubbe Rosse's little reading nook, under the sketches of famous writers and artists who were once regulars there, too. Newspapers, clamped to wooden poles, hang on the wall. The poles have bentwood supports that hold the paper so that you have a hand free to sip your espresso. On these outings, I'd read *The International Herald Tribune*, front to back, with poet Giovanni Papini, the high-spirited leader of Italian *futurismo*, peering over my shoulder from his place on the wall of fame.

Invariably, after my cappuccino at Giubbe Rosse, I'd wander past the carousel to a large bookstore on the piazza.

One evening after a movie, a cappuccino and a book browse, I was about to get in a cab at the taxi stand across from the bookstore. But on a whim, I decided instead to walk to the train station, a few blocks away, and catch a bus back to the apartment. It was a nice night for a brisk stroll.

I hadn't gone ten steps when a man walking behind me spoke to me. I didn't hear what he said exactly. I glanced over my shoulder, but kept walking. He came up alongside me. "Please, may I speak with you?" he asked.

He looked vaguely familiar. Had I seen him in the bookstore? I had gone upstairs, as usual, to the English section on the third floor and had asked a clerk about a book I was looking for. Maybe he had overheard our conversation.

The movie I had just seen that day at the Odeon was *(500) Days of Summer*, about a tortured romance that lasted for five hundred mind-numbing days. I was actually relieved that the guy didn't get the girl in the end. She wasn't worth all the aggravation she put him through. But in a sweet twist, fate takes his hand and in the last scene, he meets another girl who just may be The One. We won't know for sure unless there's a sequel. But I left the theater feeling optimistic. After all, I'm a believer that chance encounters have nothing to do with chance.

I looked at this man who so earnestly wanted to speak with me. He didn't look sinister. In fact, he had a sweet face and a nice smile. He looked to be early 40s, with graying wavy hair. He wore wire-rimmed glasses. I liked his expressive eyes.

Sometimes good things happen in a moment of hesitation. I could have easily turned my back on him and kept walking. But I stopped and turned to this man so that he could speak with me. Otherwise, I had a feeling he was going to run next to me all the way to the train station.

I was very aware of our surroundings, but not in an uncomfortable way. We stood near the arch. Behind me was the carousel and Giubbe Rosse. What was it about this spot, I thought. It had become the epicenter of seismic happenings in my life here.

His name was Lorenzo. He was a photographer. He lived in Florence, had studied English in school and liked going to movies at the Odeon. (Had he seen me there, I wondered.) He wanted to know if I was visiting Florence. I told him that I was living here for a few months more, writing a book. When he found out I was from California, his face lit up. He told me how much he had enjoyed his visit to Yosemite. He was amazed by the enormity of Half Dome and raised his arms in the shape of the majestic rounded rock that towers over Yosemite Valley. I asked him about his photography. We exchanged business cards and agreed to meet for coffee one day. He shook my hand and told me how pleased he was to meet me.

Later that night, around eleven, my phone rang. It was Marcello.

"I'm at Piazza della Repubblica, walking past Giubbe Rosse," he said.

"I was just there a little while ago."

"Really?"

I envisioned him walking past the carousel, through my trail of sparkle dust, and thinking of me. Fate has a wonderful sense of humor sometimes.

"I stopped there for coffee after I saw a movie at the Odeon," I said.

"You're seeing a lot of movies these days." Marcello had declined my invitation to see *Sherlock Holmes* a few days earlier because he was busy with a big fashion show that was in town.

"My life now revolves around the Odeon's schedule, which I've memorized," I said. "*Avatar* is playing on Monday. But it's not in 3D." (When I had inquired about that, the woman at the Odeon ticket booth said, "Sorry, *signora*, it is not possible.")

"A friend gave me a copy of *Avatar*. We can watch it on your laptop," he said. No surprise there. Marcello roams with pirates.

"No," I said adamantly. "I must see *Avatar* on the big screen. Even if it's not in 3D."

"Maybe I'll go with you," he said.

I asked how his week had been. The city was bustling with fashionistas, mostly gorgeous guys dressed in black, I noted.

"All the guys in that business are gay," Marcello informed me.

"How did you get into the fashion business?" I asked.

"I'll tell you another time," he said. "I'm freezing."

The penny in my pocket suddenly got warmer. We said goodnight.

I was heading to bed. Before I turned off my laptop, I checked my e-mail. There was a message from Lorenzo: "*Ciao Rebecca. Sono Lorenzo. We met this evening near Piazza della Repubblica. We talk about cinema, fotografia and creative writing, and I told to myself how marvelous would be to become a friend to this interesting woman. I really hope to see you again and to condivide our life activities, our passions, our ideas. Ciao e...buona serata.*"

I wondered what he meant by *"condivide."* Confide, perhaps?

29

Redemption

Kathryn returned to Florence in January and called me one evening.

We had exchanged several e-mails since her visit in the fall. In one message, she wrote: *"Hope the winter will be more fun for you. Certainly you had the hottest summer ever to live through. Don't try to understand everything. Can't be done. So don't be discouraged. Please catch me up on what you're writing about Florence. XOX."*

One e-mail exchange was especially spirited. I signed off saying I had to run to the market and how much I loved having the store downstairs. I wrote: *"The elevators in my building are designed to hold the shopping carts. I can hear you clucking your disapproval of my non-Italian lifestyle. But I must tell you this building is full of Italians who apparently also appreciate convenience."*

She replied: *"So interested to hear your Italian/American experience. Of course Italians love convenience. They invent it! They had ATM banking and EZ-pass 10 years before we did. They also are undergoing a very interesting change. Our favorite truly traditional trattoria at the corner has closed. They were the city descendants of my country life, cooking the Festival foods that the peasants ate – osso buco, coda di manzo, zampa di vitello, brains, kidneys, etc. All the parts that the padroni didn't eat and that the new generation of pizza eaters don't either. I was lucky enough to catch the chef/owner on a day when he was preparing a banquet. Just glorious. And gone. Will be fascinating to see how this ancient culture that has withstood so many invasions will survive the latest from America via the media."*

I laughed at the part about Italians inventing convenience. Kathryn and I clearly had different points of reference in this culture.

But she wasn't looking for an argument when she called in January. She was as I remembered her when we met during my apartment-hunting trip the previous spring. She was eager to know how I was getting on and was even upbeat about the prospects for my book.

"You're in that new genre that what's-her-name made popular with *Pray Love*," Kathryn said.

I gently corrected her. "*Eat, Pray, Love*," I said.

With phone in hand, I walked into my office and looked at the shelves packed with my books, many of them travel memoirs written by women. Of course, Elizabeth Gilbert's bestseller was among them. And so was the magnum opus of them all—*Black Lamb and Grey Falcon: A Journey Through Yugoslavia,* a probing historical commentary about the Balkans and its people, written by Rebecca West (née Cicily Isabel Fairfield) who traveled through Yugoslavia in the 1930s.

"But it's not a new genre," I said. "Women have been writing stories of their travel experiences and cultural perceptions for years."

"Yes, I know," Kathryn said. "I grew up reading those books, about their trips across the desert."

The desert takes many forms, I thought.

Kathryn and I spoke of many things that evening, but one thing in particular struck a chord with me. "I don't look at life as I did when I was your age," she told me. "You see things differently when there is no finite end in sight. At this point in my life, I don't know when that big truck is coming that's going to smash me."

She wasn't being morose. In fact, just the opposite. She had been telling me how rich and full her days are. She had so much to live for and so much more she wanted to do.

Kathryn's days in Florence are packed with interviews and research related to her book. She told me in the fall that she had mapped out the book's outline. But her busy schedule left her little time to write. More than that, I think she was struggling with the grim reality that many writers face: writing is a lonely endeavor that requires considerable stamina, commitment and discipline.

In my experience as a freelance book editor, I've had the pleasure of working with women who, later in life, have been inspired to write a book—or dust off a manuscript that has been sitting in a drawer for years. One of my dearest clients is a lovely woman in her 80s named Gwen. We've worked on three books together. Gwen has traveled extensively and brings great passion to conversations about sociology and world history. She taught in the Pasadena public schools for thirty years and wrote her books, for the most part, at her lectern while her students worked on their assignments. I'll never forget the first manuscript Gwen brought me. It was written longhand on lined yellow tablet paper. Pages and pages of school-issued tablet paper. What immediately worried me was that the pages—hundreds of them—weren't numbered. When I mentioned this to her, she laughed and said, "I know what order they go in, my dear." At that moment, a light breeze blew in through the window of my dining room, where we were sitting at the table, and ruffled a few pages of the manuscript. I jumped up and shut the window. My first task that day as editor was to number her pages. I soon learned that Gwen has a habit of throwing up her hands, with dramatic flair, causing pages to fly. (As a young woman, she had been a professional stage actress.) I always kept a box of paper clips handy to minimize the chaos.

It took several years for Gwen and me to work through her manuscripts. One book had a brilliant, but complicated plot, with intricately drawn characters. It was a compelling end-of-the-world fantasy that Gwen had started writing thirty years earlier. Her prescience amazed me. In her vision of the demise of the human race, she wrote about the consequences of global warming, the squandering of the earth's resources, and the obliteration of eco-systems and animal species.

Sometimes Gwen would spend several months revising and rewriting. If I hadn't heard from her in a while, I would call her to see how things were going. I didn't want her to get lost on that lonely road. As we completed each manuscript, I would print up the final copy and present it to her. It's a thrilling moment in the journey of a writer, to feel the weight of your accomplishment in your hands.

I wished I could help Kathryn in her writer's journey. I truly believed she had a great book inside her about her beloved Tuscan hillside and an era of Italian life that was fading away.

During our phone conversation that evening, Kathryn and I talked about the impact of the global recession in Italy. "My friends here aren't talking about it," Kathryn said. "But I suspect they're feeling it."

I told Kathryn about Elena and Bernardo, who resemble many American couples I know. They're well-educated professionals who work long hours and are too exhausted to enjoy what little downtime they have.

I recounted the story of a Saturday night the previous summer when I went to their apartment for dinner. A young man named Stefano, who worked with Bernardo, joined us.

Bernardo and Stefano sat through dinner with their Blackberries on the table, checking their messages every twenty minutes.

"It's Saturday night," I said to them. "Who's at the office?"

The global office has no walls and spans all time zones. "We never know when an e-mail will come that we need to answer," Bernardo replied.

After dinner, we all went out onto the balcony. Bernardo and Stefano stood at one end, with their Blackberries, discussing business. Elena and I stood at the other end, talking about life.

"I keep thinking about something you said at the apartment the other day," Elena said. It was the day she had come to meet the plumber and I'd treated her to her first margarita. "You said to me, 'You've had so much change in your life in such a short time.'" In three years, Elena had married, changed jobs, had a baby and moved to a bigger apartment that required extensive renovations.

"You've had enormous changes."

And then it all spilled out. Elena told me that night how she wished she could change her life and go back to the village by the sea where she grew up. For all her hard work—going to university to get a law degree and pursuing her career—she would give it all up in a minute. The dream she went after wasn't what she wanted after all.

"I wouldn't care if I didn't have an important job," Elena told me. "When I go to be with Giulia and my parents on the weekends, I see my friends going to the beach at lunchtime with their children. They spend the evenings there, having picnics with their families." She looked out at the block of apartments in front of us. "I don't like Florence. I don't want to live here."

"You can always make changes," I said.

"But how?" She truly wanted an answer.

I tend to be very practical in my approach to major life changes. "You could sell this place and move to your village."

Elena looked skeptical.

"If you can't sell it in this market, rent it out," I said.

"Bernardo would never leave his job."

"Have you talked to him about this?"

"I know he wouldn't," she said, shaking her head.

Since Bernardo was standing within earshot, I didn't dwell on this. But I said, "You should talk to him. Maybe he can't imagine it now, but that could change."

I looked at Elena, seeing myself at her age. "I had a successful career as a journalist," I told her. "But when my son was born, I stayed home with him. It was the greatest luxury of my life, to be with him. The financial consequences put a lot of pressure on my marriage. My husband had a lot of weight on his shoulders. It wasn't the cause of our divorce, but it was a strain."

Elena was stunned. "You're divorced?"

"Yes," I said. I realized this news came as a shock to a Catholic woman. But actually, she seemed more intrigued than appalled.

"Sometimes change is really difficult," I said to her. "But the consequence of doing nothing is worse."

I felt like the wise, older woman, twenty years down the road from Elena, dispensing advice—a bit like Kathryn, a generation down the road from me.

"I had dinner with Elena and Bernardo just before Christmas," I told Kathryn. "Bernardo looked absolutely exhausted."

At one point during dinner, I asked him how he was doing. He forced a smile and shrugged his shoulders. Elena looked at him from across the table, with what I saw to be great love and sympathy. She said that his company was going through a difficult time and that they hoped the new year would be better. I could hear the strength in her voice, but I sensed they were under tremendous stress.

I said to Kathryn, "This isn't Italian family life as you've known it."

"She truly knows what she's missing because, as a child, she had a different way of life," Kathryn said. "This is fascinating."

❦

Kathryn told me there had been a drama in the olive grove involving the man she hired to prune the suckers away from the tree trunks before the picking began. The day before Kathryn and the rest of us showed up, the pruner, named Sergio, came onto the property with his own pickers who stripped many of the olives off the low branches of the trees.

Sergio was there the day Clare, Gavin and I were in the grove. He joined us in the *capanna* for lunch. He didn't sit at the table—he sat off to the side, but was part of the conversation. At one point, he showed me photos he had on his cell phone of the olive-pressing equipment at a local mill.

He had told Kathryn that there was no need for her to take her pickers down to the lower part of the grove because there weren't enough olives down there to bother with. But to Kathryn's surprise, she later discovered the trees in the lower grove were filled with olives. She suspected he planned to come back after she had returned to the U.S., to pick the olives himself.

An olive thief had been in our midst. And he seemed like such a nice guy. Who knew.

But in an ironic turn, the thief became her ally. Just before Kathryn returned to Florence in January, part of the wall that bordered her grove collapsed onto the road below. Sergio took charge of clearing the rubble and dealing with the authorities.

"I don't know what we would have done without him," Kathryn told me. "It just goes to show that no one is all bad."

Kathryn was planning a big lunch the next day for the family of pickers who came to her aid on the last days of the harvest. "I don't know how much longer I can continue with this folly of mine," Kathryn said. "I hope I can get them all to help me next year. Even Sergio."

"It's good to keep everyone on your side of the wall," I said.

"That's true," Kathryn agreed.

Sergio had redeemed himself in Kathryn's eyes. And in a way, she had redeemed herself in mine.

Kathryn and I may not see eye-to-eye about this country she extols. But I felt very much her peer as a fellow observer of Italian life. For three decades, her reportage focused on a way of life that she had experienced with intensity and intimacy. My eye was trained on the contemporary culture that is replacing it.

And the beauty in this: the import of our equally valid and insightful stories rests one upon the other.

30

Lorenzo

I was at my neighborhood café for a late afternoon cappuccino when my phone rang. I didn't recognize the number.

"Ciao, Rebecca," the man said. "It's Lorenzo."

I had been scribbling a packing list, on the back of a crumpled receipt, of things I might ship to Edinburgh if I decided to go ahead with the move.

"Lorenzo, it's nice to hear from you," I said. My pen took on a life of its own and started doodling in the margin.

"How are you?" he asked sincerely, as if he really cared about my answer.

"I'm fine," I replied. "What about you?"

"Okay." He hesitated for a moment. Then he said, "I'd like to see you."

We met the next afternoon at my neighborhood café—good to be on familiar turf, I thought. He brought a box of mounted black-and-white photographs that he had taken at museums and churches around Florence. The images captured both the art-work and the people viewing it, in symbiotic and often humorous juxtapositions. A jowly man contemplates the bust of an equally jowly Roman emperor—they look enough alike to be distant cousins. Three young women, in cargo pants, t-shirts and sneakers, regard the erotic Venus of Urbino. One male patron regards the beautifully rounded bottom of the woman next to him as she leans over to read an inscription on the base of a statue. A young girl strikes a pose in front of a marble frieze, mimicking the hand position of the stonecut figure next to her. My personal favorite: a woman in a beautiful wide-brimmed hat stands with her back to the camera, looking at Botticelli's *Primavera*, giving the illusion that she herself is in the garden depicted in the painting.

I was impressed with Lorenzo's technical skills as a photographer and his ability to capture the humor and irony of a fleeting moment.

"Sometimes you just get lucky," he said modestly.

We lingered for two hours at the café. Lorenzo is a movie buff and loves to see Hollywood classics, dubbed in Italian, at the Odeon. We had much to talk about. I enjoyed his company.

As we were getting ready to leave, I said to him, "I have to ask you something. Where did you see me, the night we met?"

He smiled. "At the bookstore, just ten minutes before."

"You looked familiar, but I wasn't sure where I had seen you."

"I saw you upstairs," he said. "You were smiling, like this…" His imitation of my orthodontically-enhanced smile made me laugh.

Lorenzo asked if I'd like to go out into the Tuscan countryside to take photographs with him someday. "I'm always looking for new places to explore," he said. But first, he wanted to go see *Avatar* in 3D at a cineplex outside of Florence.

"Is there a bus I can take to the theater?" I asked.

"I'll take you in my car," he said.

When I got home, I called Gaya and told her I felt a little nervous about getting in a car with a guy I barely knew.

"Right. You don't want to take chances," she said. "Make an excuse. You've already seen *Avatar*."

"But not in 3D."

"This isn't about *Avatar*," she reminded me.

"Right," I said. "No getting into cars with strangers."

The next day, Lorenzo called and I told him I couldn't go see *Avatar* because I had to pick up eyeglasses from the optician (true) and I couldn't possibly watch a 3D movie without them (not exactly true). I suggested we meet at Piazza Leopoldo and go for a walk. It was a beautiful afternoon.

He called me from the piazza, and when I arrived, he was standing by his illegally parked car, with flashers on, waving at me. We clearly weren't going for a walk. If anything went wrong, I assured myself, I'd call Gaya to come rescue me.

As we raced around the first roundabout, I noticed Lorenzo wasn't wearing a seat belt. When I casually mentioned this, he said, "I don't wear a seat belt."

"Why not?" I asked. "In California, you'd get a ticket for not wearing a seat belt."

He grinned and said, "I don't like following the rules."

OMG. I should have put Gaya on speed dial.

Lorenzo's driving skills weren't great by my high California standards. Abrupt lane changes without signaling were standard for him which made traffic circles especially hair-raising. I tried to focus on the scenery as we crossed the Arno and headed, with much gear-shifting, toward the hills.

"I want to show you my neighborhood," he said.

But first, we took off up the hill toward Piazzale Michelangelo, until a police barricade forced us to turn around. Lorenzo did a figure-eight turn, something I had never experienced before. And by the looks on the faces of the drivers who witnessed this maneuver, they, too, were amazed.

We took off back down the hill and took a hard left just past Porta Romana. We were on a quiet street. Lorenzo pointed to a house that took my breath away. The stone supports of the front balcony were the heads of dragons. The house is a landmark of Italy's "Liberty" Art-Nouveau style. Two doors down, Lorenzo pointed to the front door of a large stone house.

"That's where I live," he said. "I grew up in that house."

Lorenzo has never been married and lives with his widowed mother, who's 79. Lorenzo's father had been an artisan metallurgist, whose decorative pieces were highly sought after by wealthy Florentines. But his father's passion wasn't Lorenzo's. Not long after his father's death, Lorenzo closed the shop.

For the past eight years, Lorenzo has worked on the night desk at a Florence hotel. His shift starts at 10 p.m. and finishes around 7 a.m. He tries to sleep in the mornings, but he never gets enough rest. He constantly feels tired. He says his sleep deprivation has taken a toll on his health.

"Maybe you should get a day job," I suggested.

"There are so many people not working," he said. "I wouldn't be able to find a job that would pay me even the same as I make now. I'm afraid to make a change."

Lorenzo drove the meandering streets of his neighborhood, reminiscing about his childhood. He stopped at a little piazza, near a church and an enormous house with an impressive stone-and-brick tower.

"Can you imagine when I was a child, there were no cars here like now," he said, looking around the piazza. "My friends and I would play here—twenty boys and girls. This place has such happy memories for me." He pointed to a gate of a walled garden. "We used to go in through there and climb up the hills, all the way to the top. I'll show you."

With that, we headed up a winding road to the top of the olive terraces of an area known as Bellosguardo. As the name implies, the view is incredible. He parked the car near the gates of a villa, and we walked along a low wall that revealed a stunning panoramic view of Florence and the mountains beyond.

"We would come all the way up here," he said, looking at the olive grove below us.

I could see on Lorenzo's face the joy of his summer days as a boy. I was touched that he was sharing a part of his heart with me.

Back in the car, Lorenzo was in hot pursuit of other childhood haunts. We were on a narrow lane that snaked along a high stone wall, when a car came around the curve. Lorenzo graciously yielded. He shifted into reverse, hit the accelerator and then sharply turned the wheel. It was one of those moments when you know what's about to happen before you hear the crunch of metal.

Lorenzo slammed into a parked Mercedes sports coupe.

He said something in Italian that I'm sure I wasn't supposed to understand. We both got out of the car to survey the damage. The fender of his car was scraped and crumpled. He tried to straighten it.

"It's not so bad, do you think?" he asked optimistically.

"No, it's not so bad," I said.

The Mercedes was another matter. The headlight socket was cracked. Molto euros.

Lorenzo took a business card from his wallet and left it under a windshield wiper.

"Do you want to take a photo of the damage?" I asked him.

"Thank you for remembering me," he said.

Not exactly the photo outing we had planned. As we drove on, I was surprised he didn't seem terribly upset.

"I'm sorry this happened," I said sympathetically.

He shrugged. "I didn't sleep well this morning," he said. "I'm not able to concentrate well."

When he dropped me off at my apartment, I thanked him for the tour.

"I would like to see you again. Would that be okay with you?" he asked.

I smiled at him. "As long as we don't go anywhere in reverse."

31

The other penny

One January evening, Marcello showed up with a digital receiver for me to hook up to my TV so that I could get BBC news without having to sign up for a long-term cable contract. He knew I was starved for up-to-the minute news in English. I was in the habit of downloading podcasts of U.S. news programs. But by the time those podcasts were available for download, the news was already a day old.

At one point early in the evening, as we were sipping our first margaritas, the conversation wandered to the topic of human psychology.

"I've been reading a lot about psychology," he said. "About how our brains work."

The writer-in-me grabbed a pen.

"Take this receiver, for example," he said, pointing to the box that was now on my TV stand. "I bring this to you and you might wonder, what does he want from me?"

I gave him a withering look, but he didn't seem to notice.

"It's like that in business," he continued. "If you give things away, people think they don't have value." With a glint in his eyes, he said, "But if you can't have something, you want it all the more."

I wondered if he was thinking about a hot woman who was dating a friend of his.

Although Marcello had brought me the digital receiver, it didn't actually work. He had forgotten to bring a connector so that it could be hooked up to the TV. Minor detail.

But a week later, he returned with the missing piece. I rewarded him with a pitcher of exceptionally tasty margaritas.

And then I whipped up one of my culinary specialties. I presented my creation on a Tuscan plate.

"What is this?" he asked.

"A peanut butter-and-banana-sandwich," I replied. "Goes great with margaritas."

"I have never had this," Marcello said. "But I would like to try it."

"It's my favorite comfort food," I said. "And it's very nutritious. Bananas are loaded with potassium. Peanut butter has protein. And bread gives you fiber."

He took a bite and licked his lips. "Mmm. I like this."

"Don't say I've never made you dinner," I said.

He would have laughed, except he had a glob of peanut butter stuck to the roof of his mouth.

We watched BBC news and talked about world events. Then we headed for bed.

Sex was great, as usual. So great, in fact, that we had to take an *intervallo* to catch our breath.

Our conversation during intermission covered many topics, including our upcoming travels. He was visiting friends in Cabo San Lucas, Mexico, with short stays in Chicago and L.A. en route.

I, too, was traveling to Chicago and L.A., but we'd miss each other by a few days in both places.

"I have a long layover at JFK on the way back," he said. "You should give me Tom's number. He works at JFK, right?"

Marcello knew about my rift with Tom.

"We don't call each other anymore," I said. "We send each other e-mails occasionally, but we haven't spoken in a couple of months."

Marcello was surprised. "This was really serious."

I looked at Marcello in the candlelight.

"That night when you and I had our falling out," I said.

He nodded. Marcello and I had never spoken about what happened that night.

"You apologized."

"Sure," he said.

"Tom could have diffused the whole thing by just saying he was sorry. But instead, he intentionally made it worse."

"When you look at all the friends you have in your life, there are only a few you can really count on, to be true friends," Marcello said.

I thought of all the friends who had rallied round me in recent years, as I uprooted myself to start a new life. And I thought of those few who were noticeably absent during my hours of great need.

"I can send Tom an e-mail," I offered.

"We could have a drink together, if he's free," Marcello said.

I suddenly pictured Tom in a trench coat, lurking behind a pillar in an airport lounge.

It was time to drop the penny. "You can't meet Tom until you and I have a conversation." I rolled on my side and looked at Marcello. "I need to ask you something. I don't care what your answer is as long as it's the truth."

"Yes, of course."

I took a deep breath. "Do you own the store?" I asked.

He was totally unfazed. "I'm a partner," he said.

"A few months ago, right after I got back from Greece, Nadia told me you don't own the store—that you work for the brothers on commission," I said. "She says you go around Florence looking for rich tourists. You sit next to them at the cafés and give them your card—like you did with me that day at the carousel. And if they come into the store and buy something, you get a cut."

Marcello sighed and softly said, "Oh, Nadia." But he wasn't angry. "We have a partnership. I'm not the sole owner."

"Your card says you're the owner."

"We just say that. I go out and bring in business. We're not the only store that does this."

"You don't have your own factory?" I asked.

"Everyone says they have their own factory," Marcello said. "The factory we use produces high quality merchandise."

"Is everything made in Italy?"

"The hides come from Argentina and elsewhere and are tanned in Italy. The goods are made in Italy."

"Not China?"

"Absolutely not."

Marcello wasn't annoyed. He wasn't getting dressed, looking to make a quick exit. He was lying next to me, stroking my arm. He wasn't going anywhere.

In the spirit of full disclosure, I said, "I'm going to tell you my age." I tossed back my hair and tried to look fetching. "I'm 55."

He looked surprised. "Really?"

"Nadia told me you're in your 50s." I said.

"What else has she told you?"

"That you're a skirt chaser."

He reached over and pulled me toward him. "I want to chase this skirt."

⌒

As Marcello was about to leave that night, he asked if I had something for chapped lips. I gave him a tube of lip balm. For a second, he thought it was a little tube of KY Jelly.

"I'll get a big tube when I'm in the States—but I won't put it in my carry-on this time," he said, balming his lips. "Is KY Jelly fairly new? I didn't know about it until several years ago."

"It's been around a long time," I said. "At least since the '70s."

"Really?" Then Marcello said wistfully, as if he had missed out on a good thing, "The '70s. All that free sex."

"You lost your virginity in the '70s," I said. "You told me you were 15 and she was an older woman."

"She was a hooker," he said.

"What!" I exclaimed. "Who paid for that?"

"My friends," he said. "But I didn't have sex again for several years after that. It was a long time before I became a skirt chaser." He gave me a roguish smile.

The land of full disclosure with Marcello was a minefield of surprises.

32

No place called home

I arrived in Chicago on a cold snowy day in early February. My father met me at the airport. Mom had stayed home.

It had been five months since I had had any contact with my mother. International calls from my cell phone were exorbitantly expensive. I had asked my dad numerous times to get an international phone card or add an international plan to his phone service, but he told me he didn't have time to look into it. I had tried to call them on Skype, but the connection to their home phone was poor. My dad hadn't upgraded his internet service so that he could set up Skype on his computer. He said he was too busy with my mother's care to deal with that.

On our way to the house, I asked him how she was doing. He looked at me sadly. "When I told her 'I'm going to the airport to get Becky,' she said, 'Who's Becky?'"

Ten days earlier, my dad had sent me an e-mail saying he had planned to sign a lease for an apartment at an assisted-living facility in town and had asked me to come home as soon as possible to help them get organized for the move.

I spent two hours online trying to find flights, not easy on short notice. A few days later, after everything was booked, he sent another e-mail saying he had decided not to lease the apartment, but he was happy I was coming home anyway.

I doubted he ever intended to sign that lease. In the course of the next week, I doubted everything: his intentions, his ability to close a deal, even his ability to assess his options. It was clear to him that my mother needed professional care, but he was immobilized by the prospect of leaving their home of forty-six years.

In her confused state, Mom had already left "home." She was convinced they were living in a hotel and complained about the maid service. She pointed to the clutter on her dresser and on the counter in her bathroom. "The maids mess everything up. I can't find anything that's mine."

On the first night I was there, she barged into my room at 4 a.m. wanting to know who I was and whether I was alone in the room. She said all the guests in the hotel were out in the hall, complaining about how loud I was snoring.

She was lost in the fog most of the time. One day as we were looking at photos of Colin, she didn't realize that I was his mother.

Once she asked me, "Have you called your husband since you've been here?"

"I don't have a husband, Mom."

She looked puzzled.

But on another day, she asked me sweetly, "Have you met the love of your life yet?"

I smiled at her. "Not yet."

We had conversations that made me laugh. She was getting dressed one morning and asked me to hook her bra for her. "When I was a freshman in college," she told me, "there was a boy who wanted to go out with me, but my roommate told him I only had one boob." My mother had had a mastectomy when she was 57.

"Mom, you had two boobs when you were in college," I told her.

"Oh no, I didn't," she said adamantly.

We toured two assisted-living facilities during my visit. One had an apartment that my parents had seen on an earlier tour and were interested in renting, but by the time I arrived from Italy, it had already been taken. Apparently, my dad hadn't expressed an immediate interest. Another apartment was available, but my dad didn't like the layout. In fact, he didn't like the floor plans of most of the units.

We saw an apartment at another facility that they liked. The director told us she would hold the apartment for a week with a refundable $250 deposit. My father looked at me sheepishly and said, "I didn't bring my checkbook."

Several days later, we went back to see the apartment again. He didn't bring his checkbook that day either. He walked into our meeting with the facility's director with a bulging black garbage bag tucked under his arm. When he had taken the bag from the trunk of the car, I had asked him what was inside. He told me it was a blanket that he had folded to the dimensions of a double bed mattress. "I lay this on the floor when we look at apartments," he said, "so I can get an idea of how much space a bed will take up."

I thought that was a reasonable idea until he took the "blanket" from the bag and spread it on the apartment floor. This wasn't one of the many worn blankets he could have taken from the linen closet. He had chosen an heirloom quilt, made by my great aunt Hattie, to use as his template.

"That's Aunt Hattie's quilt," I said in disbelief.

He shrugged. "I needed a blanket."

"This isn't a blanket." I looked down at the hand-appliquéd spray of lilies whose stamens Hattie had embroidered with a delicate satin stitch. My father had folded over the sides of the quilt and secured the flaps with safety pins every few inches to approximate the measurements of a mattress top.

He walked across the quilt in his street shoes. I stared at his feet crushing the pockets of batting and Hattie's beautiful handiwork.

"Get off the quilt," I said, seething with anger.

He took a few more steps on the quilt, baiting me.

"I said get off the quilt!"

The director of the facility looked at my father. "I think you should fold that up and take it to the cleaners before your daughter has a heart attack." She wisely left the room.

With the quilt on the floor between us, my father and I squared off.

"How was I to know?" he shouted at me.

"How could you possibly not know?" I shouted back. Hattie's quilt had been a gift to my mother and father when I was child and had covered their bed for many years. He acted like he had never seen it before.

On the last day of my visit, I sat down with them both. I had spent seven days pushing against their stubbornness and fear of change. My dad assured me he planned to sign a lease within a week. But I didn't believe him.

"There's nothing more I can do to help you," I told them.

My mom was so stressed and confused, she couldn't remember anything. She had no memory of seeing the apartments and wanted my dad to take her for yet another visit.

In a private moment, I told my father, "She is not able to make a decision. It's up to you."

That night, after my mom and dad were asleep, I brought Aunt Hattie's quilt to my room. I sat on my bed, with the quilt on my lap, and carefully removed the safety pins—seventeen in all. I spread the quilt on my bed and smoothed out the creases. I lightly ran my fingers over the lilies and Hattie's tiny quilting stitches.

I gently folded the quilt and wrapped it in a sheet. I emptied a dresser drawer and placed the quilt inside. Unlike me, it had a secret place to hide.

⁓

When I arrived in L.A. the next day, I was sure my guardian travel angels had heard my panicked prayers. My angels sometimes make things happen with great flourish. At four o'clock that morning, I awoke to a mild earthquake—a very rare event in Chicago. It was clearly their way of saying, *"Get up and get dressed, honey, you don't want to miss this flight."* I was in a security line at O'Hare at 7:30 a.m., with five hundred people ahead of me. Hundreds of flights had been canceled the day before because of snow. But the sun was shining that morning despite forecasts to the contrary, and my flight left on time. Five hours later, I was cruising along an L.A. freeway in my rental car, radio blaring, palm trees swaying, angels smiling. I felt like I had been catapulted into nirvana from the depths of a black hole.

The weather was gorgeous. On one 80-degree day, as I swam laps at the pool in Pasadena, I told a friend swimming next to me, "I daydream about this."

My pool pals were eager to hear tales of Italy and wanted to know when I was coming home to stay. I didn't have an answer to that.

The truth was I wasn't ready to come back. Most of my friends had been hit hard by the recession. They were out of work, taking temp and part-time jobs to make ends meet. Many were upside down on their mortgages. Food stamps were the new currency.

"You're not missing anything," one friend told me. "Life here is the shits."

I enjoyed a weekend in Berkeley with Colin. He showed me his apartment and took me on a tour of the campus. I had never been to Berkeley and enjoyed seeing the remaining vestiges of its hippie past. Across from the Rasputin Music store on Telegraph Avenue, I noticed an old guy selling macramé. Colin smiled and said, "Look, Mom—one of your people."

Colin and I spent a sunny afternoon in San Francisco. We hung out on Fisherman's Wharf, watching sea lions and sailboats, and talking about the stuff of our lives. That evening, I took Colin and some of his friends to dinner. From my vantage point at middle-age, I already knew they were going to be friends for life. They were making long-range bets about things like who would buy the other a bottle of Jack Daniels if the Dodgers won the World Series.

"You'd better put that bet in writing," I told Colin. "You might be 80 when that happens."

The next day, Sunday, was Valentine's Day. That morning, Colin met me in the lobby of the Claremont Hotel where I was staying and presented me with a box of brownies he had baked that morning. A man and his young son were sitting nearby as I opened the box. The man looked at me and the brownies. "Wow," he said.

I smiled at Colin. "Are these Berkeley brownies?" He assured me they weren't.

I had laughed at an article I read in *The Berkeley Daily Planet* about some kids who had gotten into trouble for selling pot-enriched brownies on the school playground. I told Colin, "That wouldn't have been a newsworthy story in my day."

Before he drove me to the airport that afternoon, we went back to his apartment. He wanted to show me a video of his most recent skydiving adventure. My heart was in my throat as I watched him tumble out of the plane. It was a tandem jump, but his partner, whose hair was snow-white, was no young guy.

"What if he'd had a heart attack?" I asked, trying not to sound motherly.

"Mom, why do you always think people are going to have heart attacks?"

"Because I'm nearly having one watching this."

There wasn't a shadow of concern on Colin's blissful face as he floated in the wind, arms outstretched. He looked like an angel who had just found his wings. He and his white-haired partner returned to terra firma without a misstep despite my concern during the descent that they might drop down in the fast lane of a nearby freeway.

Colin showed me photos of his Christmas trip to Lake Tahoe with his dad and the family of his dad's girlfriend. She has three grown daughters whom Colin refers to as his "sisters." I looked at a group photo of them by the lake after he and the girls had taken a chilly swim. Colin's grin went from ear to ear. He told me what a wonderful holiday they'd had together. I felt a little lump in my throat.

Colin was planning to stay in Berkeley for the summer. I told him I was looking for an apartment in Edinburgh and hoped he'd come visit. He said he might.

On the flight back to L.A., I thought about how quickly everything you know to be true in life can slip through your fingers. In less than two years, I had sold my home, given away most of my belongings and watched my son cross the bridge to adulthood. I was estranged from my parents. My only sibling was dead. My son had another family to spend Christmas with.

A few days later, I was in Pasadena, a few blocks from my old house, and bravely decided to do a drive-by. I felt a twinge of sadness as I turned down the street, seeing the enormous deodar tree in the front yard. I drove past the house slowly, then did a U-turn at the end of the block. I stopped the car in front of the house that had been my home for twenty years. It wasn't mine to call home anymore.

I realized nowhere felt like home anymore.

I had embraced a life that allowed me to pull up stakes and move my tent wherever I wanted to go. I was enjoying my freedom, yes. Like my skydiving son, I had found my wings. I had soared over the Alps at sunset and waved at the world from the top of the Eiffel Tower. I had watched the sun rise over the caldera of an ancient volcano on a Greek island that some believe had been Atlantis. I had plucked warm grapes off the vine on an autumn day in Tuscany and seen Marco Polo's house from a gondola. I had stood on Monet's famous Japanese bridge, watching raindrops create rings of ripples on the surface of his lily pond. I had walked through rows of lavender in the hills of Provence, knowing for certain I had found my corner of paradise.

My dreams were fueled by wanderlust. I had embraced the solitude of my journey. But suddenly I found myself wishing that my wanderings might take me to a new place I'd call home.

ᥩ

On my last day in Pasadena, I stopped by Distant Lands, the travel store. Daniel, my favorite sales guy, spied me immediately and came over to greet me. "You're not supposed to be here," he said.

"Just visiting," I assured him.

He wanted a detailed update of what had happened since my return to Florence, after my summer of discontent.

"Next time you're in town, would you come to the store and give a talk about your experiences in Italy?" he asked. "And when your book is published, we'd love to do a signing here. We'll do a big promotion and sell your books—boxes of them, I promise."

That evening, I met John, my former neighbor, for dinner. He was waiting outside the restaurant, teasingly eyeing his watch as I rushed toward him. He quickly forgave my tardiness when I told him about the prospect of a book signing at Distant Lands.

John and I had been friends for fifteen years. He witnessed the roughest passages of my life—the end of my marriage and the aftermath, as I found my footing as a single mom. He, too, is divorced, with a grown son. We share a love of words. John is a poet, who travels to distant lands, both in verse and in life. We used to take evening walks around the neighborhood that were always as spiritually replenishing as they were physically invigorating.

John was interested to hear about the reactions I had been getting from friends about my new life. Many were swept up with their own fantasies of what life in Italy must be like, I told him. A few friends had become noticeably silent.

"When you come back from your travels and tell your stories," John said, "some people will want to step into your shoes and try on your adventure. But some people will resent you for what you've done."

Even with some of my good friends, I occasionally sensed that admiration bordered on jealousy.

"You're challenging conventional assumptions about what a person of a certain age and means should be able to do. For some people that's very threatening," John said. "They want to experience your freedom and joy, but they can't imagine doing what you did. They're afraid of the changes they'd have to make in their lives if they were to follow anything remotely similar to the path you're taking."

One friend had been openly unsupportive about my plans to move to Italy. "You won't do it," he said. "You have no idea what it takes to let go of the life you've known and go live in another country." He clearly underestimated me.

"Cut the naysayers loose," John advised me.

"I don't want to cut some of them loose," I said. "Just because they're struggling with their own fears and doubts doesn't mean I don't value their friendship."

John smiled at me. "Just don't let them make you lose your footing. What you're doing is very inspiring to many people. When we see someone who has found their freedom or has realized their dream, it gives us the gumption to wonder if we could do it, too. People may step into your shoes and realize they wear a completely different size, but that's okay. They're gaining a vicarious experience that will help them learn from you."

As we said our good-byes that night, John said to me, "People will be drawn to you like moths to a flame—both because they want what you've found and because they fear it."

At the end of our evening together the previous summer, John had sent me out to sea in my rocking boat, telling me to hold on tight. As he pushed me out to sea on this night, I felt exhilarated by the pull of the tide.

More than ever, I knew the universe was willing me to tell this story.

༄

My last port-of-call before returning to Florence was Glen Rock, New Jersey, where Carol was waiting for me with open arms.

It was my first visit to her apartment. I was amazed by how much it reminded me of her house, on a smaller scale. Her antiques, paintings, knick-knacks and mementos were all so familiar, and her flair for filling every nook made the rooms feel like the home she left behind. I took great joy in seeing the treasures she had kept from her mother's house, where I used to go for my voice lessons as a teenager. Her mother was a world-traveler and the souvenirs from her trips came with wonderful stories that I still remember in every detail.

Letting go of things was something Carol and I understood. We each had purged and sold our homes as we began new chapters of our lives. We had watched strangers walk out the door with possessions we had once valued. But we both had experienced the relief and joy that comes when you are no longer encumbered by stuff.

I told her the story of my fabric sale.

Quilting had been my hobby for many years. It was Aunt Hattie who introduced me to quilting one summer when I visited her home in the Smoky Mountains of Tennessee. As a souvenir for me, she pieced, by hand, a Grandmother's Flower Garden block from clothing scraps that she had cut into little hexagons. Hattie's quilts won blue ribbons at the county fair. A few of her blue-ribbon beauties were on the bed in her guest room. I loved turning down the covers at night, one quilt at a time, marveling at the lovely patterns and fine stitching.

A couple of years before Colin was born, when I was in my early 30s, I signed up for a quilting class at the recreation center in South Pasadena. I met a group of women through that class who became soul sisters and wise aunts to me, in times of sorrow and joy, for the next twenty years. Week after week, we shared our quilts and our stories. They mothered me during my pregnancy. They made a baby quilt for Colin and loved bouncing him on their knees. They consoled me during my divorce. They sat in the audience crying tears of happiness when Colin became an Eagle Scout. Ever since he was little, Colin fondly has called them "the quilting ladies."

In those twenty years, I had amassed an extensive collection of quilting fabrics, far more than I could ever use. I spent days sorting through my stash, keeping only my absolute favorites. I printed up flyers and sent them to the local quilting guilds. When the word got out that I was selling off the bulk of my collection for only $2 a yard, I called on the quilting ladies to help me with crowd control.

The sale was a huge success. As I bagged up the purchased fabrics, I wistfully thought of the quilts I had planned to make. But I was pleased to hear about the new quilts that were springing to life.

Prior to the sale, I had invited each of the quilting ladies to come take whatever fabrics they wanted, at no charge. One woman in the group named Daphne brought her 9-year-old granddaughter, who was already an accomplished sewer. They left with twenty grocery bags of fabric that they intended to share with the children in a sewing class Daphne taught.

Before I moved to Italy, Daphne invited me to tea with the quilting ladies. Many of the women in the group were now in their 70s and 80s, but they still met every week to work on their quilts. Daphne had told me that a visiting Nigerian missionary couple, sponsored by her church, would be there, too. She said they wanted to meet me.

Kari greeted me at the door. He grinned as we shook hands, looking like a kid who could barely contain a surprise. He proudly held the hem of his tunic-style shirt. There was something familiar about the fabric. I looked closer and smiled. I had used that fabric in the first quilt I ever made.

"You like my shirt?" Kari asked, beaming.

His wife Rikwe stepped forward and embraced me. I was the honored guest at an extraordinary surprise party.

As I sat on the living room sofa, I witnessed an amazing show-and-tell. Daphne had been teaching Rikwe how to make blouses and dresses, using simple adjustable patterns, for the women in her village in Nigeria. Rikwe took the garments, one by one, from a large bag to show me. Most of them were made from my fabrics.

Daphne told me that women who live in Nigerian villages usually are dependent on the local tailor to make their garments, from a limited choice of patterns and material. Rikwe and Kari wanted to set up a sewing school in their village to teach women how to sew their own clothes. When word of this had reached women in neighboring villages, they, too, wanted to learn to sew. Rikwe and Kari were hoping to find enough sewing machines to make this possible.

Twenty bags of fabric had given a group of women in Nigeria the possibility of making their own garments, allowing choices that would encourage their creativity and personal expression. They could make their own patterns, sized to their bodies, and choose whatever fabrics captured their fancy.

I told Carol, "I couldn't have imagined that letting go of something I prized would come back to me in such a wondrous way."

On the night before my return to Florence, Carol's family gathered at an Italian restaurant for a dinner in my honor. In a toast, Carol's son informed me they all were coming to visit me in Italy over the summer.

I winked at Carol. She knew about my hopes to move to Edinburgh, which she wholly endorsed.

As we said good-bye at the airport, I told her, "There's a non-stop flight from Newark to Edinburgh."

"Really?" Her eyes lit up.

We hugged each other. "I love you and your wonderful family," I whispered.

"I love you, too." She held me tight. "You'll always have a home here with us."

33

A change of season

A few minutes after the plane pulled away from the gate at Newark, an Italian woman on the flight had a panic attack and threw up on everyone in her row. Attendants escorted her off the plane to a waiting ambulance, while a cleaning crew removed her seat and hosed down the floor. The pandemonium delayed our departure an hour, causing me to miss my connection to Florence. I spent eight hours at the Rome airport, cursing the genome that makes Italians so high strung. *Madonna mia!* In Italian, that's one notch up from *Mamma mia*.

Marcello phoned that night from southern Italy where he was visiting his parents. The conversation was short. "My mom is calling me," he said before we hung up. I thought maybe she was calling him because she needed his help. "No," he said, "she's calling me to dinner."

He returned to Florence two days later and came to my apartment directly from the airport. He looked great. He still had the glow of his Cabo tan. I had never seen him so happy.

I made margaritas, as usual. He told me that he'd had a margarita in Cabo that was *almost* as good as mine.

Later that night in bed, I asked him how he liked the señoritas. "I didn't have sex," he said. "I didn't feel horny when I was in Mexico."

Of course, I wished he had said, "*I only had thoughts of you, bella.*" Turns out, he did have thoughts of me. "I fantasized about your ass," he confessed. (When I later recounted this conversation to Gaya, she said, "I give him a ten out of ten for honesty.")

Marcello regaled me that night with the advice he gives to his female friends about men.

"I have one friend who didn't hear from a guy after they had sex the first time. I told her not to call him. 'He'll think you're easy,' I told her. She took my advice. A month later, he called her." Marcello clearly was pleased with himself in his role as counselor to lovelorn women. "I'm like a consultant to them."

I put my face in my pillow to smother my giggles. I was in bed with an Italian Dr. Phil.

"What's so funny?" he asked, perplexed.

I looked at him, lying next to me in the candle glow. "Do you think I'm easy?" I asked.

"No!" He seemed stunned by the question.

At that moment, I found Marcello irresistibly endearing.

"You're adorable," I said.

He sighed and shrugged. "Sometimes I am."

༺ঙ༻

A few days later, after a matinee at the Odeon, I went looking for a scarf vendor who usually parks her cart near Marcello's store. She wasn't there. As I turned the corner, looking for her, I stopped in my tracks. The front window of the store was covered with paper. Scrawled in white letters on the glass: *Saldi fino al 70%.* Final sale, 70 percent off.

I peered through a tear in the paper on the window. The merchandise was gone. The racks and shelves were gone. The interior was a concrete shell. A man I didn't recognize stood in the middle of the store, which was lit by a dangling light bulb.

There was a notice on the window that all mail and packages should be delivered to the restaurant where I had gone to see Kamil about the apartment key.

After the holidays, I had asked Marcello how sales had been for the year. "We're down 30 percent," he said. "Even our rich customers aren't buying like they used to."

As soon as I got back to the apartment, I called him. He seemed happy to hear from me and asked what I had done that day.

"I walked past what used to be your store," I said.

"Were you coming to see me?" I could hear the smile in his voice.

"When did this happen?"

"About ten days ago," he replied. "A big cosmetics company expressed an interest. It's a great location. You know the saying—anything is for sale if the price is right."

"Does this mean you're out of business?"

"We're looking for a new location," he said.

He seemed upbeat, but over the phone, I couldn't tell if he was just sounding brave.

"Are you all right?" I asked.

"I'm fine."

❧

Turns out Marcello wasn't totally fine. The unpredictability of the weather in March and April affects his moods. "I hate when it goes from warm and sunny in the morning to cold and windy in the afternoon," he told me one day when the temperature dipped from spring to winter in the course of a few hours.

He wondered if he should try an antidepressant. "Everyone in America takes them," he said.

"Antidepressants can have side effects, so you have to gradually increase the dosage to see how you're feeling," I replied. "You shouldn't expect results right away." I suggested he talk to a doctor.

He had just told me about a party he had attended the previous night for the launch of a new line of watches. It had been a celebrity event, with drinks and dinner.

"You'll need to be careful about alcohol if you take an antidepressant," I cautioned him.

"I don't drink that much." He was getting testy. "I think you're jealous."

"Jealous of what? I want you to feel better," I said. But suddenly I realized another raw nerve was exposing itself.

I had told Marcello a few days earlier that I was looking for a flat in Edinburgh and hoped to move by May. I had thought about discussing this decision with him, but I didn't think there was much to talk about. It soon would be time for me to leave. And he hadn't given me reason to stay.

Marcello seemed eager to come visit me in Edinburgh. But that night in bed, he made a comment about Scottish men that made me think he was feeling jealous of potential competition.

Clearly his remark about what he perceived to be my jealousy of his social life went to the heart of what we were denying each other.

Our phone conversation about alcohol and antidepressants ended with me saying, "This is none of my business. Do what you want."

Gaya called a few minutes later. She could tell I was upset and asked if I'd like to come over.

"I'm going to the movies," I said. "I've gotta run or I'll miss the bus."

A half-hour later, I hadn't yet sunk into my velvety seat at the Odeon when my phone rang. It was Marcello.

"Rebecky-bekina," he said teasingly. "Do you know what *becchina* means in Italian?"

I wasn't in the mood for an Italian lesson, but I played along. "Bikini?" Knowing Marcello, I thought that was a pretty good guess.

"No," he said. "*Becchino* means gravedigger. *Becchina* is the feminine form."

I sat looking at the Odeon's big screen, imagining if this book is made into a movie how wonderful this scene will be. I saw myself up on the screen in a black veil digging Marcello's grave, yelling, "*Madonna mia! You should have listened to me!*"

As if reading my mind, he said, "Tell me what kind of doctor I should see." Then sounding like a kid on the verge of a tantrum, he declared, "I'm *not* giving up your margaritas."

❧

In March, James and Fiona flew in from Edinburgh for a weekend visit. I gave them the grand tour of Florence, with James reading aloud from the guidebook as we marveled at Renaissance frescoes, ornate church facades and the exquisite anatomy of David. I took them to Giubbe Rosse for cappuccino and to Vivoli for gelato. And as we were sipping hot chocolate at an outdoor table at Caffè Rivoire, Marcello appeared.

"What a coincidence," Fiona said.

I smiled at him as he made his way to our table. I had lost count of my coincidental meetings with this man in the streets and piazzas of Florence.

Later that evening, Marcello joined us for dinner at La Giostra. He was engaging and funny. Conversation and laughter flowed easily among the four of us.

At one point, I sensed Marcello was looking at me from across the table. I was looking at James, directly opposite me, who was telling a story. But I could feel Marcello's eyes on me, like that day at the carousel.

Sometimes I envision myself at a dinner party, a year or two after I've left Florence, and Marcello is there. He sits on the other side of the table, not directly opposite me, but slightly to my left. I'm turned toward the person on my right, telling a story that everyone is enjoying. I look at Marcello and he's smiling at me, with an expression of amazement that says, *I didn't know the half of you.*

Though I could feel the pull of his gaze at La Giostra that night, I didn't steal a glance at Marcello. I wanted him to take me in. There was so much of me he was only beginning to appreciate.

34

The lady abroad

My internet search for a flat in Edinburgh had turned up some interesting prospects in Stockbridge. One I especially liked shared a wall with the upstairs lounge of the Starbucks I had frequented over the holidays. I wondered if I could cut in a pass-through window for my "skinny" lattes.

The flat that quickly rose to the top of my list was on St. Stephen Street, known for its galleries and restaurants. Starbucks and The Bailie sit at the bottom of the street; the high end of St. Stephen curves toward Edinburgh's New Town. The flat I had my eye on was on the curve, in a new block of buildings situated with a view to the north, toward Fife.

James viewed the flat with the property agent, whose name was Mitch. When the Asian tenants asked that James and Mitch remove their shoes, it was revealed that Mitch had holes in his socks—a male-bonding moment for James and Mitch.

For all their fuss about shoes, the Asian tenants weren't exactly tidy housekeepers. There was so much clutter that I couldn't see the furnishings in the photos James e-mailed me. But overall, I liked the flat. It had two bedrooms and two bathrooms, with an eat-in kitchen and a large living room where I envisioned putting my desk by French doors that opened onto a faux balcony.

The only snag was that Mitch didn't think the agency would allow me to sign a lease without viewing the flat myself. I told him I didn't anticipate a problem as long as everything was in good condition and working order. He said he'd check with the owner.

About a week later, Mitch forwarded a letter from the owner, stipulating her conditions.

She wrote: *"I understand that the lady in question is currently living in Florence, making it impossible to view the flat herself and making it difficult to take up the usual references. I know it is your policy only to let to Tenants you have met and with full references, neither of which criteria you can fulfill on this one."*

A possible resolution to this dilemma, she said, would be for me to pay the full six months' rent in advance, along with a hefty deposit. Only when Mitch was in receipt of the funds would she take the flat off the market. She was willing to let me out of the lease if I didn't like the flat, but I would have to pay the rent until a new tenant moved in, along with the cost of re-advertising it. In an e-mail to Mitch, she wrote: *"I do not wish to prejudice or be difficult with the lady abroad and if she is interested and happy to proceed as above, I have no objection."*

I can't say I was "happy" about having to fork over $9,000 to cover the deposit, six months' rent and the agency fee. But I rather liked being called the "lady abroad."

Fiona and James quickly dubbed me "the broad abroad." They thought the owner's demands were unreasonable and were happy to supply references. Fiona offered her sister Liz as another reference. Liz, who also lives in Edinburgh, is a lawyer who specializes in real estate contracts.

I sent Mitch a very ladylike reply, which I asked him to forward to the owner: *"I'm willing to proceed, though I think asking for the full amount up front is unusual. I could provide several references, including an Edinburgh lawyer who is a property specialist. James and his wife Fiona are both highly regarded physicians in Edinburgh and also could provide references. (I've known them for thirty-five years, since our university days.) I could also provide a reference from my current landlady in Florence as well as a letter from my banker in California verifying my assets."*

As I waited for the owner's reply, I remembered the day I went to see an apartment in a guest house at a villa outside Florence, in Bagno a Ripoli. My agent, Sofie, had sent me out with her assistant because she had to pick up her daughter from school. As we drove out of Florence to Bagno a Ripoli, the assistant was amazed that I knew all about the historic landmarks along the way. Kathryn had taken me on the same route when we had gone out to see her beloved Tuscan hillside. I gasped when we turned up a long winding road through an olive grove. The villa was one Kathryn had asked me to photograph for her book.

What I didn't know until later was that the woman who owned the villa was concerned about renting to me because I was a "foreigner." She had insisted that Sofie find out about my background and financial resources.

I knew none of this as I greeted the Signora on the front steps of the villa. The coincidence of this was astounding to me. I explained to her that Kathryn had given me a tour of the area and had told me the history of the house and the property. The Signora was surprised I knew Kathryn. She introduced me to her son, a well-known olive grower in the region, whom Kathryn had interviewed for her book. He had worked as a consultant at UC Davis where they're cultivating olive trees to be grown in California. The Signora was impressed that I was from California and that my son went to Berkeley.

After she gave me the tour of the two apartments in the guest house, she pointed to the wing of her villa. "I have a home theater," she told me. "You would be welcome to watch movies there." I thanked her. And then she showed me the villa's laundry room, where the maids do the wash. She told me that they would launder my sheets and towels and that I could have access to the washing machine one or two days a week. The guest house didn't have a washer or a drying rack.

The Signora invited us up to the villa for tea, prepared by her Romanian housekeeper. The Signora's son joined us and we spent an hour, at the long wooden table in the villa's kitchen, talking about country life in Tuscany and the art and science of growing olives.

"I can grow the same tree here and on the next hill a few miles away and the olives will be very different," he told me.

"The soil makes a big difference," the Signora explained.

"Like grapes," I said.

"Yes, like grapes," she said. "Tasters describe olive oil like wine. They say the olive has a hint of artichokes or the flavor of almonds."

The Signora gave us a tour of the villa. The dining room ceiling was a work of art—a fresco of the four seasons in Tuscany. The same artist had painted a scene with a wisteria-draped garden arbor and birds in flight, on the walls and ceiling of the grand stairwell.

As we were about to leave, I stood on the villa's front steps, mesmerized by the view. In the distance, the domes and towers of Florence were silhouetted in the twilight. The setting sun had created a band of fiery orange at the ridgeline of the mountains. The Arno River looked like a strand of metallic ribbon, reflecting the golden sunlight.

I'd need a car to live in such a remote location, which would break my budget. But for a few minutes it was fun to imagine what life at the villa would be like.

We had been gone for two hours by the time we returned to the office. Sofie was waiting there, wondering what had happened to us.

"We had tea at the villa," I said.

Sofie thought I was joking.

"No, really," I said. "The amazing thing is that I photographed that house a few days ago with my friend Kathryn who has interviewed the landlady's son for the book she's writing."

"I don't believe this," Sofie said, shaking her head.

"It's an incredible coincidence," I said.

"You don't know what I've been through with that woman," Sofie said. "For two hours I have been on the phone with her before your visit. She wanted to know all about you, your background, why you wanted to come to Bagno a Ripoli. I wasn't sure I should send you there. I was afraid she would be rude to you."

"She was very gracious," I said, surprised. "She even said I could watch movies in her home theater."

"No!" Sofie burst out laughing. She was baffled by this turn of events. "This is a very difficult woman and you have made us look good to her. Rebecca, I think it is your destiny to come here. You are like a witch—a very good witch."

I had never been called a good witch before, but I liked that Sofie thought destiny was at play in my wild scheme to move to Italy.

And there I was, exactly one year later, submitting myself for approval to a very British woman, who was fretting that I didn't have "full references." But I felt undaunted.

I had grown into my persona as a lady abroad, known for her charm and personality. In fact, in the days after my visit to the villa, the Signora called Sofie several times telling her how much she hoped I would come live in her guest house.

Destiny took me to Via Tavanti instead. I was embraced by Elena, Bernardo and little Giulia, who brought much joy to my stay in Florence. With great fondness, Elena once said to me, "Rebecca, you are a piece of our family."

A few days after I e-mailed Mitch about my references, he wrote back saying that the owner of the flat was "adamant" about her conditions. (He mentioned she was a lawyer—no surprise there.) She also refused to speak with Fiona's sister, Liz, who had called Mitch on my behalf to supply a reference. Mitch noted that his agency and the owner were "falling over themselves" to secure my tenancy, which made me laugh.

Liz advised me not to proceed. We both agreed I'd have no leverage if I paid the entire rent in advance and found out later there was a problem with the flat.

I sent Mitch this reply: *"Thanks so much for your efforts on this. The owner is asking me to bring a lot of good faith to the table when she's not offering any in return. So I'm afraid I'll have to pass. Best regards."*

That was the ladylike way of saying, *"Stuff it."*

35

Perception and deception

My dispute with the Italian cell phone company dragged on for nine months. Although I had returned the phone in September, with the understanding that the contract would be voided, the phone company debited $700 in fees and penalties from my bank account. My bank agreed to dispute the charges, but informed me that if I lost the dispute, I would have to pay another $30 in service fees.

I filed the paperwork in November. I received a letter from the bank in December saying that the phone company had until March 10 to respond. By mid-March, I had heard nothing more from the bank or the phone company, so I e-mailed my banker, Isabella. She wrote back: "You won the dispute!"

The next day, I showed up at her office to close my account. I wasn't going to risk giving the phone company another chance to come after me.

The only snag was that my most recent bill for internet service, from the same company, had not been debited from my account.

"The bill will not be paid until April 10," Isabella told me. "So I can't close your account until then."

The Italian government assesses a tax on personal bank accounts, which the bank deducts directly from your account every two months. The bi-monthly tax on my account was roughly €10. On top of that, my bank collected €15 in quarterly service fees, in addition to an annual fee of €50. In nine months, I made about €10 in interest and paid roughly €135 in taxes and fees. Saving money in Italy is a challenge.

By keeping my account open for another two weeks, in order for the internet bill to be paid on the tenth, I would have to pay an additional €25 in government taxes and bank fees. So I suggested, "Let's just pay off the internet charge today and close the account."

"You mean pay the bill early?" Isabella asked, shaking her head. "That is not possible."

"You can't pay a bill in advance of the due date?" I asked.

"No," she said. "It must be on the tenth, not before."

She agreed to reverse the bank fees, but said that I had to pay the government tax. I put my head in my hands.

I then walked across the street to the phone store, to hand-deliver a letter that Isabella wrote for me in Italian, giving the required sixty days' notice that I would be canceling my internet service.

Lucia, the shop manager, and her male sidekick looked at me with their usual disdain as I placed the letter on the counter. The sidekick shrugged when he read the letter. Although he had been conversant in English on the day I set up my internet account the previous summer, he must have suffered a cerebral hemorrhage in his foreign language lobe because he looked at me blankly and said (in English), "I don't speak English."

He handed me pre-printed instructions, saying I had to notify the phone company by registered letter.

I looked at him with equal disdain. "I will never do business with you or this company again," I said calmly. "Do you understand that?"

"No," he replied.

I left the store and returned to the bank to sign the final papers. In all, I had signed more than fifty pages of documents—none of which I could read because, of course, they were all in Italian—to open and close my bank account.

I went to the teller window and collected my money, less the funds on hold for the internet bill and the tax payment.

I said good-bye to Isabella and thanked her for all her help during my battle with the phone company.

She once had told me how Italians regard Americans as being naïve. "Americans are so trusting," she said. "When Italians go to Turkey, we're afraid the Turks are going to take advantage of us because they think we're naïve. Italians look at Americans that way."

Isabella asked what I would do next. I told her my book was nearly finished and I would be submitting it to agents and publishers soon.

"You will be famous?" she asked. "I would like to read your book. But I can't read in English."

I told her I would send her the link to my recently published book of photos from my travels in Italy.

Although Isabella knew that I was a writer, she seemed impressed. "Rebecca, I didn't know all this about you," she said, wide-eyed. "You've never said anything about this."

Literally at the last moment, as I stood at the exit, she saw me in a new light.

I pushed a button and the door to a glass security chamber opened. Italian banks are big on state-of-the-art security systems. I stepped inside. Sealed in my glass cylinder, I felt like I was teleporting to my next destination. I waved good-bye to Isabella. When the door opened, releasing me to the world outside, I felt a rush of relief. I could take my money and run.

❧

That afternoon, Marcello called. "Rebecca, I have a question I want to ask you," he began. "We're printing up new cards for the store and I want to know if it would be better to put 'owner' on the card or 'principal.' Or should we say 'co-owner' or is there such a thing as 'co-principal'? I want to know what the meaning is in English."

I thought about the irony of this question for a moment. His business card and the story that went with it had already inspired me to write a few thousand words.

"If you're not the sole owner, then putting 'owner' on the card is misleading," I said.

"Why do you think it's misleading?" he asked.

"Because it's not true," I replied. "If you have partners, then you should say 'partner' or 'co-owner.'"

"What do you think we should say?" he asked.

"That's up to you and your partners."

"What about 'principal'?" he asked.

"Are you the principal owner?" I asked. "Call me back in ten minutes. I want to check something."

I flipped open my dictionary, to the definition of "principal," just as my phone rang again. This time it was Gaya. When I told her Marcello was asking me about how to identify himself on his business card, she said, "Isn't it interesting that he wants your opinion about this."

Gaya, an attorney, agreed that it was misleading for him to call himself the owner if he's not the sole owner. But bottom line, if someone sued the store, he personally wouldn't be held liable just because his card said "owner." Regardless, she said, he was potentially discrediting himself and hurting the reputation of the store by claiming to be someone he's not.

Six months earlier, after Nadia had told me Marcello wasn't the owner, I had done a little investigative googling about the store that led me to a lengthy and contentious conversation on a travel website about whether the owners were conning their customers. According to one traveler, the store's owners told him they manufacture goods for well-known designers and sell the same items, a lot cheaper, at the shop. Marcello is not mentioned in the posts, but a few of his partners are.

I was about to send Marcello an e-mail recounting my conversation with Gaya, when he called me back. I asked him if he knew about the travel site's posts. He said no, so I sent him the link, along with a message saying if his relationships with clients are based on false claims, his credibility is on the line.

At the risk of plunging a needle into a nerve, I wrote: *"The day you and I met, you told me you and your six cousins owned the biggest leather factory in Florence, remember? You misrepresented yourself to me and quite honestly, it affected my perception of you, when many months later, you told me it wasn't true."*

"Wow it seems you wanna sue me," he wrote back. *"Don't know why u don't have a good idea of our company. U think we are dishonest."*

I responded: *"My friend Gaya was taking the legal angle regarding what you say on a business card. You asked my opinion about the wording and I also gave you some input about how clients (especially Americans) might react if you're not totally honest with them."*

Gaya's take on all of this was insightful. "I think you intimidate Marcello—you make him feel small," she said. "You're relentlessly walking toward your destination and leaving him behind. Now he wants to redeem himself in your eyes." And then she said prophetically, "I hope he doesn't pick a fight with you right before you leave."

36

Hell on earth

A few days before Easter, my friend Peg from San Diego arrived for a visit on her way to a conference in Kenya. Her work as a microfinance consultant literally takes her around the world: Amman, Bali, Bangkok, Beirut, Belgrade, Bhutan, Cartagena, Colombo, Dehli, Dubai. And that's just the top of the alphabet. I love listening to her travel tales. She had just been at a meeting in Jordan and, during a day trip to Petra, was befriended by a Bedouin who gave her a ride on his burro.

Peg and I have been friends since the fifth grade. She has been a pillar of support for me during my struggle with my parents. Part of her empathy stems from her memories of my mom and dad when they were in their prime.

On Easter morning, she and I went to services at Santo Spirito church, which dates back to the 1400s. As a young friar, Martin Luther visited Santo Spirito on his pilgrimage to Rome in 1510.

Before Easter mass began, I lit a candle for my sister. It was her birthday. She would have been 53. I said a prayer for my parents. I sent greetings up to friends and relatives who've left this world but whose spirits are still close to me.

I am not an overtly religious person. I'm not a churchgoer. In fact, I've grown to dislike organized religion. I was raised in the Protestant faith. I sang in church youth choirs and was active in youth fellowship programs. I've read much of the Bible and have studied the teachings of Jesus. My belief in destiny and the forces of the universe are directly linked to my sense that there is a divine realm somewhere. Despite what Dante says, I don't believe there's a Hell. There's enough hell on earth.

I must admit I was feeling strongly anti-Catholic during Easter service at Santo Spirito. The Papacy had spent Easter week dismissing the growing priest pedophilia scandal as "petty gossip." It was incredible to me that the scant few priests who are ever found guilty of their sex crimes against children are punished with banishment from the priesthood and not with prison sentences.

I thought a lot about hell on earth during Easter service that morning. I thought about my poor mother who slowly was losing her mind and my father who was losing his grip with reality.

A few days after my visit with them in February, my father e-mailed me that the assisted-living apartment we had decided would be a good fit for them was no longer available. He said it had been rented out to someone else, but I later learned that he had postponed their move-in date beyond the deadline set by the facility, so essentially he knew he was jinxing the deal.

I sent him a reply saying I had done all that I could do to help them.

I was determined not to let myself be pulled into their swirling vortex. I had spent a week with them, immersed in all the problems and issues that were pulling them under. I had a clear sense of what needed to be done and who to call if I needed to take action in a crisis.

I kept in frequent touch with my dad, as usual. I didn't ask about his plans. After a few weeks, he was in serious talks with another local facility. He set a move-in date, but postponed it a week. Then to my amazement, he sent me an e-mail saying they had "checked in," as if they were at a hotel. His first comment was that half the residents were in wheelchairs.

They stayed at the facility for four days. My dad then took my mom to their vacation home in Wisconsin. According to my father, my mother became confused and agitated while they were there. One night after they returned home from dinner, she refused to get out of the car. She told him she didn't know who he was and that she was going to walk down the highway to call the police. He left her in the car and went in the house. A little while later, he told me, he heard her trying to open the garage door. He says he went outside, brought her into the house and put her to bed.

The next day they were driving back to the assisted-living facility and stopped at a McDonald's. My dad says he took Mom inside and got her seated at a table. He went out to park the car and when he returned she had disappeared. Turns out she had gone to the manager to tell him two men were in the car threatening her. The manager called the police, who questioned my father for forty-five minutes at the restaurant. The police checked the car and saw that the back seat was down and filled with stuff. There wasn't room for a third person. My mother claimed that the other man in the car had run away after they pulled into the parking lot. At my father's suggestion, the police called the assisted-living facility to verify that my mother suffered from dementia. Finally, they told my father they believed his story and let them go.

My father told me that ten minutes later, after they were back on the road, my mother had no recollection of the incident.

After they returned to the assisted-living facility, my mother had two more episodes in the span of two days, asking the staff to call the police because a strange man was in her room, threatening her and trying to poison her. The director of the facility's dementia-care unit later told me that it took the staff three hours to calm her down after the first episode. After the second episode, they admitted her to dementia care. The next day, my father terminated the apartment lease and moved back home.

My mother stayed in dementia care for three days. The director of the unit told me by e-mail that Mom was comfortable and lucid some of the time. She wanted to go home, but she was wasn't panicky or agitated and actually was very pleasant with the staff.

I e-mailed my father and asked him to call me on the international phone account I had set up for him. We spoke for an hour. His speech was slurred, but I couldn't tell whether he had been drinking or whether he was exhausted. Perhaps both. I took notes because it was difficult to sequence the events. He rambled a little and repeated himself. He kept saying, "Your mother doesn't know me more anymore. This can't be reversed."

He told me the staff had advised him not to see my mother for five to seven days. He said they were afraid his presence would trigger another episode or that if she did recognize him, she would want to go home. I later learned that the staff hoped that during their time apart he would steel himself emotionally to tell her that she couldn't come home.

When I spoke with him, he was calm, but he was struggling with his grief. He had gone online to find a local Alzheimer's support group, which I thought was a good sign. I encouraged him to follow up on that. "You are not alone," I told him. "Everything you're feeling is part of this horrible disease. It would be good for you to talk to other people who are going through the same thing."

He said he was sleeping well. In fact, he said he hadn't had such good sleep in months because he wasn't waking up every time he heard my mom get out of bed.

I worried that Mom might feel abandoned, but I knew she was getting the professional care she needed.

Peg skyped me from Nairobi. She had a bad cold and could barely speak to begin with, but my story left her nearly speechless.

I was trying to keep it all in perspective. "They've been on a runaway train for a long time," I told Peg. "But they didn't go over a cliff. They made a spectacle of themselves at a McDonald's in Wisconsin. But nobody died or ended up in the emergency room. Mom acted up and got herself into the dementia unit and my dad moved back home. She's okay. He's okay, sort of. So we'll take it one day at a time from here."

Two days later, my dad told the director of the dementia-care unit that he wanted to bring my mother home. The director e-mailed me, telling me of his plans. He told her he'd hire home help or his daughter in Italy would come live with them.

I immediately sent him a message: *"Dad, I realize you and mom are in extreme distress. But I cannot come home and take care of you. I'm not a nurse or a caregiver—and neither are you—and that is what Mom desperately needs at this point. I know you feel grief and guilt about this. But you need to accept that she has a brain disease that is progressing quickly. Do you want her calling the police every day and reporting that you're abusing her? If you end up in jail, where does that leave her? She's not in her right mind! Her brain is dying. Let her have the care and treatment she needs. This is the most loving thing you could do for her. Don't feel guilty about this. If you allow her to come home and something horrible happens, you'll have a lot more to feel guilty about."*

He didn't respond. The day after he brought my mother home, he sent an e-mail saying that when he went to visit her in the dementia-care unit, the scene was shocking, "like *Cuckoo's Nest*," he wrote. He found my mother in her room, crying.

He assured me he was going to get home care and find a support group. But despite his intentions, I feared the runaway train was back on track.

37

Escape to Umbria

One morning in mid-April, I set off for Umbria, desperately wanting to get lost for a few days.

I had re-booked a room at the villa in Montefalco that had been the retreat of Gabriele D'Annunzio, the oversexed fascist poet who allegedly liked to give himself blow jobs. Montefalco is 140 kilometers from Florence, via Perugia. However, I zipped past the exit for Perugia because I was driving an E-class Mercedes that liked to go fast, with a GPS system I was ignoring because it stubbornly wanted me to go back to Florence. No worries. Somewhere between the Perugia turnoff that I missed and the aqueduct of Spoleto that took my breath away, I morphed into Grace Kelly, scarf sailing in the breeze. The missed turn, however, added about two hours to the trip.

I arrived late afternoon to a crackling fire in the salon of the villa, which is secluded on park-like grounds under towering cypress trees, on a hillside overlooking the expansive Vale di Spoleto.

Montefalco is known as "the balcony of Umbria" because of its high perch above the valley. From my upstairs room at the villa,

I felt like I was standing at the balcony railing, with a sweeping view of the olive groves and vineyards below and snow-capped mountains in the distance.

Sabina, at the front desk, gave me a local map and circled the locations of the two Pardi linen shops in the village. The shop closest to the villa was just inside the ancient wall of the village, at the main gate, Porta Sant'Agostino. I wasted no time.

I was delighted to see a sign in the shop window, inviting customers to inquire about tours of the Pardi factory. A friendly saleswoman, Manuela, who spoke English, called the factory to arrange a tour for the next day. She handed the phone to me.

"I don't speak Italian," I said apologetically to Manuela.

Manuela smiled. "Augusta speaks very good English."

The woman on the line was Augusta Pardi, whose father was one of the founding partners of the company.

"Rebecca, I am so happy to speak with you," she said, "I heard you might be coming to Umbria in December." Francesco, the shop owner in Florence, had told her of my planned visit at Christmas. I hadn't heard from him after our conversation at his store that day, so I thought he hadn't been able to reach anyone on my behalf.

"My Christmas plans changed at the last minute," I explained. "So I decided to postpone my visit here until spring."

Augusta and I arranged to meet at the factory the following afternoon.

I spent the next hour at the shop. The shelves were stacked with table linens, bed coverings, pillows and fabric bolts. I asked Manuela about the pattern I had seen on the tablecloth at Francesco's shop, of the woman playing the harp. She took an identical tablecloth from the shelf and carefully opened the folds. It was as exquisite as I remembered. Manuela told me that the pattern was inspired by an Umbrian tablecloth, on display at the museum in the village, from the early 1400s.

She asked what size my table was. I smiled at her. "I have no table." She looked surprised. I told her I had sold my home in the States and given away most of my furniture before moving to Italy. "I think I should buy a tablecloth first and then find a table to put under it," I said. That made her laugh.

Manuela showed me a bolt of pure linen, about 27 inches wide. The design band, with the harpists, ran crosswise and was repeated every 19 inches, forming a panel that was intended to be cut precisely on a trim line woven into the fabric.

"Is this meant to be a table runner?" I asked her, fingering the cloth.

"No. You would use it as a bath towel," she replied.

I imagined drying myself with a swath of linen decorated with women playing harps. Heavenly.

A strikingly elegant woman in a flowing red cape walked into the shop. In English, she greeted an Australian woman, who had just purchased a tablecloth, and then said something in Italian to Manuela.

"I'm sorry to speak in Italian," the woman in red said apologetically to the Australian woman.

"It's your country," the Australian woman replied. I giggled from the corner of the store where I was poking around in a basket of napkins.

Manuela said something to the woman in red, who turned to me and smiled. "Rebecca!" she exclaimed.

For a split second I wondered how I could be so well known in this village when the woman in red introduced herself as Augusta Pardi. "It's such a pleasure to meet you," she said, shaking my hand. "I'm so looking forward to your visit tomorrow."

She had to rush off, but scribbled her cell number on a scrap of paper. "Call me if you get lost," she said. "Keep to the right once you cross the bridge." She waved good-bye and was out the door in a blur of red.

That night, as rain pelted the tile roof of the villa, I dreamed about harps and sheets of linen flapping in the wind. I woke up before dawn feeling very cold. The window next to the bed was open. A cool breeze was ruffling my hair and a bird was singing in the darkness. The ghost of D'Annunzio? Such a rascal. I closed the window and snuggled deep under the covers.

The next morning, Sabina showed me around the villa, which her uncle had purchased as an inn in the 1940s. The room D'Annunzio used during his visits to the villa in the 1930s is now the bedroom of Sabina's aunt.

"Would you like to see it?" Sabina asked, motioning for me to follow her down a short hallway off the salon. The room, which D'Annunzio had furnished, still has two matching bamboo chairs and a night table that had belonged to him.

"He liked Asian influence," Sabina noted.

I couldn't help myself. "Would you mind if I sat in one of the chairs?" I asked.

"Of course you may," Sabina said.

I sank into the cushion and rested my arms on the slanted sides of the chair. Later that day, I e-mailed a friend: *Now I can say I've lap danced with D'Annunzio.*

Sabina took me out to the garden to show me the spot where German-Swiss writer Hermann Hesse, also a frequent guest at the villa, used to sit on a bench and admire the view. He wrote: *"Montefalco is one of the most peaceful places on earth."*

I hadn't mastered the GPS system yet in my Mercedes, which I should mention was the only automatic available at the rental car location (poor me). But Sabina told me I'd have no trouble finding the Pardi factory if I just followed the signs to Bastardo, apparently named after an infamous "bastard" who once owned a tavern in the vicinity.

I couldn't find the road out of Bastardo to the factory and had to call Augusta, who told me to wait for her at the bank across from the Esso station. She showed up minutes later and waved for me to follow her. This was a guided tour in every respect.

Augusta was the perfect hostess. She introduced me to her cousin Alberto and his 26-year-old son, whom she fondly called Albertino, who has a doctorate in oenology. The Pardis' well-known Sagrantino winery is in Montefalco, just down the road from the villa. Albertino's cousin has a degree in textiles. Clearly the family's next generation is poised to take the reins.

The Pardis' venture into textiles began in 1949. Augusta's father and his two brothers returned from World War II to find the family's vineyards badly damaged. They knew it would take time and money to re-cultivate the vines and resume wine production.

According to family lore, the three brothers were walking in the countryside one day and met a beautiful young woman carrying a heavy basket, filled with tablecloths woven by her mother and sisters that she was hoping to sell. The brothers were so impressed with the beauty and the quality of the hand-woven fabrics that they decided to manufacture textiles using patterns from ancient Umbrian designs. They eventually bought several shuttle power looms and hired an expert weaver from northern Italy named Giovanni Battista. Today, Giovanni's grandson and namesake is the keeper of three generations of weaving secrets that make Pardi textiles unique.

"The designs are inspired by the countryside—the olives, the sunflowers, the grapes," Augusta explained, as we toured the factory's showroom where fabric samples hang on racks and bed-and-bath linens are displayed.

Augusta handles the company's public relations and gave me a press kit about the history of the company and its textile designs. "I am the poetry of the weaving mill," she said. "I write the brochures." The men of the family run the company, she told me. "When I offer an opinion, they say, 'Augusta, this is business. You are the poet.'"

The poetry of the looms is part of her DNA. "I grew up with the looms," she told me. "Our production still adheres to traditional methods. We use computers in the office, but not in the factory."

The power looms are massive and so loud that only a few can be operated at the same time. The cotton and linen fibers are guided through holes punched in cardboard panels that move above the looms and determine the jacquard designs. I was mesmerized by the process, threads flying through the punched cards as each thundering thrust of the *pettine*—the comb-like bar that pushes the threads into place—gave shape to a woven cluster of grapes, a honey bee or a sea shell. I stood in awe for a moment watching a loom give birth to an intricately woven border of women playing harps.

Augusta calls the harp pattern—known as the "Lira" design—the jewel of the company's textile collection. Every detail of the design is authentic to the period of the original cloth from the fifteenth century. The lyre players wear a "pellanda," a fashionable dress that was imported from France during that time. Their hair is upswept in the style of the day.

The next day I went to the Museum of Saint Francis in Montefalco to see the original cloth that had inspired the design. It was in amazingly good condition, given its age. The Pardi design is a close copy of the original, which is so finely woven that the fingers of the women are intertwined with the harp strings.

I returned to the shop in Montefalco to make a request of Manuela. I wanted to have a table runner made from the harpist panel. Manuela laid the panel on the cutting table and turned under the selvage edges to approximate the width of the runner, making sure the hemline wouldn't chop off a harp or the billowing skirt of a harpist.

She made a quick phone call to a seamstress at the other shop in village. I braced myself for the usual "it is not possible, *signora*" reply I've heard so often during my time in Italy.

Maybe it was because I was in a village known for its convents, monasteries and churches. But a miracle happened.

Manuela hung up the phone and smiled at me. "It will be ready for you tomorrow evening," she said.

"*Grazie mille*," I replied with delight. I couldn't imagine a better souvenir of my visit to Montefalco.

৵

The next day was my last day in Umbria. After breakfast, I decided to drive to Deruta, famous for its majolica ceramics. Sabina's cousin Alessandra, who was working at the reception desk that morning, gave me a card for a ceramics shop in Deruta.

"We know the owners," she said. "They may even show you their workshop."

I was under the impression there was one big ceramics factory in Deruta, but Alessandra said that there were many majolica producers in the area.

The ancient village of Deruta sits on a hill overlooking the town's business district where the main street is crowded with ceramics stores. On my first pass through town, I couldn't find the shop Alessandra recommended, so I turned around and doubled back. No luck. On a whim, I pulled into the parking lot of a small shop that looked inviting. The front door was open, so I went inside.

An American couple were thanking a woman for her help as I entered. I looked around in amazement. I was in a gallery of the most exquisite majolica—*maiolica*, in Italian—I had ever seen. Elegant amphora vases, pitchers, pedestal bowls and apothecary jars lined the tall display shelves. As I turned slowly in a circle, I was in a whorl of hand-painted floral garlands, birds in flight, pastoral landscapes, winged man-beasts and ripe voluptuous fruit.

"Welcome." The voice startled me. I turned to see a strikingly handsome man with tousled gray hair, smiling at me. "Where are you from?" he asked.

"California."

"Where in California?"

"Pasadena."

"Pasadena! I know Pasadena. I had a client there for many years."

I had just met the gallery's owner, Renato Mancini.

We hit it off immediately. He was pleased to know I was writing a book about my life in Italy.

"You will be inspired to write about Deruta," he said, smiling. "I will make sure of that."

I noticed several framed magazine articles on the wall near the entryway. One, with a large photo of Renato, caught my eye. The caption read: *When he took over the family business in 1980, at the age of 30, Renato Mancini says, "My life changed overnight."*

"It sounds like you were quite the playboy," I said, scanning the article. I could easily imagine it. There was something very alluring about Renato.

He smiled. "I was always foolishing around, all over the world," he said. "But I couldn't escape my destiny."

"Are you an artist?"

"No," he said. "I was too busy foolishing around."

I loved his favorite expression. I wanted to hear the Playboy Chronicles.

But first, Renato told me the story of Spanish traders who came to Italy in the thirteenth century with brilliantly colored tin-glazed earthenware that, according to ceramics lore, Italians called "majolica" because they believed it came from the Mediterranean island of Majorca, which was a major port for trading vessels traveling between Spain and Italy at the time. Italian potters eventually mastered the glazing technique and elevated majolica painting to an art form during the Renaissance. By the early 1500s, Deruta was a thriving ceramics center, ideally situated on a major trade route between northern and southern Italy and surrounded by the rich clay beds of the Tiber River valley. The Catholic Church became one of Deruta's biggest patrons, selling ceramic religious items to pilgrims visiting Saint Francis' tomb in nearby Assisi.

The Mancini gallery features majolica pieces, inspired by forms and designs rooted in Deruta's history, that are made on the premises by local artisans. "I want to honor Deruta's legacy in the work we do here," Renato said. "So we look to the past for our inspiration."

During the Renaissance, Deruta was known for its production of majolica "loving cups" that were presented by the groom to his bride at their wedding celebration. The cups typically were decorated with an idealized portrait of the bride or with romantic motifs such as Cupid carrying a heart pierced by an arrow. Wedding cups had two handles—one for the groom, the other for the bride—and often were inscribed with words of love and longing.

It was customary for the groom to sip from the cup first, Renato explained, showing me the groom's inscription on one of the cups on display. "This amorous gentleman was at the end of his patience," Renato said.

I couldn't make out the ornate scroll of the inscription. "What does it say?" I asked him.

"Drink fast, I'm horny."

I burst out laughing.

"It's a loose translation," Renato said, trying to look serious.

I liked Renato. "So what was the inscription on your loving cup?" I asked.

He chuckled. "No loving cup for me."

I noticed Renato didn't wear a wedding ring.

"Come," he said. "I'll show you the studio."

Renato led me through a small office behind the gallery and down a hallway to a studio lit by large windows and sky lights. Several artists sat at long work tables, cluttered with colorful paint pots and plates propped on stands.

"We have a writer visiting us from California," Renato announced. The artists looked up from their work and smiled.

Renato picked up a brush perched on a paint pot. "Look at this," he said, holding it for me to see. The tip was almost as thin as an eyelash.

He walked over to a table where one artist was painting a decorative plate with a delicate design of tiny birds in a swirl of fruit and flowers. Next to the plate in progress was a plate of the same design that had cracked in the kiln. There was no way to salvage it.

"All that work," I said sadly, inspecting the intricate pattern.

Renato shrugged. "You never know what will happen in the kiln. Sometimes there's a bubble in the clay or a defect in the glaze."

I was puzzled by the pastel shades of the new plate in progress, which were nothing like the rich hues of the fired plate. "The artist must know how the heat will change the color," Renato said. "We use pigments and glazes from the old recipes. We are one of the few producers in Deruta still making majolica the traditional way."

Renato's grandfather, who had worked in one of Deruta's ceramics factories in the 1930s, set up his own studio after World War II. "He was a master artist whose work became well-known," Renato told me. "Collectors from all over the world came to see him."

During the 1950s, as the commercial export market expanded, Renato's father opened a factory to produce modern designs that would appeal to an international clientele. "The business was successful for many years," Renato said. But the Mancini factory fell on hard times in the 1970s. "We nearly lost everything," Renato said. "My father was very ill, so I had to step in and quickly make big changes. It was a very difficult time. I had to let go of many people who were like family to me."

Renato halted the company's tableware production and focused on creating high-end majolica art pieces inspired by Deruta's age-old designs. "My father had many contacts with museum curators and private collectors in the U.S., who knew of our reputation for fine artistry. That opened many doors for me."

He ran his finger around the rim of a vase sitting on a work table. "Life sometimes takes us in a circle," he said. "We have come back to where we started, back to the old ways."

"I think your grandfather would be pleased."

Renato smiled at me. "I do, too."

❦

It was almost lunch time. I had intended to spend the afternoon in the village of Todi before returning to Montefalco. But my plans quickly changed.

"Would you like to have lunch with me?" Renato asked as I was getting ready to leave. "My house isn't far from here."

"I'd be delighted," I replied.

"Good," he said. "But we'll have to take your car."

I wondered why he didn't have a car of his own, but I later found out that Renato commutes by motorcycle.

We walked out to my Mercedes. Renato was impressed. "Would you like to drive?" I asked him.

"Well, I do know the roads. Maybe I should."

I handed him the keys. I sensed imminent adventure.

After I helped him shift from park into reverse (a tricky maneuver), we were off, along a winding road that took us up above the village.

"I can't get out when it snows here," Renato said as we neared the top of a steep hill.

He turned down a gravel road that ran alongside a stream. Two golden retrievers greeted us as we approached a stone-and-timber house. They were happy to see Renato and quickly took a liking to me.

We walked to the back of the house, where Renato removed a key from its hiding place.

I followed him inside, into a large living room with a stone fireplace and glass doors that opened onto a terrace.

"Close your eyes," he said.

I stood in the middle of the room, eyes closed, and heard Renato open the terrace doors. Then I felt his hand at my back.

The sun warmed my face as we stepped outside.

"Careful here," he said, steering me around something in my path. "You are very trusting of me."

I laughed. "Maybe too trusting."

"No, no. I have a wonderful surprise for you." We took a few more steps. "Okay, now you must look," he said.

I opened my eyes and took a sharp breath. "We're on top of the world."

"Incredible, isn't it?"

The pastoral Tiber River Valley stretched to the Apennine Mountains in the distance. Renato pointed out the path of the river, marked by an undulating line of trees, as it meandered through the fields of Umbria on its way to Rome. Below us was the ancient heart of Deruta, where the fires of the kilns had kept a legacy alive for half a millennium.

Renato smiled at me. "Welcome to *paradiso*."

❦

Renato filled a pot with water and put it on the stove.

"So you're a cook," I said.

"My housekeeper prepares everything for me," he said. "I just make the pasta."

He grated a wedge of pecorino and handed me a piece.

We took turns stirring the pasta as we talked about his upcoming trip to the U.S., which would take him to New York and Chicago.

Renato poured wine and set the table with majolica dishes, naturally.

He drained the penne pasta and sprinkled it with the grated cheese before he added the sauce.

"Cheese first?" I asked, wondering what Marcello would say about this.

"Yes," Renato said. I peered into the pot. He carefully tossed the pasta as the cheese melted from the heat of the penne. My appetite was whetted for a sensual feast.

The pasta course was followed by plump round beans, *fagioli*, from Renato's vegetable garden, that the housekeeper had prepared in a seasoned tomato sauce.

We spoke of many things. I asked him about his playboy days.

"Until I was 30, I traveled the world and followed the girls," he said.

"And you never married?"

"I was engaged a few times," he said. "But—what is the expression—I got wet feet."

"I think you mean cold feet."

"Yes, very cold feet."

He wanted to know more about why I came to Italy. When I told him I had sold my house after my son went to college and set off for Europe, he smiled and said, "You're a typical American. Go west. Except you went east."

At one point he said to me, "You are very brave and strong."

"I've dealt with tragedy and great sadness," I said. He looked pained when I said that. "But I try to be positive and see the good in life."

"I see that in you," he said. "You're a very positive person. I like that."

As we talked, Renato eyed the beans left in my bowl. "They're getting cold," he said. My belly was full from the pasta.

"You finish them," I said, passing the bowl to him. "It was a wonderful meal. When you eat on dishes like these, food tastes even better."

We lingered at the table. I sensed Renato was in no hurry to get back to work.

He reached over and took my hand. "You make me so happy," he said. "Stay with me."

I looked at my watch. It was a little after three. "When will they miss you at the shop?"

"Three thirty."

"I don't want you to lose your job," I teased him. I stood up to clear the table.

I was at the kitchen sink when I felt his arm slip around my waist. He turned me toward him and kissed me.

It was all too fast. True, I had been seduced by Marcello's charms on our first date. Maybe my experience with him made me hesitate with Renato.

"We really should go," I murmured. And then he kissed me again.

He stroked my shoulders. "You are so soft. I could die on you."

"Oh no," I said, wide-eyed. "No one is going to die here."

He smiled. "I mean I could die of happiness."

"C'mon," I said, tugging his arm. "We have to go."

We left the beautiful dishes in disarray on the counter. Renato locked the door behind us and tucked the key back into its hiding place. "You are always welcome here," he said. "You know where the key is." I knew he meant it.

As he drove down the mountain, Renato looked over at me and smiled. "You are my *passerina*."

"What does that mean?" I asked.

"It means sparrow," he said. "But it has another meaning, too."

I waited expectantly.

"It also means pussy."

I laughed. The playboy was alive and well. "You're bad."

"I used to be bad—so bad," he said. "But now I'm like a baby."

※

Renato pulled into the parking lot and turned off the engine. "Don't leave," he said. "Have dinner with me tonight."

I was quiet for a minute, weighing my options. I was returning to Florence the next day, though I could have extended my stay. The scale in my mind tipped side to side. Stay or go, stay or go.

Finally, I said, "I should go."

"But first, come inside." he said, squeezing my hand. "I want you to see something."

As we walked in the door, a few customers were already waiting for him. He immediately was in salesman mode.

I wandered through the display rooms, thinking about the hairpin turns of this journey of mine.

It wasn't long before Renato came looking for me. "I was afraid you had flown away." He leaned toward me and whispered, "My *passerina*."

He led me to the back of the shop and up a staircase.

"Where are you taking me?"

Renato unlocked a door at the top of the stairs. "I do this only for special visitors," he said, smiling.

I stepped into the inner sanctum of an ancient world—the private collection of the Mancini family. The room was small but the walls were lined with floor-to-ceiling display cases filled with ceramic treasures, some dating back to the Renaissance.

"Where did this come from?" I asked incredulously, trying to take it all in.

"My father was a passionate collector. He loved the thrill of the hunt and especially liked finding something extraordinary in an unlikely place." Renato showed me an elaborately decorated apothecary jar. "This is a seventeenth-century *albarello*, for storing herbs. My father found it at a flea market right here in Deruta."

One case contained a colorful array of pottery shards. "They came from the kiln dumps around Deruta. Some of these are 500 years old." Renato said. "My father used to take me out on digs when I was a boy. After a big rain, he'd give me a bucket and a little shovel and we'd go out along the riverbed, looking for ceramic pieces. The soil around Deruta is filled with them." He smiled at me. "I felt like I was a pirate digging for treasure."

He pointed to a painted majolica bead in the case. "My father and I found this on one of our digs. It's a *fuseruola,*" Renato said. "It was used in spinning, to balance the spindle. They were made in Deruta in the 1500s. It was the custom for an Umbrian man to give a *fuseruola* to a woman as a token of his love. You see, this one has a woman's name on it."

"I had no idea Umbrian men were so romantic," I said.

"You can't imagine." He gave me a smoldering look, which made me laugh.

In the center of the room stood a glass case containing one object—the prize of the collection—a Deruta loving cup. I recognized it immediately as the "drink fast, I'm horny" cup that I had seen downstairs.

"The reproduction in the shop is nearly exact because we own the original," Renato said.

"When was this made?"

"The fifteenth century," Renato said. "Before Columbus sailed to America."

I inspected the writing on the groom's handle. "Tell me, what does this really say?"

Renato stepped behind me and put his arms around my waist. He whispered in my ear, "Not being able to is putting an end to me."

"Not being able to," I repeated slowly, "is putting an end to me."

"I'm glad we agree."

I looked at him skeptically.

"Truly, that's what it says."

We stood there for a moment, not speaking, barely breathing. I channeled the spirit of a newly married Renaissance maiden: I gulp the wedding punch, which tastes like a margarita, and say lustily to my horny husband who's breathing hotly down my neck, "Take me—all of me, darling—but first, get me another drink."

"What are you thinking about?" Renato asked.

"I'll tell you another time."

"Another time?" He smiled. "There will be another time?"

"It's possible."

"That makes me very happy." He kissed my cheek.

☙

We said good-bye in the parking lot and exchanged cell phone numbers. He promised to call me that night.

It was late afternoon. I abandoned my plan to go to Todi. I had a table runner waiting for me in Montefalco.

Manuela smiled as I entered the shop. She pulled a bag from under the counter and walked over to the cutting table. She took the runner from the bag and spread it out for me to see.

"*Bellissimo,*" I murmured.

"I am so happy you are pleased," she said.

I thanked her for her kindness and for letting me hang out at the shop and play with the linens.

"It's been a pleasure having you here," she said. "Usually, we need to help customers with their selections, but you already know so much."

She tucked my harpists into the bag. "*Se li goda,*" she said. "May this bring you joy."

᠙

I had just put my hotel room key into the lock, when my phone rang. It was Renato. "Why didn't you stay with me?" he asked.

I asserted my prudent, practical side. "First of all, I don't like driving at night on roads I don't know," I said. "I enjoy the freedom of traveling on my own, but the reason I enjoy myself is that I don't take unnecessary risks."

"I understand," he said.

I opened my window. The sun was setting, turning the sky a rosy peach above the cobalt-blue mountains. Church bells chimed.

"I don't want you to think bad of me," he said. "I have a great attraction to you."

I sighed. "Of all the ceramic stores in all of Deruta, I had to walk into yours."

Renato laughed. "It is our destiny."

"I believe in destiny—absolutely," I said.

"When will I see you again?" he asked.

"Well, I might surprise you," I said. "I know where the key is."

"The key is always there," he said. "I will spend this night alone, but I will be with you, my *passerina*."

I gazed at the afterglow of the sunset and thought, *I'll never forget this day.*

38

Eruption and disruption

On the day I met Renato, the Eyjafjallajokull volcano erupted in Iceland.

I received an e-mail from Carol that evening. She was worried I might be in Edinburgh looking for an apartment. An immense ash cloud was moving toward Britain and northern Europe.

I drove back to Florence the following day as planned. I stopped in Todi for a walk around and a bite to eat. While I was at the café, Renato called. He sounded sad. "I miss you," he said.

I had intended to take a leisurely drive back via the beautiful Val d'Orcia of Tuscany. But when I arrived in Orvieto, it started to rain. I set the GPS for Via Tavanti and hopped on the *autostrade* in a deluge. I suddenly had an urgent desire to get back to some place familiar.

For the next two days, a cloud of melancholy descended over me. The news about the volcano crisis grew worse by the hour, as the air space above Europe closed, stranding millions of passengers. I was glad I wasn't traveling, but the reality was I couldn't leave if I wanted to. The president of Iceland, in an interview with the BBC, basically said—Heads up everyone, volcanic eruptions in Iceland can go on for weeks, months, even years.

I felt physically and emotionally stranded. My search for a flat in Edinburgh had spun out. Fiona and James had viewed at least ten flats on my behalf. Several were in locations where security and street noise would be an issue. With the others, there were problems with leasing terms, deposits and references.

The night I returned from Umbria, I discovered my internet connection was down. I could pick up a weak wi-fi connection if I put my laptop on my kitchen table, but I had no internet access from my spare bedroom, which I used as my office.

Steeled for battle, I went to the phone store in the city center, near Piazza del Duomo, a few days later. This was the same company I had gone to war with over the cell phone. Before I left for Umbria, I had mailed the letter that I had tried to deliver to the shop of horrors across from the bank.

The staff at the Duomo store speaks English. A sales person accessed my account and then made a call. "You closed your account," she said.

I showed her a copy of the letter. "I asked that the account be closed at the end of May," I said. "I was giving the required sixty days' notice."

"The account is closed," she said.

The store manager looked at my letter. "We can't reopen your account," he said. "It is not possible."

"I asked for my account to be closed in sixty days," I said.

"Too bad," he replied. "There's nothing we can do." With that, he walked away.

I left the store, seething.

I walked across the street to another phone store. I had to buy a new mobile internet key and had the option of an automatic re-charge plan if I gave them a credit card. No way. I wasn't going to be twice burned.

The saleswoman, who spoke a little English, presented a form for me to sign. It was all in Italian.

"What am I signing?" I asked.

"Take it home and translate it," she replied. "This is Italy."

"I know what country I'm in," I said, my anger roiling.

"We don't give contracts in English," she retorted.

"When you do business with English-speaking customers, you should explain the forms you're requiring them to sign," I said.

She shrugged and marked an X where my signature was required.

"Is there a penalty for canceling this agreement?" I asked.

"This is a re-charge plan," she said.

"Is there a penalty for canceling the agreement?" I asked again.

"No."

Under my signature, I wrote: "Per salesperson, there is no penalty for canceling this contract."

She looked at what I had written. "What does this say?" she asked.

I smiled at her. "Take it home and translate it."

I left the store, with my new key, and walked toward the Duomo. It was a sunny spring day. The tourists were returning. Students roamed around the piazza in packs.

I stopped by the leather shop where Nadia works. I hadn't seen her since before Christmas. She had invited me to her son's birthday party a month earlier, but I wasn't feeling well that day and had sent her my regrets by text.

I could tell she was a little miffed with me when I walked in the shop. She was pleasant and friendly, but she remarked sarcastically, "Your life is busier than Obama's."

Predictably, she asked if I was in touch with Marcello. I shrugged off the question. She told me that the store had moved to a smaller location. I said I had been surprised when I saw the sale signs in the window. She said, "I don't think Marcello will work there anymore."

"What will he do?" I asked.

"I don't know," she said. "He's rich."

Nadia said that business was very slow and that her boss was always in a bad mood.

"I'm working six days a week," she complained.

"You have a job at least," I said.

"I hate this life. I hate Florence. I want to move away from here."

"What's stopping you?" I asked.

"My house," she said.

"Sell your house."

"I can't find anyone to buy it."

"Then rent it," I said.

"I need to find someone I can trust," she said. "I need to know they will take care of my things. I have a plasma TV."

"Take your plasma TV with you and put a less expensive TV in the house," I suggested.

"I already have another TV."

"So what's the problem? Leave that TV at the house and take the plasma."

She changed tacks. "I don't want other people sleeping on my bed."

"If you come back, you can buy a new mattress."

"People are dirty." She wrinkled her nose. "The walls will be dirty," she said.

"Wash them. Paint them."

I'm always intrigued by the obstacles people put in their own way that keep them from going after what they want—or at least, what they say they want. Nadia wanted a less stressful life in a quiet place where she could enjoy more time with her son. She was confident about finding work. "I can find a job anywhere," she told me. But she was emotionally rooted to her house and the things in it, even though she could take most of her belongings with her.

After I left Nadia, I walked to Francesco's store. He wasn't there, but his wife was. She remembered me from my visit to the shop in December. I told her I had just returned from Umbria and wanted to thank Francesco for calling the Pardis on my behalf. She promised to tell him and gave me his e-mail address so I could thank him personally.

Across the street was the leather shop where I had met Alex, the funny guy with the lighter, and his brother Tito. As I left Francesco's store, Tito saw me and waved. He and another brother, Mido, whom I had met during my apartment-hunting visit, were happy to see me.

"We remember your smile," Tito said to me. He invited me to sit down and asked Mido to make me a macchiato.

Tito and I had a long chat. Alex had found a girlfriend in Cairo. "He will marry later this year—we hope," Tito told me. I wondered if Tito was trying to find a wife for Mido. "He's my little brother," Tito said, smiling at Mido. "I carried him in my arms when he was a baby." Mido, who's about 6'3", towers over Tito. Tito is the eldest of nine children—six boys and three girls.

The shop had suffered some water damage from a broken pipe. The repairs were almost finished. Tito told me this was a very difficult time for him financially, but he was making changes in his business that he hoped would "make it easier for me to breathe," he said.

"I try to be positive, to see the good in life," Tito told me. "Sometimes I feel alone, far away from my family." Tito has lived in Italy for nine years. He tries to see his family in Egypt once or twice a year. "I miss seeing my nieces and nephews. They grow up so fast."

Tito showed me his new line of handbags. I saw one I especially liked, an ivory bag with a dark brown strap. He gave me a "special" discount. We exchanged e-mail addresses. "If you ever need help, let me know," he said. I think Tito is a big brother to everyone he meets.

From there, I followed the magnetic pull of Giubbe Rosse. Claudio seated me at a table and went inside to order my cappuccino. We talked about Gavin's watercolor exhibition that would be held at the café in September. I told Claudio that Gavin was retiring in August. "I think this exhibition will be the perfect start to the next phase of his life," I said.

That night, I met Gaya and her friend Ashanti, who was visiting from Brussels, for a drink. Ashanti had spent the previous two days trying to find a way back to Brussels by train—planes were still grounded because of the volcanic ash. She had waited in line for four hours at the Florence train station to get a ticket to Basel, Switzerland, but had no guarantee that she could get on a train from Basel to Brussels.

"I will sit on the floor of the train if I have to," Ashanti said. I liked her determination.

∽

Later that night, I set up my new internet service and e-mailed Renato a photo I had taken of him in the studio.

He called the next day and sounded tired. He had just been skyping with contacts in the U.S. "I'm not looking forward to this trip," he said.

I tried to cheer him up. "It will be good," I said. "You'll see old friends."

"Yes, it will be good if it's a success. But the economy is so bad."

Later that night, he called again. "I'm just getting ready for bed and thinking of you," he said.

"I was just thinking of you, too."

He told me he had picked wild asparagus that evening. "It grows next to another plant—I don't know the name in English," he said. "You find it in a sunny place. But you look for the other plant first and then you find the asparagus hidden beneath it."

He told me how he would prepare it—with butter and garlic.

"So you do cook," I said.

"I cook very simple things."

"I go down to the market, buy a roasted chicken, bring it home and put it on a plate," I told him.

He laughed.

"Do you have truffles where you are?" I asked.

"I've never looked for them," he said. "They're hard to find. You need dogs. Sometimes they use pigs."

I smiled. "But the pigs like to eat the truffles."

I sensed he wanted to talk about more than asparagus and truffles.

He was quiet for a moment. "Rebecca, I have such desire."

I took a deep breath, then said softly, "I have desire, too."

"There's nothing better in life," he said.

I thought he was talking about sex.

But then he said, "There's nothing better in life than love."

39

Gaya

"There's never a dull moment with you," Gaya said when I called her the next morning.

"What the hell am I doing?"

Gaya said she would help me find the answer to that rhetorical question over a pot of tea that afternoon on her balcony.

Forget the tea, I told her. I needed a stiff drink.

Gaya was full of metaphors that afternoon, most of them related to ceramics. "Renato is not like Marcello and your other knick-knacks," she said.

"Knick-knacks?"

"Renato isn't like the other characters in your book," she said. "What you have with Renato is evolving. Go to him. See what happens. You don't know. Jump in his teapot."

"His teapot?" I burst out laughing.

Gaya, who had recently purchased the complete works of Lewis Carroll, was tumbling down the rabbit hole. "You can hide in his teapot. He'll lift the lid and say, 'Rebecca, are you there?'"

Gaya poured me a cup of cardamom tea from Sri Lanka. "Drink this," she said. I didn't dare look in the teapot for fear Renato might be there.

I was in a tempest in my own teapot. I looked at the calendar on Gaya's kitchen wall. In six weeks, my Italian visa would expire and I still had no exit plan.

"Go to Edinburgh," Gaya said. "But go to him before you leave. You have a man on a mountaintop picking wild asparagus and thinking of you. How wonderful is that."

This is how women get into trouble, I realized. They listen to their Alice girlfriends who have estrogen-enhanced views of Wonderland.

∞

The best thing that happened to me during my year in Florence was meeting Gaya.

I didn't know until a few months after we met that she just happened to stop in at my neighborhood coffee bar that day, to pick up some pastries for a friend.

"I had never been there," she told me. "I was passing by and decided to pop in."

The loving hand of destiny.

I can still see Gaya struggling with her stroller on the shop's steps, looking around for someone to hold the door for her. I was happy to help, remembering the many times that I, too, had struggled with a stroller.

One of the things I enjoyed most about my time with Gaya was watching her baby son, Dani, grow. He was so much like my own son, in his colicky early months, screeching and fussing from intestinal distress. I recalled how I learned to burp my son by putting him high on my shoulder so that pressure on his diaphragm would help him expel the air in his tummy. The same technique worked for Dani.

I loved my time with Gaya's daughter, Anjou, who at age 4, was already multi-lingual, speaking English, German and Italian. Anjou loved to draw and decorated my fridge with pictures she made for me. My favorite of her artworks was a tea towel on which she drew a portrait of her and me together.

Anjou is a beautiful girl, with dark eyes and straight dark hair that falls around her face "like a J," she pointed out to me.

"What letter of the alphabet is my hair like?" I asked her, twirling one of my curly locks around my finger.

She considered this for a moment and started to draw me on the tea towel. First she drew large green-rimmed eyes, a bright red smile and a pink nose. Then she drew my hair—loops of yellow filled in with reddish brown. I loved the hands she drew for me— they were big blue flowers.

"This is much too precious to use as a tea towel," I told Gaya. "It's going on my wall."

Anjou signed the towel with a backward, upside-down J. "That J will be the hallmark of her early works when she's a famous artist," I predicted. "This tea towel will be a hot item on eBay someday." But for as long as I live, the towel is mine to treasure with heartwarming memories of an adorable 4-year-old girl.

Gaya, Anjou and I had a favorite expression that became our motto. When we'd get cozy on the sofa to watch a DVD (*Mary Poppins* was a favorite) or pull up our chairs to the kitchen table to have a snack together, we'd look at each other, enjoying each other's company, and say, "We are girls!"

We three girls especially liked to climb on Gaya's bed in the evening to sing Dani to sleep. We had discovered that the way to stop his crying was to sing to him. He quickly would go quiet and listen to our songs. One night, we sang the entire *Mary Poppins* songbook to him. Somewhere between *Let's Go Fly a Kite* and *Feed the Birds*, he drifted off to sleep with a sweet smile on his face.

One night, as Gaya nursed Dani to sleep on the bed, I softly started singing an old folk song my father had sung to me as a child.

My grandfather's clock was too large for the shelf, I sang.

Gaya jumped in. *So it stood ninety years on the floor.*

I looked at her in amazement, as we sang together: *It was taller by half than the old man himself. Though it weighed not a pennyweight more.*

We sang all the verses together, not missing a word. Only when we got to the "tick tocks" of the clock did our rhythm differ slightly: *Ninety years without slumbering, tick tock, tick tock. Life seconds numbering, tick tock, tick tock. But it stopped short, never to go again, when the old man died,* we sang quietly.

The last note hung in the air for a moment. Dani was asleep.

"How do you know that song?" I whispered incredulously.

"My British upbringing," she said. "We grew up on British and American songs." Her mother used to sing the old standards, including American songwriter Stephen Foster's greatest hits, *O Susanna, Swanee River* and *My Old Kentucky Home.* "I've never been to the U.S.," Gaya said. "But I've heard of Kentucky and old Virginny."

৵

Although I am eighteen years older than Gaya, I think it's interesting that her parents are older than mine. She's the youngest of six. Her eldest sibling is my age. My parents were in their mid-20s when I was born. Gaya's parents were already middle-aged when she came into the world.

Gaya looks at me, as a middle-aged woman enjoying her freedom, and says, "You are my avatar—my guiding light. When I'm your age, I want your life."

She has a long way to go, at 37, with two small children to raise. When her baby boy is my son's age, she'll be 57.

Gaya has great professional aspirations and won't be content being a full-time mother for the next eighteen years. A recent snafu in her application for European nationality threw her plans of pursuing a doctorate into doubt. It also ripped open a stress fracture in her marriage that had been worsening with the daily demands of family life with two small children.

She called me one morning, asking if she could come over with the baby. Her housekeeper had taken the key by mistake and Gaya had no way to get back into her apartment after she took Anjou to school.

Gaya spent several hours with me that day. She was in tremendous distress. Her professional plans hinged on becoming an EU national. As a legal resident of Belgium at the time of her application, she fulfilled the requirements for nationality, but her application had been delayed by a two-year bureaucratic logjam. The only clear way for her to make an appeal was for her to re-establish residency in Belgium.

With no money of her own, she felt totally dependent on her husband. And worse, she doubted that he had her best interests at heart.

"Rebecca, look at me." She was on my sofa nursing her son. "I'm stuck. Totally stuck."

"You are not stuck," I said adamantly.

We went round and round about her options, but the more we talked, the deeper we sank into the mire.

Finally, I got up and went into my office to get a blank piece of paper.

I came back into the room and sat down at the table. "We're going to play a game," I said, grabbing a pen.

At the top of the paper, I wrote: "Gaya's Map of Possibilities."

"Let's pretend that you're going to leave your husband in a week," I said. "And you're going to take your children to a place where you can re-group until you figure things out. Where will you go?"

She decided against Sri Lanka. She considered Rome. But in the end, she said, "I would go to Brussels."

I wrote down the reasons why Brussels was a good destination: job prospects, good schools for Anjou, friends and contacts who could be her support group.

"What are your goals?" I asked.

I made a list: to re-establish residency in Belgium, become financially independent from her husband and re-start her career.

"What belongings will you take with you?" I asked her.

"Oh, no," she protested. "I can't do this."

"It's just a game, Gaya."

Her to-take list was short: her grandfather's desk and chair, her mother's tea set, a John Constable print that belonged to her mother (that Gaya's husband didn't like and had insisted that she keep in storage), and her books, DVDs and CDs.

"What conversation will you have with Anjou about this?"

Gaya thought for a minute. "I would say Mommy needs to go to Belgium to see about a job. Daddy will stay in Florence, but will come to visit."

"What do you think your expenses will be?" I asked.

We did a budget together, itemizing rent, utilities, food, clothes, childcare, miscellaneous expenses. I added an item tagged "F&G."

"What's F&G?" Gaya asked.

"Fun and Games."

She laughed. It was the first time she had laughed since she walked through the door that morning.

We talked about how she was going to pay her bills for the first month. She could live with Ashanti to defray expenses while she looked for an apartment. She could possibly borrow money from her family. I reminded her that her husband would be obligated to pay child support, which would give her some wiggle room.

We made a list of immediate tasks: She needed to collect financial/tax records as well as bank and credit card account/ PIN numbers and call an attorney to help her navigate legal channels with her nationality application. Gaya was perking with ideas. She knew a woman who could help her find a nanny. She had a friend who could help her find an apartment. She had contacts at the university who could get her proofreading jobs.

Gaya wasn't stuck anymore.

We did a timeline, six months out. Gaya planned to spend five weeks in Sri Lanka during the summer. She would return to Brussels in August, in time for Anjou to start school in September.

She said to me, "You're doing this because you're leaving, aren't you?"

I thought to myself, *No, I'm doing this because you may be leaving.* But instead, I said, "When I have decisions I'm struggling with, I always draw myself a map like this." I have drawn many maps in my life.

I didn't want to push Gaya toward a divorce. But I wanted to help quiet her confusion and make her feel empowered.

I put her map in an envelope and handed it to her. "If you have a map, you will never get lost," I told her.

She smiled, with tears in her eyes. "Rebecca, you are a very good friend."

෴

A week later, Gaya's crisis had passed. She and her husband had called a truce of sorts and had stopped talking about divorce.

They were trying to find a workable solution and were committed to keeping their family together.

I knew that could change. Marriage is hard work. But for now, Gaya and her husband had survived a major conflict, tattered but intact. If anything, Gaya's map of possibilities had helped her clarify what was at stake.

I had dinner with Gaya and her husband one evening, during the first days of the truce. We laughed and drank wine until the kitchen grew dark in the twilight. It was a lovely spring night.

Gaya walked me partway home.

"Look!" I exclaimed, pointing to a huge golden moon that seemed to be sitting on a red tile roof. "It looks like a pepperoni pizza."

Gaya laughed. "I'm going to miss you so much," she said.

"We're going to be friends for a long time," I assured her. "We've shared a very special chapter of our lives."

As I walked alone up Via Tavanti, I heard Dean Martin, who's much loved in Italy, crooning from somewhere beyond the moon: *When the moon hits your eye like a big pizza pie, that's amore.*

40

The beginning of the end

A few nights later, Nancy called. She had found, in the bottom of an old purse, a diary she had kept while we traveled through Europe on our spring break in 1975. We were in the same study abroad program. She was doing a vocal music course at the Guildhall School of Music in London while I was studying art history, English literature and Greek archeology in Edinburgh.

The diary was a tiny book, she said, just big enough for her to jot down the abbreviated highlights of our grand tour. Next to notations such as Colosseum, Sistine Chapel and Spanish Steps, she had written things like "Marvin and guys." Neither of us could remember Marvin or his buddies.

Her entries for Florence: Il Duomo, pizza, David, Vivoli's, Santa Croce, Vivoli's, San Lorenzo, Uffizi, pizza, Ponte Vecchio, Vivoli's, bought purse.

Vivoli's, now world famous for its gelato, and a pizza place around the corner were our favorite dining spots.

Our quest for the Perfect Purse took us to the stalls of the street markets. We looked at scores of handbags during our three days in

Florence. On our final day, after much discussion and deliberation, we made our purchases. Nancy's bag was the color of espresso. Mine was the color of honey and cost about $30—my most expensive souvenir during my year abroad. I still have that purse.

From Florence, we traveled to Venice, where we stayed at a *pensione* owned by a woman named Mamma Leone. Venice was under water. Our shoes didn't dry out for days.

We took what was to have been an overnight train from Venice to Vienna. Somewhere in the Dolomites, an avalanche buried the tracks. We had to get off the train and onto a bus that got us down off the mountain—a potentially life-threatening adventure that was noted in the diary simply as "avalanche on tracks." I remember a crush of passengers trying to board that bus. I was very good with my elbows and managed to get on first, with Nancy behind me, clinging to my backpack. I turned to her as we boarded and said, "Where would you like to sit?" Nancy couldn't stop laughing. We were in the middle of an evacuation and I was concerned about our seat selection.

As culturally-astute young ladies abroad, we enjoyed more than pizza, gelato and shopping for handbags. We hit all the major museums and historical sites. And we attended operas: *The Barber of Seville* and *La Traviata* in Vienna, *Manon Lescaut* in Zurich, *Le Nozze di Figaro* at Convent Garden in London. We were young ladies abroad on tight budgets, so we bought SRO or restricted-view tickets. My job was to scope out the empty orchestra seats and at intermission, we'd claim them. Seat selection was my specialty.

It was after 1 a.m. when Nancy and I finished the diary, sides sore from laughing. Thirty-five years later, we were both living in Europe. Our year abroad had changed the course of our lives. Nancy became an opera singer whose career took her to Germany and I became a journalist and writer whose stories have taken me everywhere.

As I clicked off Skype, I decided to check Gumtree, Edinburgh's version of Craigslist. For two months, I had been checking Gumtree's apartment listings at least twice a day. Since my search began in December, I had made inquiries on at least two dozen flats.

There was a new listing on St. Stephen Street in Stockbridge, in the same building where James had seen the flat owned by the arrogant attorney who wanted $9,000 up front. This flat had the same floor plan, but the furnishings and décor looked much nicer. I immediately sent an e-mail request for a viewing and made note of the phone number. The next morning, I left a voicemail message explaining my situation, describing myself as a responsible, respectable middle-aged woman with verifiable assets and excellent references. I got a text message from the owner who was boarding a plane to Spain. He said he'd get back to me when he landed.

For the next several hours, text messages flew between Florence, Spain and Edinburgh. The owner and I had a brief phone conversation. He said there was a viewing that evening at 6:15 and he was expecting at least two other people. "It's first come," he said, suggesting that I leave a deposit of one month's rent with his tenant, who would be handling the viewing.

I reached Fiona and we mapped out our strategy. She would arrive a few minutes early and do a quick look-around to make sure everything was in order. At 6:20, she called to say, "Becky, it's perfect." She wrote a check on the spot. I texted the owner to say I wanted the flat just as the tenant texted him to say he had received the check. The owner then texted me back to say that Fiona had called him to confirm the details and that the flat was MINE!

The deal was closed in five minutes, with four people in three countries. It would have made a great smart-phone commercial.

On Skype that evening, Fiona, James and I toasted our success at last—they drank wine and, of course, I had a margarita.

❧

Later that night, Renato called and asked about my day. I regaled him with the tale of my smart-phone real estate transaction.

"Edinburgh is a beautiful city," he said. "What will you do after your six months there?"

"I have no plans," I replied.

The next day, Lorenzo, the terrible driver, called. I hadn't heard from him in a few months and hadn't seen him since that day we slammed into the Mercedes sports coupe. He wanted to see me, so we arranged to meet at my neighborhood café.

He was waiting out front, with his car parked in the street, blinkers on. I thought we were going to have coffee at the café. I reluctantly followed him to his car. I surveyed his fender, which still had a few telltale scrapes.

"I fixed it myself," Lorenzo said proudly.

"You did a good job," I said. After I got in the car and strapped in, I asked, "So how much was the bill for the Mercedes?"

Lorenzo cut the wheel hard as we rounded Piazza Leopoldo. "They never called me," he said, downshifting with a lurch.

"Aren't you lucky," I said, secretly hoping luck would stay on our side of the street for the rest of the evening.

Lorenzo took me to a trattoria in his neighborhood and nearly plowed into two moving vehicles as he backed into a parking space. I couldn't wait to get out of the car.

The trattoria is owned by a guy Lorenzo had grown up with, so we got a table without a wait. The restaurant was crowded and lively. We were seated at a long table between an Italian couple and tourists from New York.

Lorenzo enjoyed my friendly banter with the guy sitting next to me, a physician from Brooklyn.

"You have different ways of speaking," Lorenzo said to us.

"It's our accents," I explained.

Dr. Brooklyn said, "I don't have an accent."

"Oh yes you do!" No way was I going to let a New Yorker get away with that outrageous claim.

Our *primo* course was spicy penne pasta. The *secondo* was a thick cut of rare Florentine steak, served with a side platter of fried zucchini flowers.

Lorenzo and I walked around the neighborhood after dinner. During the quiet hours of his night shift at the hotel, he told me he had been learning tai chi, to keep up his energy. He showed me a few moves in the middle of the street, which made me laugh.

He took my hand as we turned down the street to his house. He invited me inside and introduced me to his mother. He showed me their back garden where a pergola was laden with huge pink roses with ruffled petals. I reached up and touched one. "I miss my garden," I said.

Lorenzo took me to his bedroom, which was at the front of the house. It had been his room since he was a child. He pulled out the chair at his desk for me to sit down. He took his guitar from the case and sat on the bed. He sang to me for quite a while. I didn't miss the message of the lyrics. One of the songs was Keith Carradine's *I'm Easy*.

As we walked back to his car, he put his arm around me and kissed my cheek. "I like you so much, Rebecca."

"You're very sweet," I said.

I closed my eyes and held the dashboard as he threw the car into reverse.

He dropped me in front of my neighborhood café, at the foot of Via Tavanti, and we said good-night, with plans to meet again before I left for Edinburgh. I stood on the corner and watched him speed off into the night.

I was beginning to feel that the universe was staging the events of my last weeks in Italy just so I could write about them. As Kathryn had once said to me, marveling at my experiences here, "You are a magnet for happenings."

∽

As my time in Florence was ending, a main character of this story disappeared. I suppose it was his way of detaching. Or maybe he was still pissed off about the needle I sank into his spine about his bogus business claims.

The last time I had spoken to Marcello was a few days before my first trip to Umbria. He had called about 8:30 one Friday evening as I was skyping with Colin. I didn't answer, but I called him back a half hour later. No answer. In a few minutes, my phone rang. It was Marcello and he was laughing.

"What's so funny?" I asked.

He told me that a woman from Slovenia he knows had just arrived in Florence that afternoon with her new husband. "She got him drinking grappa beer," Marcello told me, "and now he's really fucked up." He said she took him upstairs, to their hotel room, and put him in bed. "He told her, 'Go out to dinner with Marcello.'"

I could hear a woman laughing in the background.

As if to corroborate his story, Marcello said to her in English, "I haven't seen you in two years, right?"

She replied, in English, "Yes, two years." She didn't sound Slovenian.

"I'll call you tomorrow," Marcello said to me, about to hang up.

"Marcello," I said, "You called me, right?"

"Yeah," he said.

I clicked off my phone.

In fairness—though I had no reason to be fair at that point—when he called at 8:30, the woman and her husband probably had just gone up to their room. When I called him back at 9, she may have just returned to tell him she was free for dinner. Or…not. Marcello's one lie to me had sown many seeds of doubt.

Regardless, he plainly was poking at a raw nerve in me, the woman he had never taken anywhere, except for a drink at an Irish pub.

I remembered as we left the pub that night, he noted I'd had only one drink and said, "You're a cheap date." My fate with Marcello had been sealed from the start.

∽

I e-mailed Elena to let her know I had finally found a flat in Edinburgh and would be leaving Florence June 1. She was happy for me, but sad to see me go. She wrote back: *"I don't think we will rent the flat immediately: where could we find another Rebecca??"* She put a smiley face next to the question marks.

I wondered if they would try to sell the flat. Bernardo had just quit his job, after eleven years with the accounting firm.

Elena and Bernardo invited me to lunch at the popular neighborhood trattoria, Fratelli Briganti, one Saturday before I left.

"Sometimes you have to try something new," Bernardo said to me. He was working as an independent consultant for an accounting service with corporate clients.

I thought about that conversation Elena and I had on their balcony the previous summer. She had insisted Bernardo would never leave his job, that there was no way to escape their life in Florence. I knew this was a courageous step for them.

Elena handed me a little black bag with a silver bow. Inside, there was a pair of dangly earrings, made of garnet-colored glass beads and filigreed silver balls.

"I notice you like long earrings," she said. "I want you to have a pair from Tuscany."

I hugged her. "They're beautiful, Elena. I will think of you every time I wear them."

I removed the earrings I was wearing and put on my new Tuscan danglies.

Bernardo went looking for Giulia, who had wandered off to see a little girl at another table.

"Elena, I hope you get your wish someday of returning to your village by the sea," I said.

"Me, too," she replied. "Bernardo and I are talking about starting a business together. We are a bit scared because it's not easy to start everything again from nothing, especially in this bad economy. But I want to be positive."

I smiled at her. "Anything is possible."

41

A dream

One May afternoon, I boarded a train for Umbria.

I gazed out the window, at the blur of vineyards and wild red poppies. I tried to read Frances Mayes' travel memoir *A Year in the World*, but I couldn't concentrate. When the train pulled into the station at Terentola-Cortona, not far from her famous Tuscan home, I savored the irony of my journey in a parallel universe. But her destination wasn't mine. The Umbrian sun was my beacon.

I had sent Gaya an e-mail with all the details of my intended whereabouts, with Renato's mobile and office numbers and a rough description of how to get to his house if she needed to come looking for me. She texted me the emergency numbers for ambulance, police and fire. I called her from the train and promised to keep her apprised of my movements.

Renato was waiting for me on the platform in Perugia. But I didn't see him at first. In fact, I looked around as the crowd thinned out and, for a moment, I thought he wasn't there.

I noticed a distinguished-looking man, in a dark blue blazer that set off his wavy gray hair, standing just ten feet from me, and suddenly I realized it was Renato. He was smiling at me.

"Did you forget what I looked like?" he asked, folding me in his arms.

"How could I forget this handsome face." I kissed him on the cheek.

His car—a red Alfa Romeo—was parked in front of the station. "What would you like for breakfast?" he asked.

It was 6:30 p.m. "Is that the first meal I'm going to get?" I asked.

He laughed as he put my bag in the trunk.

We didn't stop at a store for breakfast provisions or at a bar for a pre-dinner drink. We headed over the Tiber River to Deruta and then up the winding road above the ancient village.

It was a lovely spring evening. I looked out at the familiar landscape that had turned bright green from all the spring rain. "I didn't imagine I would be back in Umbria so soon," I said.

He took my hand and smiled. "My *passerina* from Pasadena."

His two dogs bounded toward us as we pulled up at the house. With my bag in hand, Renato led the way to the back steps. I removed the key from its hiding place, which made him laugh. He unlocked the door and I followed him inside.

The early evening sun poured in through the terrace doors of the living room.

"Let me show you your room," Renato said.

Renato put my bag by the guest bed, where there were bath towels laid out on the fluffy duvet.

"This reminds me of the bed in the movie *Under the Tuscan Sun*," I said to him. I looked closer at the medallion in the center of the scrolled iron headboard. "Except that the bed in the movie had the face of the Madonna here." My bed had a painted scene of a sailboat on a lake, with mountains in the distance. It reminded me of the views I had seen from the train of Umbria's Lake Trasimeno.

He opened a bottle of wine and filled my glass. We went out to the terrace to enjoy the last of the evening light. His dogs and one of his cats joined us. They were eager for his attention. One of the dogs snuggled up to me; his fur warmed my feet.

Renato leaned over and kissed me. The cat meowed and the other dog whined, which made us laugh. "They're jealous," he said.

We watched the darkness descend over the valley below.

As the wind shifted and the air turned cool, we went back inside. Renato took me to a sofa by the fireplace.

He gently cupped my chin in his hands. "Not being able to," he whispered, "has nearly put an end to me."

And with that, he swept the Renaissance maiden off her feet.

ᖇᖇ

For dinner we ate prosciutto, cheese and lentil soup topped with bread slices, which Renato drizzled with oil from his own olive trees.

The house had grown cold. We didn't realize until later that the housekeeper had left a window open in the guest room.

Renato lit dry twigs stacked in the fireplace. We sat by the crackling fire, drowsy and content.

Stroking my cheek, he said, "I knew the moment I saw you."

Neither of us realized it just then, but our paths in life had crossed even more times than we knew. Why had we been given this one chance when we had missed so many others? For one precious night on a mountaintop, we were living a dream of what might have been. Was destiny cruel or kind—I couldn't decide.

"You will sleep like a baby," Renato promised as he closed the window in my room.

Before I went to bed, I tiptoed into the kitchen to get a glass of water. The TV was flickering in Renato's bedroom at the end of the hallway. I could hear him snoring.

I went back to the guest room. As I crawled into the big iron bed, I took a close look at the sailboat on the lake above my head before I turned off the light.

∽

The next morning I woke up a little after seven to the sound of a radio. I heard water running in the bathroom. A short while later, Renato opened the door to my room. He was in his bathrobe.

"Good morning," he said. He walked over to the bed and smiled at me, snuggled in my cozy nest of covers and pillows. "How did you sleep?"

"Like a baby." I truly had slept well.

"The bed is nice, yes?" he asked.

"I felt like I was sleeping on a cloud."

Renato lay down next to me and held me close.

"You smell good," I said.

"I just took a shower."

I ran my fingers through his damp hair.

With each tender kiss, my heart broke a little. The teapot I had jumped into was cracking and crumbling.

"This has been like a dream," I said.

"Yes," he said. "A dream."

Outside the bedroom windows, birds welcomed the day.

"Listen to them," he whispered. "Isn't it beautiful?"

In that moment, I knew what I longed for. For all my solo wanderings and adventures, for all the freedom I had embraced in my celebration of a new life, at the end of this journey what I longed for was someone to hold me in the morning as we listened to the birds sing.

Renato kissed me one more time. "We have to get up," he said, swinging his legs to the floor. He put on his slippers and padded toward the door. He turned and looked at me, with a boyish grin.

But sadly I knew the teapot was in pieces.

⁖

I showered, dressed and packed up my bag.

Renato was standing at the stove making me an espresso. The radio news, in Italian, mentioned U.K. Prime Minister Gordon Brown.

"What's happened?" I asked. It had been four days since the U.K. general election had resulted in a hung parliament.

"He resigned," Renato said.

"I don't believe it." Gordon Brown was a student at the University of Edinburgh during my year there. As president of the student union, he had pulled off a still-talked-about maneuver that landed two students (including himself) on the university's board of regents. He was a political animal even then.

Renato served me toast with jam made from wild plums that grow on the mountain.

I looked out the window next to the table, memorizing the view. The valley was shrouded in mist. It had started to rain.

I carefully rinsed my breakfast plate. I noticed that Renato had piled the dishes from our dinner the night before precariously in the sink.

"It makes me nervous to see these works of art stacked like this," I said.

He laughed. "Leave them."

Renato suggested I spend part of the morning exploring the village, which I had seen only briefly the day he brought me to the house for lunch, and told me the places I should visit. He dropped me off at a café-bar near the village church.

"Come down to the studio whenever you'd like," he said. He pointed to a narrow street across from the café. "Take that street down the hill." He had booked a lunch reservation for us at a restaurant in the village.

I went into the café to escape the rain. I ordered a cappuccino and sat down at a table. I sent Gaya a text: *"All is well. I'm at a café in the ancient village of Deruta enjoying the local color. I'll call you from the train tonight. Hugs, R"*

She wrote back: *"Am relieved that I don't need to go looking for a teapot that looks like you in 2 weeks when search fails ☺ hugs back."*

I took out my journal and started writing the tale of my return to Umbria. I wrote for about an hour. The rain stopped, so I headed out to see the sights. I visited the church, where, Renato told me, a tile floor had been discovered during a renovation in the early 1900s that was the work of one of Deruta's master artists in the sixteenth century.

I saw fragments of the floor at the ceramics museum next to the church. I lost track of time as I roamed through the rooms, filled with extraordinary ceramic pieces, dating back to the fifth century B.C. I was intrigued with devotional plaques that depict scenes of divine homage. One was of a woman in labor, her bare legs apart as a midwife kneeled on the floor, ready to receive the child, with Saint Anthony looking on. Another showed a young couple in bed, hands raised in prayer to the Madonna and child, who looked down on them from a cloud. The description on the card next to the plaque indicated they were a "married" couple.

Renato called while I was at the museum. "Where are you?" he asked.

"I'm lost in the museum."

"Good. Stay there. I'll meet you at the restaurant in about thirty minutes. It's next to the museum."

I arrived at the restaurant before he did and told the hostess I would wait outside. A few minutes later, the hostess and an older gentleman came outside to speak with me.

"I am Giuseppe," the man said to me. "You are waiting for Renato, yes?"

I nodded.

"Please come inside and wait at the table for him," he said kindly.

I later learned that Giuseppe's father had worked as a Mancini potter for thirty years.

I was writing in my journal at the table when Renato appeared. "Is this book going to be the end of me?" he asked, kissing my cheek.

Giuseppe appeared at the table and spoke with Renato in Italian about the feast that was about to be served.

"I never see a menu when I come here," Renato told me as a waiter poured our wine. "I let Giuseppe decide."

The meal began with marinated chickpeas, prosciutto and beans in tomato sauce, eggs scrambled with truffles, baked eggplant and a mound of fluffy ricotta cheese topped with sundried tomatoes. The main course was pasta with artichokes in a pesto sauce. Dessert was a warm chocolate tart that, when pierced with a fork, oozed fudge sauce onto the plate, like lava from a volcano.

We drank a beautiful *vino rosso* from Montefalco called Arquata. At the end of the meal, Giuseppe appeared with a bottle of Sagrantino Pastino.

"You must savor every drop of this," Renato said. Two months after the harvest, he explained, the grapes left on the vine, which by then are saturated with sugar, are picked one by one to produce this particular vintage. "This is the sacramental wine that priests drink during Mass."

I took a sip, which was a near-religious experience.

Giuseppe came to the table as we were getting ready to leave.

"This was the best meal I've had in all the time I've been in Italy," I told him.

"*Grazie, signora,*" he said with a big smile.

༄

When Renato and I arrived at the studio, his assistant was discussing a custom order with a couple from Chicago who had a home in Cortona.

"Would you like to look around?" Renato asked me. On the phone a few days earlier, I had asked him if he would help me select a thank-you gift for Fiona and James, for all they had done to help me find a flat in Edinburgh.

I was eager to explore the display rooms again and wandered off, as Renato greeted the American couple from Chicago-Cortona.

I made several tours of the rooms, waiting for a lovely piece to speak to me. A pitcher with a lush floral design called out. It would look perfect in James and Fiona's drawing room, where a big bay window looks onto their gorgeous garden.

I returned to the room where the Chicago-Cortona couple were still customizing their order. Renato sat at a long display table, laden with vases, pedestal bowls and spouted jars. He didn't notice me looking at him. He was staring at nothing, not engaged in the conversation his assistant was having with the Americans.

I sat down at the table next to Renato. "This is a beautiful table you're sitting at, *signore,*" I said.

He smiled.

I looked around the room. "This is what I think heaven looks like," I said. "Actually, my heaven has two rooms—one like this, filled with beautiful ceramics, and another filled with beautiful fabric and quilts."

I told Renato about a quilt store in Manhattan I used to visit, back in the early '80s when I was working for *People*. "It was called The Gazebo."

"I know that store," he said. "It was on…"

"Madison, I think."

"Or was it Lexington? I knew the owner," he said. "She died of cancer."

"Really?"

"The store closed soon after she died," he said.

It was surreal to me that I was hearing this news from Renato. "She was always kind to me. She knew how much I loved quilts," I said. "Some days I would go to the store just to escape the stress of my job. I used to tell her that when I walked through the door, I felt like I had entered heaven."

✺

I waited for Renato in front of the studio while he went to get his car. As we pulled out of the parking lot, I couldn't believe my eyes. Directly across the street was the shop I had been looking for on my first visit to Deruta, the shop I couldn't find.

We arrived at the train station with a few minutes to spare. As we stood on the platform, Renato reached into his jacket pocket and took out a tiny black velvet sack tied with a gold drawstring.

"This was made especially for you," he said.

I could feel a lump swelling in my throat. I untied the string and opened the sack. Inside was a *fuseruola*, decorated with tiny flowers and inscribed with my initials.

"Renato…it's beautiful."

"A token, to remember me." He took me in his arms one last time.

The train to Florence was announced. We crossed over together to Track 3.

I boarded the train and quickly took a seat by a window near where Renato stood. I blew him a kiss. He raised two fingers to his lips. I leaned forward, to catch one last glimpse of him as the train pulled out of the station.

∽

With the train gathering speed, I felt like a cannonball being shot out of a rabbit hole.

The writer-in-me sat in the seat next to me and patted my arm. *"Don't do this to yourself,"* she said quietly. For once, she wasn't taking notes.

I stared out the window. The scenery seemed bleak, not like I had remembered from the day before. My eyes filled with tears as the train sped past the misty islands of Lake Trasimeno.

This was a year that had begun with a fantasy and ended with a dream. But both had been fleeting.

I closed my eyes and imagined a summer's day in Manhattan in 1983…

I'm walking down Madison Avenue—or was it Lexington? At 29, I'm at an early zenith in my career as a journalist. I have a bylined entertainment column in a magazine read by 20 million people every week. Life is good. I walk into my favorite store— a quilt shop called The Gazebo. The woman who owns the shop is talking to a man, with long wavy dark hair, who has his back to me. His English carries an Italian accent. As he turns to leave, he and I nearly collide. "*Mi scusi*," he says apologetically. I smile at him. He's strikingly handsome. With his hand on the door, he looks back at me.

I savored the daydream for a moment, thinking of the intersecting circles in life that connect one person to another. In the 1980s, Renato and I were walking the same streets of Manhattan, visiting the same stores, even talking to the same woman. He had visited Pasadena many times during the twenty years I lived there. His client in Pasadena was one of my favorite shops. No wonder we felt each other's magnetic pull the day I walked into his studio.

As the train rocked on the tracks, I felt Renato's hand stroking my face. *I knew the moment I saw you.* His words would haunt me for a very long time.

42

The crisis

The volcano in Iceland was spewing ash again. Two days after I returned from Deruta, I received an e-mail from my father, written at 1 a.m. Chicago time, saying that an ambulance had just taken my mother to the hospital. He had found her semi-conscious at the bottom of the stairs. She hadn't fallen down the staircase. Apparently she had collapsed as she was about to go up the stairs to her bedroom.

My internet service with the new key I had purchased was limited. Even though I had been told at the phone store I would have five hours of internet access daily, that turned out not to be exactly true. No surprise there. (I found out later that the time was allocated in quarter-hours, so that if I was online sixteen minutes, I was charged for thirty minutes.)

When I read my father's e-mail, it was 11 a.m. my time, 4 a.m. Chicago time. I couldn't get a strong enough internet signal to make a Skype call—another problem with the key—so I called Gaya and asked if I could use her computer.

As I rushed out of my apartment building, I looked at the sky, which was bright blue with big puffy clouds, and wondered, *Mom, are you there?* For the next hour, I braced myself for the news that she was dead.

From Gaya's laptop, I made a Skype call to the emergency room of the hospital where my mother had been taken. The attendant assured me that she was okay. She had complained of neck pain from her fall, but he told me they examined her and that she had no broken bones or other injuries. "She was able to get up and walk around," he told me. "We told your father there was no reason to keep her, so he took her home." The attendant was aware of her dementia.

My relief was short-lived. I returned to my apartment and was able to get back on the internet. My mother's sister, Aileen, had sent me an e-mail account of two phone conversations she'd had with my mother the preceding day, one just hours before my father found her at the bottom of the stairs. My aunt told me that during the second conversation my mother was crying hysterically. During the first conversation, my mother said a strange man was with her and she wanted to go home. Aileen could hear my father in the background, yelling, "I'm your husband!" Aileen tried to calm my mother, telling her she was at home and the man was her husband. "No, he isn't!" my mother cried. "So long." My mother hung up the phone.

I tried to call my parents' home phone on Skype, but the call wouldn't go through. I then tried my aunt's home number. I nearly jumped out of my chair when I heard her voice.

"Aunt Aileen, it's Becky. I'm calling on my computer. Can you hear me?"

Miraculously, we had a clear connection. "Yes, yes. I can hear you fine," she said.

She recounted the details of the phone conversations. I asked her to call my father. "Please tell him to call me right away."

About a half hour later, my dad called. He sounded exhausted. He said that the night before, he had gone up to bed, but Mom had stayed downstairs because she was watching a program on TV. "That was a mistake," he admitted. "She usually comes upstairs with me and watches TV in her room." He got up at 1 a.m. to check on her and found her at the bottom of the stairs. He immediately called 911.

I asked my dad about her mental state. "She says she wants to die and keeps asking me why this is happening to her," he said.

We were in the bowels of hell on earth. "Is she still having delusional episodes?" I asked.

"She hasn't had episodes lately where she doesn't know me," he said.

I could feel my diaphragm tighten. Either my father was lying to me or he, too, was suffering severe memory loss.

"Has she been in touch with her friends and Aileen?" I asked.

"I encourage her to make calls. Sometimes I have to dial for her," he told me.

"Do you know if she tried to call Aileen yesterday?" I asked.

"I don't recall," he said. "We had a crew here yesterday taking down that tree by the patio. I was busy with that."

He couldn't "recall" my mother's hysterical call to her sister the day before. Aileen said that after her first conversation with my mother, she tried several times to call her back. Finally that evening, my father answered and forced my mom to get on the phone, even though she was crying. According to Aileen, he shouted at her, "Get on the phone! It's your sister." Sobbing, my mother told Aileen, "I fell. I broke my hip and both knees and my feet." Aileen told her, "You can call me back when you feel like talking." My mom said, "Okay." Aileen didn't hear from her again.

I could barely breathe.

My dad said he needed to get some sleep and would call me later.

After we hung up, I went out on my balcony to get some air.

❧

I spent that entire day trying to deal with my parents' crisis. I e-mailed Aileen about my conversation with my father. *"I don't want my father ending up in jail or my mother throwing herself down the stairs,"* I wrote to her. Something had to be done quickly.

A month earlier, just a few days after my father brought my mother home from the assisted-living facility, he received a call from the county department of senior services. I surmised that the facility had contacted the county. My father had e-mailed me to say that a county case manager would be making a home visit. I was concerned what the outcome of this might be. But the home visit turned out to be an outreach gesture to help my parents assess their needs and to inform them of the resources available to them. The case manager, a woman, was very helpful, according to my father, and he greatly appreciated her suggestions.

Gaya urged me to get in touch with the case manager, as did Aileen.

A daughter should never have to go to the authorities to essentially blow the whistle on her parents. But at that point, I couldn't see any other way to ensure my mother's safety and to provide her with the professional care she so desperately needed.

❧

Gaya and I had become regulars at an indoor pool in the neighborhood. I liked doing my laps during the early afternoon aqua-gym classes. The instructors played pop music with molto amplification. I flew through the water during Disco Swim, as I called it, burning enough calories to justify a gelato afterwards. Or so I reasoned.

During the fomenting crisis with my parents, Disco Swim saved me. One day, I cried as I swam. My tears were hot and angry, but the cool water washed them away. The pounding music cleared my brain. After an hour of Disco Swim, I pulled myself out of the pool, feeling invigorated and cleansed.

I had been back from Deruta for three days and had not heard from Renato. After Disco Swim, on my third day back, I went for a pedicure at the neighborhood beauty spa, popular with the fake-tan crowd. Many Italian women are as deeply tanned as their handbags.

I had just dipped my feet into a basin of warm water when my phone rang. It was Renato.

"It's nice to hear your voice," I told him. I was so happy to hear from him.

"It's nice to hear you, too," he said.

He sounded upbeat. "Business has been very good these past few days," he said. "We've had many American visitors."

I told him that was a good omen for his upcoming trip to the States.

He asked how I had been. I told him about my parents.

"I'm so sorry to hear this, Rebecca," he said.

After we said good-bye, I rested my head against the back of the chair and closed my eyes. I couldn't stop the tears.

Gaya called the next day, which was Saturday, and invited me over for dinner. Her husband and a friend of his were going out for the evening.

She and I were at the kitchen table, eating chicken curry and bacon rice, when sleepy Anjou came into the kitchen saying she heard a bell ringing. It was my phone, tucked in my purse, which I had left in the living room.

I didn't get to the phone in time. There was a message from an unknown caller. I wondered if it was Renato. I'm not good at retrieving voicemail messages. The prompts, which are in Italian, are mind-numbingly loquacious and illogical. To hear the first message, you press 1. To hear the second message, you press 6. Go figure.

Gaya found the message, which was from my father. He had called to tell me that my mother had been in the hospital since Thursday, after another fall, and would be moved to a rehabilitation care facility. "No need for you to come back," he said. "There's nothing you can do." He said he was going back to the hospital and would call me the next day. He made no mention of her condition.

I looked at Gaya, bewildered. "My mother has been in the hospital since Thursday and I'm just now finding out about it."

As I was trying to re-play my dad's message, two unheard messages popped up. Both were from Renato. The first was from the previous week, before my trip to Deruta. The second was from the day after I returned. Renato had called to say hello and to make sure I was safely back in Florence.

"Oh, Rebecca," Gaya said. "The poor man is probably wondering why he didn't hear from you."

I listened again to my father's message. He sounded calm and in command of the situation. I sent him an e-mail from Gaya's laptop, telling him I would expect his call the following day.

I then sent a text to Renato. It was about 10 p.m. *"Are you awake?"* I wrote.

A few minutes later, a little text bubble appeared on my phone with no words inside. I giggled and typed *"Si?"*

A minute later my phone rang. Renato sounded sleepy.

"Did I wake you?"

"I was asleep on the sofa," he said.

"I called to wake you up to tell you to go to bed," I said.

He laughed.

I told him I had just discovered his message on my phone from Wednesday, the day after I got back. "I didn't know you had called," I said. "I'm sorry."

"It's okay."

"How are you?"

"We had another good day today," he said. "I think it's a good sign."

"I do, too."

He asked about my mother. I told him what I knew.

"Your mother needs care," he said. "She is only going to get worse."

"I know, but it's a difficult situation. My sister died two years ago, so I don't have an ally in this."

"My god, Rebecca."

"I'll let you get to bed," I said.

We said good-night. "We'll talk again soon," Renato promised.

Gaya came into the room. I played back his message from Wednesday, on speaker.

She smiled at me. "I like Renato."

The next day, my father called to say that my mother had been admitted to a rehab facility, at the recommendation of two doctors who had examined her in the hospital. They said she was losing her strength and coordination because of her lethargy and prescribed a physical therapy program for her. She would be staying at the facility for twenty days.

I urged my father to move quickly, while he had this opportunity, to find a dementia-care facility in town and to arrange to move her there directly from rehab when her treatment was finished.

"You need to seize this moment," I told him. "You have a team of professionals who can help you find a good place for her and help you get her there. Do not bring her back home."

He was silent for a moment. "Let me get this phase behind us," he said. "You don't know how hard it is to convince your mother…"

I cut him off. "She is not in her right mind, Dad," I said. "She has no say in this anymore. You have to take action. She needs professional care. You cannot bring her home."

"Your mother wasn't happy about going for rehab," my father said. "You know how she gets…"

"Dad, I know about Mom's frantic conversations with Aileen the day before she went to the hospital," I said.

He was silent.

"I don't know what is going on in that house, but do you want to end up in police custody if Mom calls 911, sobbing and saying she has broken bones?" My voice was hard. "You say she wants to die—what if she throws herself down the stairs and tries to kill herself. You could be accused of criminal neglect. She could leave the house and get hit by a car. She could get behind the wheel and kill somebody. Don't you understand the crisis you're in?"

With that, he said, "Okay, dear, thanks for your advice. I need to go now."

I hung up the phone, resolved to take action.

I sent an e-mail to the county, saying that I urgently needed to reach the case manager who had visited the house. And I e-mailed the rehab facility, explaining that I had concerns about my mother's long-term care, and asked for an administrator to contact me.

∽

The next day I received an e-mail from the county case manager. She informed me that the purpose of her visit to the house a month earlier had not been just to help my parents evaluate their needs—she had gone there to investigate allegations of elder abuse. She didn't say who had waved the red flag, but I assumed it was the assisted-living facility where my parents had spent a tumultuous ten days. She told me she had closed the case because she could see no evidence of abuse, but she asked me to inform her of my concerns.

I hadn't been the first to blow the whistle, which gave me some consolation. The case manager said that only a few days earlier, a social worker at the hospital who had been assisting with my mother's move to rehab, had also called the county expressing her concerns about my mother's situation.

A few days later, I received an e-mail from a family friend saying that my father was in the hospital. He had suffered a mini-stroke, called a TIA, that had caused some weakness in his left hand. He was okay and in good spirits, she reported. He underwent tests and was put on a blood thinner. He had told her that he planned to take mom home as soon as he was discharged from the hospital, even though she still had two weeks remaining of her prescribed PT program.

I spoke with my father and I told him as gently as I could about the abuse allegations. I told him that nothing had come of the county's investigation, but that he could face neglect charges if he brought Mom home. I contacted the director of skilled nursing at a dementia-care facility in town, to discuss transferring my mother directly from the rehab facility.

I could not leave Italy. The volcano was still spewing, affecting trans-Atlantic flights. Even if I could get to Chicago, there was no guarantee I could get back in time to make the move to Edinburgh on June 1. If I were delayed much longer than that, my Italian visa would expire and I could face problems trying to re-enter the country.

Divine intervention was at play, I told myself. Both of my parents were getting the medical attention they needed from professionals who could help them make good choices for their long-term care. I would not honor my father's wish for me to come live with them and take care of them. But I had done what I could to help them through this crisis.

I didn't know what the coming weeks would bring. But I had reached a point of resignation. I had done everything I could to stop the runaway train from going over the cliff.

Basta, basta, basta.

43

Final days

As I gathered up my things, I made a little stack of mementos I had collected during my year in Florence. Ticket stubs from the Odeon and the Galleria dell'Accademia, where Michelangelo's David resides. A Lamborghini postage stamp. A postcard of Dante admiring Beatrice. My recipe for Italian-style margaritas. Business cards from Claudio at Giubbe Rosse; Lorenzo, the photographer who can't drive in reverse; Augusta Pardi, the poet of the looms; Francesco, who called Augusta on my behalf; Guido, my osteopath; Tito, big brother to everyone; Nadia, the Moroccan shop girl with a big heart and a mouth to match; Sofie, my real estate agent; Enrico, the hotel manager who welcomed me to Florence; Isabella, my banker who helped me go to war with the phone company; Elena, who shared her lovely apartment on Via Tavanti with me. On top of the stack, I put Marcello's card, thinking I should frame it someday. I took Renato's card and tucked it into my wallet.

I savored my last days on Via Tavanti. I went to the corner coffee bar and said my good-byes. I thanked the staff for their kindness. I had spent many hours writing this book at their tables. Luan gave me a big hug: "*Ciao, bambina.*"

On my way home from Disco Swim every day, I enjoyed walking past the little carousel in Piazza Leopoldo—a big attraction with the *bambini* crowd. A grandfatherly gentleman in the control booth calls out "Ciao! Ciao!" to the children, riding in seats in the shape of swans, smiling dragons and ninja turtles. Savvy toddler customers are poised to grab a puppet—usually Pinocchio or Jiminy Cricket—that dangles on a string, just above their heads. The man in the booth controls the string, allowing Pinocchio or Jiminy to fall within reach of eager hands.

I was intrigued the first time I witnessed this game. The tiniest boy on the carousel, who had incredible hand-eye coordination, snatched the puppet (it was Jiminy that day), beating out much bigger children who easily could have reached it. But the little guy was focused and determined. It took him three passes, but he was triumphant in the end.

The amazing thing to me about this game was that at the end of the ride, the child who grabs the puppet returns it to the man in the booth, who reattaches Pinocchio or Jiminy to the string for the next ride. It's not about the prize. The satisfaction is in a job well done, not the trophy for it.

A profound life lesson, I thought.

Peg had asked me what I would miss most about Florence. "The sense of awe I feel when I walk around this city," I said.

I hadn't caught the "disease" of Florence, as Nadia had predicted. But I truly was in awe of the city's beauty and history. How could you not feel inspired when walking in the sandal steps of Dante, Michelangelo, Galileo, Machiavelli and Leonardo da Vinci.

I had survived my year on Via Tavanti, blowing a fuse (literally) only once, when I turned on my new electric kettle while the dishwasher was running. I learned to live without a clothes dryer, a microwave and a freezer bigger than a blender pitcher. For a year, I slept on two twin mattresses unevenly butted together—the European version of a queen-size bed. I'm not sure my spine will ever recover. But the rest of me fondly will remember all those midnight soaks in my Jacuzzi tub. The Jacuzzi brothers are high on my list of influential Italians, right up there with Galileo.

In one of my Google searches, I discovered that the Jacuzzi brothers emigrated from Italy to the U.S., eventually settled in Berkeley and became machinists whose many inventions included an agricultural hydraulic pump that they adapted for the bathtub when one of the brother's sons developed rheumatoid arthritis. The Jacuzzis hired Jack Benny as their spokesperson and, in 1968, introduced the "Roman Bathtub" for home use.

As candlelight baths are my habit, I lit a few extra votives for the Jacuzzi brothers during my last nights on Via Tavanti. Alas, my tub in Edinburgh had no whirlpool jets.

ᘒ

The week before I left Florence, Gaya returned to Brussels for several days with her husband and children, to deal with issues related to her EU nationality application. She was focused on her goal and her husband was on board—the alternative for him was the gangplank, but never mind.

On the eve of her trip, she asked me to take a cab with her into the city center so that she could pick up something for her Sri Lankan friend Ashanti. By the time the cab arrived, Dani was crying in his car seat. The cries turned to screams as we headed off. For some reason still unclear to me, I ended up in the back seat with Dani, so it was my job to placate him. I started singing our *Mary Poppins* favorites. Gaya, in the front seat, was shouting out requests. "Try *Summertime*," she yelled. Dani usually liked my soft rendition of the George Gershwin lullaby, but on that day he was screaming so loud he couldn't even hear me.

In an act of desperation, I segued to…*When the moon hits your eye like a big pizza pie, that's amore*…

The cab driver, who was on the verge of a nervous breakdown, howled with laughter. It was quite a scene, as we sat in rush-hour traffic, baby screaming and me singing gustily about *when the stars make you drool just like pasta fazool.*

All the while, on the ride into town, I thought we were picking up a high-end gift item, like a designer handbag. But when Gaya asked the driver to stop in front of a Sri Lankan take-out restaurant, I said, "Surely, you're joking." Gaya's hostess gift was Ashanti's favorite foods from home.

While Gaya was inside collecting her to-go order, I sang all the verses of *That's Amore* to Dani, with the driver humming along, and by the time Gaya returned, her darling son was fast asleep.

ॐ

I celebrated my fifty-sixth birthday with a massage at the neighborhood spa/tanning salon.

I called Gaya when I got back to the apartment. "I've just had a massage and released a lot of toxins," I said. "I'm having second thoughts about leaving Marcello's digital receiver with you. I think I should return it in person and say good-bye to him. What do you think?"

"I think that would be good of you," Gaya replied.

"So I'll send him an e-mail saying I'm leaving and would like to return the receiver—we could meet for a drink or I could drop it off at the store or I could leave it with a friend."

"That's too many choices for an Italian," she said. "Just say, 'Things worked out and I'm leaving for Edinburgh next Tuesday.

By the way, I'd like to return your receiver.' Say *by the way*. Then say you could meet him for a drink or you could leave it with a friend."

I sent Marcello this message:

> *Ciao bello,*
> *I'm leaving for Edinburgh in a few days—all the pieces finally fell into place. I'd like to return your digital receiver. Thank you so much—it saved my sanity! If you'd like to meet for a drink, I could return it in person. Or I could drop it by the store.*
> *Rebecca*

I didn't take Gaya's advice about saying "by the way."

Gaya and I went out to dinner that night to welcome my new year. We promised to become Skype pals. She planned to bring Anjou for a visit to Edinburgh in the fall.

Gaya and I had shared a special time of our lives. As her much older "sister," I looked forward to seeing where her life's journey would take her. I already had a sense of where her path would lead.

"I have an idea where you'll be in five years and in ten years," I told her.

"Tell me."

"No, no," I said. "I'll write it down and we'll see if I'm right."

"Tell me!"

I smiled at her. "That would spoil the surprise."

❦

Elena stopped by to say good-bye. She was bursting with good news: she was eleven weeks pregnant. She said I was the first person outside her immediate family whom she had told.

"I feel like it's a female," she said, stroking her tummy.

I wondered how she'd manage everything that was coming her way. I knew she was already dealing with a lot of stress with her job and Bernardo's decision to start a new venture.

"I feel confident," she said.

"Good. I'm very happy for you."

We exchanged Skype addresses. I hoped we'd stay in touch. Elena has never been to the U.S. and would love to visit California.

I gave her a copy of my Italy photo book and thanked her for her kindness to me.

She asked me to send her a copy of this book when it is published. "What is the title?" she asked.

"*Tales from Tavanti.*"

"Really?"

"If it hadn't been for you, this book would have another title," I said.

I could see the emotion in her eyes. "Rebecca, this is such a beautiful story."

৩৯

Renato called a few days before I left Florence. He wanted to know how the packing was going. I promised to send him my new phone number when I got to Edinburgh.

"Summer in Edinburgh will be beautiful," he said wistfully.

He was leaving for the U.S. two days after I arrived in Scotland.

"Send me texts about your trip," I said.

"I will."

Just before we hung up, I said, "Big kiss."

And back to me, he said the same.

৩৯

I stopped by the leather store to say good-bye to Nadia. She was happy to see me, but soon started needling me. "You never called me. You never came to my house for couscous. We never even went out for pizza," she complained. "You are so bad."

An American woman from Tennessee wandered into the store. She was recently divorced and had come to Florence to study Italian for a month. A new chapter of her life was beginning, at age 54.

"*Brava*," I said to her.

We talked about men, motherhood and the bonds of friendship.

"Rebecca has been a wonderful friend to me," Nadia told her. Nadia put her hand to her mouth. "I'm going to get emotional."

I was stunned by what she said next.

"One day I got very upset with my son," she continued. "I was so angry, he hurt me so much. I thank God that Rebecca was there." Nadia started to cry. "She stayed with me. She talked to me. She helped me so much."

I went to Nadia and hugged her. She said to me, "Even though I haven't seen you very often, it makes me so happy to know you are here in Florence. I will be so sad when you go."

I had been a friend to Nadia in her darkest hour as a young mother. I was just back from Greece and had gone over to her house. It was the day she told me that Marcello didn't own the store.

We had walked a few blocks from the house to pick up her son at school. He was tired and irritable. We went across the street to a park and he had a tantrum on the playground there. Nadia told him he had to go home.

As she took him in hand, he cried, "I have no family!"

She turned on him in a fury and grabbed him by the shoulders. "What did you say?"

He was only 3 years old, but he already knew how to push Nadia's hot button. He ran on ahead with Nadia close on his heels. I trailed behind with Nadia's 4-year-old niece.

When I got to the house, Nadia and her son were already inside. Through the closed front door, I could hear her shouting at him.

I banged on the door. "Nadia! Nadia!" I yelled. Her niece held my hand tight and looked up at me, frightened.

When she opened the door, Nadia was flushed and wild-eyed. Her son sat on the sofa, wailing.

"How could he say such a thing to me?" she ranted.

The boy cried himself to sleep within minutes. For the next hour, I sat with Nadia and tried to calm and console her, sharing some of the lessons I had learned as a mother. "I never imagined he could hurt me so much," she said, sobbing. I knew the pain of this wound would be with her for a long time.

When the American woman left the store, I turned to Nadia. Part of me wanted to simply say good-bye. But the question that had been gnawing at me for six months demanded an answer: How could this woman, who claimed to value my friendship, have betrayed my confidence?

"Nadia, I need to ask you something." I steeled myself. "Marcello told me that while I was in Greece last fall, you saw him at the store with a group of friends and said, 'So you fucked my friend.'"

"What?"

"I asked him how he knew you were referring to me and he said just before that, you asked if he knew I was in Greece."

"He's a liar. I never talked to Marcello about you. Never!" She looked at me, her eyes burning. "Do you think that I am that kind of person, Rebecca? That I call you my friend and then say such things? He's a fucking liar!" She paced behind the counter. "Rebecca, who do you believe—me or him?"

"I don't know."

"You don't know? How could you believe him?" Nadia grabbed her purse and took out her phone. "We will see who's the liar here. You will come with me and we'll confront Marcello."

"I'm not going anywhere with you."

"What are you afraid of?"

"Nothing."

Nadia scrolled through her phone contacts.

"Put that phone down right now or I'll walk out of here," I said.

"Why would I say such a thing?"

For a moment, I considered the possibility that Marcello had lied to me.

"I've never told you anything about Marcello or his problems," Nadia said.

That wasn't true. Nadia had just tripped herself.

Still holding her phone, she punched a key. "I mean it, Nadia," I warned her again. "I will walk out."

"As soon as you leave, I will call him," she said defiantly.

"Okay," I said. "Good-bye, Nadia." She looked as if she wanted to spit in my face.

There were a half dozen customers in the store, staring at Nadia and me as I turned to leave.

As I walked to the bus stop, I thought about texting Marcello to warn him. But I knew Nadia would get to him first.

A few minutes later, my phone rang. It was Marcello. "Are you still friends with that bitch?" That was hello. But his anger wasn't directed at me. "The unbelievable thing is that she denies she said that to me," he fumed.

I told him what had happened at the store.

"She will never work for us again," he vowed. "The problem is she will go tell all my friends about this."

"I'm sorry, Marcello. I truly am sorry." I wasn't offering an apology for confronting Nadia. I was sorry he was incurring her wrath.

"I thought you had already gone to Edinburgh," he said. "I was going to e-mail you to find out how you were doing there." (When

I recounted this conversation to Gaya later that evening, she said, "He's so full of shit.")

"I e-mailed you a few days ago and told you I was leaving," I said. True to form, he hadn't replied.

"Yeah, I got that message," he said.

My bus pulled up. "I've got to go."

"I'd like to say good-bye to you," he said. "Call me tomorrow."

No chance of that, I thought.

"Or I'll call you," he said.

He didn't call. No surprise.

On my last night in Florence, Gaya invited me for dinner at her place. I arrived with wine and presents. For Anjou I brought an orange flower to be worn in her J-shaped hair, just above the ear. It had been made by a tango-dancer friend of mine in L.A. I also gave Anjou my well-worn Fossil wallet, which I had filled with Euro copper in one-, two- and five-cent denominations. As Anjou opened the wallet, I stressed to her the importance of girls having their own money—a message that made Gaya laugh.

I gave Gaya a silk pashmina in spruce green, a color she especially likes, and a copy of my Italy photo book. The inscription made her cry. (It began: *"You have been the best part of my year in Firenze."*) I also gave her a little pouch of Euro coins, in ten- and twenty-cent denominations.

"Between you and Anjou," I told her, "you have enough money to get to the airport."

After dinner, Gaya and I sang Dani to sleep. It was a beautiful evening. Swallows swirled outside the bedroom window that looked out on the top boughs of an enormous magnolia tree.

I lay at the foot of the bed in the late evening light, looking up at the slowly spinning ceiling fan.

"My father used to sing me to sleep every night," I said. "Hymns and camp songs mostly."

"What did he sing?" Gaya asked.

I remembered his favorite hymn. I began singing: *On a hill far away, stood an old rugged cross…*

Gaya joined in: *The emblem of suffering and…*

She sang "pain" and I sang "shame."

She giggled. "It's pain."

"Are you sure?" I asked.

"I'll call my mother. She wants that hymn sung at her funeral."

I rolled over on my side and looked at Gaya, propped against the headboard with Dani asleep in her arms.

"I don't believe this," I said. "We grew up on opposite sides of the world and we both know this hymn."

Together we sang *The Old Rugged Cross* through to the end. (I later googled the lyrics. I was right—it's shame, not pain.)

I sang my father's repertoire, starting with *I've Been Workin' on the Railroad.* Gaya liked the verse about that mysterious someone who's in the kitchen with Dinah, strummin' on his old banjo.

Gaya sang *Home Sweet Home*, which left a little lump in my throat. *'Mid pleasures and palaces though we may roam, be it ever so humble there's no place like home.*

Our finale was *Loch Lomond.* We sang softly as Gaya laid Dani in his bed: *I'll take the high road and you'll take the low and I'll be in Scotland before ye. For me and my true love will never meet again on the bonnie, bonnie banks of Loch Lomond.*

Gaya and I walked back to my apartment. We filled a couple of bags with items I was leaving behind—pasta, jars of sauces, books, toiletries, Marcello's receiver and a basil plant.

We said good-bye at the crosswalk on Via Tavanti, in front of my building. I watched her walk away, with her bags of goodies, memorizing the moment—wondering when we'd see each other next, knowing we'd never have this time in our lives again.

About an hour later, she sent me this text: *"I went onto the balcony and watered the basil and said a prayer to the stars for you…an Irish blessing hung on our veranda…May the road rise up to meet you, may the wind be always at your back and may the sun shine warm on your face. And til we meet again, may God hold you in the hollow of his hand. I'll never forget your singing, tilt of the head and gutsy smile. Hugs and a big kiss."*

A blessing hanging on a veranda. I couldn't imagine a better send-off than that.

44

Red rose, dead rose?

The last item of unfinished business was how to say *arrividerci* to my neighbor, the Mafia princess.

There hadn't been any more screaming fits since the night she held her finger on my door buzzer for a half-hour. But she had an annoying habit that involved a power drill.

I sent my e-group this message:

> *I'm packing up my tent in Firenze and moving to Edinburgh on June 1, volcano willing.*
>
> *For those of you who have followed my e-Tales from Tavanti, I have a request.*
>
> *You may remember my neighbor, the Mafia princess, who terrorized me one fateful night when I accidentally parked in her spot in the parking garage. Her Papa from Palermo got into the act, and one morning, a few days after my parking gaffe, I found my apartment door wide open. A Don't-Mess message, according to my Italian friends here.*

The Princess and I have lived in tentative peace since then.
If I play my music a tad too loud — or if she doesn't like the music
I'm playing — she drills into the wall that we share. (I no joke
you.) When the power drill starts, I've tried to imagine the scene
on her side of the wall. Images abound. Usually, my immediate
response is to crank the volume even higher. Then I grab my cane
(a relic from my sprained ankle days) and thump the wall until
she stops. This happened today, in fact. She capitulated within
minutes. (I blasted her with Bette Midler's "Mambo Italiano.")

So here's the big question: What should I leave her as a fare-
well gift?

I considered fish heads and horse heads, pig snouts and boar
snouts. (I'm told by Italians in the know that if the Mafia really
doesn't like you, they bring in the pigs.)

All that seems a little messy. I want to go out as the Class
Act that I am.

So here's the choice: Shall I leave on her doormat a RED rose
or a DEAD rose? Red rose, dead rose – please cast your vote!!

If you want your vote to count, I must have your response
no later than Monday, May 24 (in order to allow the rose to die
in time for my departure).

Grazie mille,
Your Friend in Firenze (with a pig oinking at her door)

I clicked the SEND button and went to the bathroom. I came
back to my laptop about five minutes later and couldn't believe
what was happening. The early responders, on their smart-phones,
were already casting their votes.

The first reply was from a woman of Italian descent—southern
Italy, I should mention: "*Dead rose by all means. And to make it*

even more of a 'memento mori' (you too will die) find a recently dead worm and perhaps some funky charm bracelet from the flea market." And for all the years I had known her, I thought she was such a sweetheart.

Another sweetheart—a devout Irish Catholic—sent a reply on her iPhone: *"Dead rose. I'll write more later. Miss you!"*

"I vote dead rose," another friend wrote. *"But please give her no time for retaliation. I do want you to arrive in Edinburgh with all your appendages."*

And then came the red roses: The resounding refrain was "Class Act—has to be red." One friend worried there might be a Cosa Nostra implication to red and suggested I do some research first.

Tom suggested a black rose.

John, the poet, wrote this verse:

> *If roses are right, they must be white,*
> *To set you and her free, they must be three.*
> *To show that you are hardly a wimp,*
> *They are neither red nor dead, but languidly limp.*
> *One white rose to remember your name,*
> *One white rose for her, the same,*
> *And one to show you've transcended her game.*

Steve, who time-traveled with me to the student house in Edinburgh thirty-six years earlier, weighed in. He's now a minister. On his iPhone, he wrote: *"I just happen to be studying Proverbs for summer sermons and I thought I'd leave you with this little gem: Proverbs 26: 4 & 5. If you can figure it out, let me know."*

Jeez, all I wanted was a vote for red or dead.

I googled Proverbs and considered the conundrum. Verse 4: Answer not a fool according to his folly, lest thou also be like unto him. Verse 5: Answer a fool according to his folly, lest he be wise in his own conceit.

I replied to Steve: *"Sounds like a no-win to me. The latest vote was a dead rose in the hands of a headless Barbie doll. Send me your sermons. I'll forward them to my e-list. They're a flock that apparently needs tending!!!"*

His response: *"You know that 5 minutes after you leave that headless doll and vanish happily into the distance, you're gonna realize you left your phone/wallet/passport in the room, and as you creep back up the stairs, you'll hear her open the door...THEN WHAT???"*

The final tally:
Red – 15
Dead – 4 (one with headless Barbie)
Black – 1
White – 1
Bleeding pig snout – 1
No rose – 2

As one friend wisely advised, *"Leave nothing and go in peace—one piece, that is!"*

45

My good-bye

I went to Piazza della Repubblica one last time, returning to the place where it all began. I sat down at the table by the carousel where I had been writing that day, when Marcello said those fateful words: *"It's like a fantasy."* I thought of Marcello as I gazed at the triumphal arch. Instead of Charlton Heston in his chariot, I envisioned Paul Newman as The Hustler, sauntering into the piazza, twirling his cue stick.

My life in Italy had been like a fantasy in a way. A fantasy gone wrong some days. But I had realized my dream of living in Europe and writing about it, while sharing a part of me with the people I met here. There are a few lucky souls in Florence whose lives have been forever changed by my margaritas.

To my friends in Florence, if I call you one day and say "I'm here…" and we're disconnected, you'll know where to find me. If you come to Piazza della Repubblica, I'll be at my favorite café by the carousel, writing in my journal.

In the piazza that final day, I wrote the last entry about my life in Florence and closed the book on a story—well-told, I think—called *Tales from Tavanti*.

Oh and by the way, I left no rose—red or dead—on my neighbor's doormat. I slipped away quietly, class act that I am.

Grazie mille...

To Nora, my first reader, who laughed and cried in all the right places,

To Peg, my second reader, who kept me from jumping off my desk in despair during a rewrite crisis and helped me find a creative solution to my dilemma,

To John, for his gentle voice of wisdom, his keen eye for detail and his generous heart,

To the A-listers (Mary, Pat, Christopher and Marty), who cheered me on at every white-knuckle turn,

To Dan and his clan, who helped me build an author platform, plank by plank,

To Caroline, for her publishing expertise,

To Adriana, my Italian guardian angel,

To Elena, who made me a piece of her family,

To Claudio, who always had a table waiting for me at Giubbe Rosse,

To Gaya, for her friendship and her teapot,

To Mark, for giving the Renaissance maiden a margarita,

To Elizabeth, for her inspired cover design,

And to my adorable son, Colin, who, at the age of 14, gave me this sage advice: "Mom, if you don't take a shot, you won't make a basket."

A thousand thank-yous, indeed.

91231787R00208